Forensic Aspects of Paediatric Fractures

Rob A. C. Bilo
Simon G. F. Robben
Rick R. van Rijn

Forensic Aspects
of Paediatric Fractures

Differentiating Accidental Trauma
from Child Abuse

emma kinderziekenhuis AMC

Springer

Rob A. C. Bilo, MD
Department of Pathology and Toxicology
Netherlands Forensic Institute
P. O. Box 24044
2490 AA The Hague
The Netherlands
r.bilo@nfi.minjus.nl

Rick R. van Rijn, MD, PhD
Department of Radiology
Emma Children's Hospital/Academic
Medical Center Amsterdam
P. O. Box 22660
1100 DD Amsterdam
The Netherlands
r.r.vanrijn@amc.uva.nl

Simon G. F. Robben, MD, PhD
Department of Radiology
Maastricht University Medical Center
P. O. Box 5800
6202 AZ Maastricht
The Netherlands
s.robben@mumc.nl

With contribution of
George J. R. Maat
Department of Anatomy
Leiden University Medical Center
Leiden
Netherlands

Nina M. Huls
Department of Pathology and Toxicology
Netherlands Forensic Institute
The Hague
The Netherlands

Titel of the original Dutch edition: Foresische aspecten van fracturen of de kinderleeftijd.
2009, Isala Series nr 58, ISBN/EAN: 978-90-74991-58-2

Translation by D.M. Schenck, Kampen, The Netherlands

Artwork by I. E. M. Kos, Medical Photography & Illustration, Academic Medical Center
Amsterdam, The Netherlands.

ISBN: 978-3-540-78715-0   e-ISBN: 978-3-540-78716-7

DOI: 10.1007/978-3-540-78716-7

Springer Heidelberg Dordrecht London New York

Library of Congress Control Number: 2009938952

© Springer-Verlag Berlin Heidelberg 2010

Cover design: eStudio Calamar, Figueres/Berlin

Printed on acid-free paper

Springer is part of Springer Science+Business Media (www.springer.com)

Maxima debetur puero reverentia
A child should be given the greatest respect

Foreword I

Child abuse is a shocking social problem. Every time when we are confronted through the media with stories regarding child abuse, we react with abhorrence. Every time we hear that children have suffered serious injuries and fractures that have been inflicted by adults, sometimes with lethal results, there is a wave of indignation and social unrest. It is an evil that every right-minded person would like to combat; however, the (knowledge) infrastructure to recognise these cases swiftly and accurately is not adequate.

Childhood is a playful journey of discovery with at times painful consequences. During this journey children may get hurt, due to a lack of certain specific skills or because they are not able to anticipate the danger of their actions. It requires specific forensic knowledge to distinguish between injuries that result from normal behaviour and injuries that result from child abuse. Since most physicians and social workers do not have this specific knowledge, there is a risk that child abuse will not be recognised as such. It is also possible that injuries are unjustly labelled as resulting from child abuse and that innocent people will be branded for life.

This book by Bilo, Robben and Van Rijn discusses in an accessible manner how a physician can recognise fractures that result from child abuse, and distinguish those from fractures due to other causes. Hence it fulfils a great need.

Forensic paediatrics is a branch of forensic medicine, which in itself is again part of forensic science. For a number of years, forensic medicine has been provided by the Netherlands Forensic Institute (NFI). In 2008, forensic paediatrics was added. The NFI would like to continue contributing to this field, since the demand appears to be larger than anticipated. Unfortunately, the cases of child abuse that have been discussed in the media represent only the tip of the iceberg. The NFI would like to invest in forensic paediatrics in two ways: by treating concrete cases and by organising education and training for physicians. In this manner the NFI will be able to contribute to the early recognition of child abuse in children.

It is my firm believe that the book lying before you will become a standard reference in forensic paediatrics. Hence I hope that it will be widely read, not only in the field of health care, but also within the field of forensic science. This will most certainly be in the interest of the many thousands of children that each year fall victim to child abuse.

Tjark Tjin-A-Tsoi, PhD
Netherlands Forensic Institute
February, 2009

Foreword II

As a retired Consultant Paediatric Radiologist at Great Ormond Street Hospital for Children, London, and having specialised in skeletal disorders in general and in physical child abuse in particular, for the last 30 years, I welcome this important reference book. It draws together the available medical literature in an accessible form and provides a benchmark for good medical practice in relation to childhood fractures and physical child abuse. It will be a valuable addition to this largely neglected area of medical literature.

The authors are eminently experienced clinicians from three academic centres in the Netherlands. They bring important insights into the relatively common situation of children presenting for medical attention with fractures, whether these are occult or overt. The question of child abuse inevitably will need to be addressed if only to be excluded. This diagnosis is more pertinent the younger the child and understandably is a highly emotive subject both for the physicians caring for the child and more especially for the parents. In Western cultures the welfare and protection of the child are of over-riding importance and legal frameworks are in place to enable adequate child protection.

This text with its numerous illustrations will provide a valuable resource for effective and timely evaluation of the child by clinicians, especially casualty officers, paediatricians, paediatric radiologists, pathologists and orthopaedic surgeons. It will also be of value to other workers in the field of child protection and inevitably to lawyers involved in judicial processes.

There is detailed description of individual fractures sustained by children. Of particular value are the discussions of the mechanisms and biomechanics responsible for the causation of the fractures. Correlation with the history given by the carers is emphasised and may result in corroboration of the accidental nature of an injury, or, if inconsistent with the mechanism, will increase the possibility of child abuse.

Numerous peer-reviewed papers are cited, both from the more historical aspects of child abuse, but more importantly to justify the current accepted teachings on physical child abuse. Many up-to-date references are summarised and overall conclusions presented. When data are insufficient or incomplete this is stated. It is this meta-analysis from available research and more anecdotal case reports, which will prove of value in cases of suggested child abuse pursued through the courts.

The role of the paediatric radiologist in assessing the radiographic skeletal survey and supervising the imaging protocols is emphasised. A detailed understanding and knowledge of the normal appearances of the growing skeleton is essential when assessing normal variant findings in childhood and in their differentiation from bone injuries. Also the question of pathological fractures resulting from localised or generalised underlying alterations in bone structure as a result of medical conditions with increased bone fragility is addressed comprehensively.

Fracture dating is of consequence when child abuse is suspected for better evaluation of the history of specific trauma given by the carers of the child. This is of no consequence when factures are caused by more common well-documented and witnessed accidental trauma. The authors recognise that more research is needed in the area of fracture dating. There is imprecision about the rate of fracture healing resulting from variables that are sometimes indefinable. Also, defining landmarks in what is a continuous process may be quite subjective. The section on histology also details findings relating to fracture healing in addition to other autopsy findings.

I wish that this book had been available when I was actively involved in child protection.

Christine M. Hall, MBBS, DMRD, FRCR, MD
Institute of Child Health
London University
January 2010

Contents

General Aspects of Fractures in Child Abuse

1

1.1 Introduction

The incidence and prevalence of child abuse is unknown. The reason for this is that in nearly every study to establish the incidence and prevalence, researchers use their own definition. Sometimes this is a 'broad definition,' such as that of the World Health Organisation (WHO): '*Child abuse, sometimes referred to as child abuse and neglect, includes all forms of physical and emotional ill-treatment, sexual abuse, neglect, and exploitation that results in actual or potential harm to the child's health, development or dignity. Within this broad definition, five subtypes can be distinguished – physical abuse; sexual abuse; neglect and negligent treatment; emotional abuse; and exploitation*' [1]. In other cases a much narrower definition is used by preference. This makes it impossible or nearly impossible to compare the research results for incidence and prevalence. In his report on the occasion of the violent death of Victoria Climbié on 25 February 2000, Lord Laming writes on the incidence and prevalence of child abuse: '*I have no difficulty in accepting the proposition that this problem (deliberate harm to children) is greater than that of what are generally recognized as common health problems in children, such as diabetes or asthma*' [2].

During the postmortem investigation of Victoria Climbié, the pathologist established that her body counted as many as 128 injuries. In his report he declares: '*There really is not anywhere that is spared – there is scarring all over the body.*' Lord Laming's report mentions in particular external visible injuries. In children that suffer a trauma, the skin is – in accidental as well as in non-accidental injury – the organ that is most frequently damaged [3]. However, the presence or absence of injuries is not conclusive in establishing physical child abuse when the parents/caregivers or other persons show particular physically aggressive behaviour. That kind of behaviour itself determines whether you can speak of child abuse. The severity of this behaviour can range from a single very serious life-threatening or even lethal incident to regularly returning occasions of aggressive behaviour, such as beating, burning, biting and kicking, in which there is no life-threatening situation with or without injury. Injury (internal as well as external) is the visible result of that kind of behaviour. The severity of the injuries can range from superficial abrasions and bruising to injuries incompatible with life (Table 1.1).

Physical violence does not have to lead to injury. Yet, it appears that up to 90% of victims of physical child abuse sooner or later sustain injury [4, 5]. However, these injuries are seldom severe, and as a result medical treatment or admittance to hospital is required in only 3.2% of abused children [6]. Only a small proportion of these injuries is pathognomonic for the use of violence, resulting from a recognisable kind of injury pattern, such as a bite injury or the identifiable print of, for example, the sole of a shoe (Fig. 1.1) or 'tramline' bruising (Fig. 1.2). Other injuries can only be objectified based on context and other specifics, such as the child's story or a statement that does not correspond with the child's level of development; a remarkable medical history that is in sharp contrast with the nature, localisation and the extent of the injury; a relation with other older and/or unaccounted for injuries; or conspicuous behaviour of the parents.

In other words: usually it is only possible to differentiate between non-accidental and accidental injury by a detailed answer to the clinical question whether this specific child in these specific circumstances can sustain these specific injuries.

R. A. C. Bilo et al., *Forensic Aspects of Pediatric Fractures*,
DOI: 10.1007/978-3-540-78716-7_1, © Springer-Verlag Berlin Heidelberg 2010

Table 1.1 Injuries in child abuse

Directly visible external injuries	
	Haematomas and contusions
	Excoriations and lacerations
	Burns
	Scars
	Other anomalies, such as traumatic alopecia
Indirectly – through additional examination – visible injuries	
• Radiology	Fractures
	Intracranial haemorrhages
	Intra-abdominal injuries
• Fundoscopy	Retinal haemorrhages and retinoschisis
• Laboratory tests	Intra-abdominal injuries
• Forensic light sources	Old and new superficial and deeper subcutaneous injuries

After haematomas, contusions of the skin and burns, fractures are the most prevalent injuries in child abuse [7, 8]. Often (maybe even in one in five children) fractures are the first sign of child abuse [9]. Fractures are nearly always the result of the more severe forms of child abuse. Approximately 10% of children under the age of 5 who are seen by a physician in the emergency department in the United States as a result of injury have non-accidental injuries. In other words: anomalies and/or injuries that do not result from an accident, but from child abuse or neglect [10]. In children evaluated in the emergency department

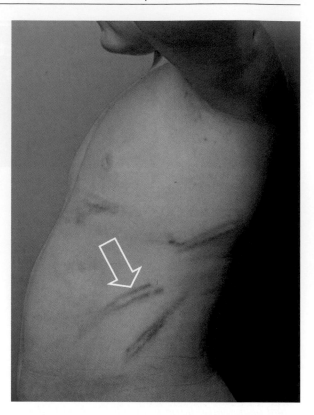

Fig. 1.2 Seven-year-old girl beaten with a stick. On the left side typical tramline haematomas can be seen (*open arrow*)

on suspicion of child abuse, >30% appears to have fresh or healing fractures [11]. In a study on deceased children between the ages of 1–15 years (average 3.9 years) of air force personnel in the United States, it was found that 55% of these children had been seen by a physician as a result of physical trauma in the month prior to their death [12].

1.2 Incidence of Fractures in Children

Irrespective of the aetiology, fractures are a regular feature in children. Landin carried out several large studies in Sweden [13, 14]. In 1983, he reported on a retrospective study regarding 8,642 children. It concerned all fractures in children treated over a period of 30 years in Malmö (between 1950 and 1979). In 1997 he added the most recent data to his original study.

In this period, the chance to sustain a fracture between birth and the age of 16 was 42% for boys and

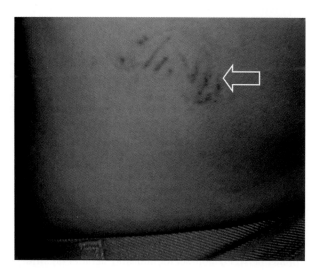

Fig. 1.1 Shoe print (*open arrow*) on the right side in a victim of physical violence (With permission of D. Botter MD, The Netherlands Forensic Institute)

27% for girls [13]. This means that there is a 2.1% chance for all children to sustain one fracture per year (2.6 for boys; 1.7 for girls). This is regardless of the type and location of the fracture and the treatment required (clinical or outpatient). This percentage does not differ significantly from the reported incidence of 1.6 reported for boys and girls in an English study of children with fractures treated clinically as well as in the outpatient clinic [15].

Of the fractures sustained by children during the first 16 years of their life, 6.8% is severe enough to require admittance to hospital. Recalculated to the chance of one hospitalisation per year, this gives a chance of 0.43%. Slightly less than 20% of children who visit a hospital for sustained injuries appear to have sustained a fracture [16].

1.3 Difference Between Fractures in Children and Adults

1.3.1 Fracture Type and Location

From an anatomical, physiological and biomechanical aspect, the skeleton of young children differs from the adult skeleton. These changes make that growing bone in children reacts differently to subjected forces than fully developed bone.

The main difference between the still developing skeleton of a child and the fully grown adult skeleton is the presence of growth plates in the long skeletal bones. Growth plates consist of cartilage and make a person grow taller. This cartilage is among the weakest parts of the still developing skeleton of the child, and the weakest part of the long bones in the child's skeleton. Due to this weakness and being localised near the joints, the growth plates are the most vulnerable place when the joint is subjected to force. Only when ligaments and tendons are stronger than bone, which is often the case in growing bone, fractures can occur in this location. The damage then consists of a fully or partially torn off metaphysis (resulting in the 'classical metaphyseal lesion', see Chap. 5). When the fully grown skeleton is subjected to the same forces, it more likely results in damage to the ligaments around the joint.

The presence of larger and more extensive haversian canals make the child's bone more malleable than adult bone. Consequently, immature bone (in particular the shaft of the long bones) can bow instead of break. This means that in children specific types of fracture of the shaft are found that are typical for growing bone. This concerns in particular the so-called incomplete fractures (see also Chap. 5):

- 'Bowing' fractures: in very young children there can be such plastic deformation of the bone that it bows past the point at which, based on the elasticity of the bone, spontaneous recovery is feasible. In these cases, there is no radiologically visible damage in the cortex, neither to the tension nor to the compression side. The fracture will only be visible by the bowing of the diaphyseal segment (Fig. 1.3a and b).
- 'Buckle' fracture or torus fracture (damage to the cortex at the compression side): In axial compression of a bone that has very limited ability to bow, a child can sustain a torus fracture at the shaft-metaphyseal transition (Fig. 1.4). These fractures are stable by nature and when immobilised will heal within 2–3 weeks.
- 'Greenstick' fracture (damage to the cortex at the tension side): this type of fracture can occur when the bone is bowed past the point that spontaneous recovery is possible. It concerns an incomplete fracture on the tension side of the bone and plastic deformation with an intact cortex and intact periosteum at the compression side (Fig. 1.5). In these cases, the force that caused the damage of the cortex on the tension side is insufficient to cause a complete fracture.

In adults, the impact of a comparable amount of energy will cause a fracture as a result of the compression and bowing components, resulting in damage to the cortex on the tension and the compression side, a so-called complete fracture. Complete fractures do occur in children (see Chap. 5). Complete fractures of the shaft can be classified with the aid of the direction of the fracture line in respect to the long or central axis of the bone:

- Transverse, possibly with fragmentation: the fracture line occurs more or less perpendicular to the long or central axis of the bone.
- Oblique: usually the fracture line occurs oblique at an angle of 30–45 degrees in relation to the long or central axis.

Fig. 1.3 (**a**) Bowing fracture of the left radius (*open arrow*) in a little girl with a healing fracture of the distal ulna (*arrow*). For comparison, a view of the healthy right side which shows anatomical alignment. (**b**) Five-year-old girl with unknown trauma. There is a transverse fracture of the distal tibia (*open arrow*) and a bowing fracture of the fibula (*arrow*)

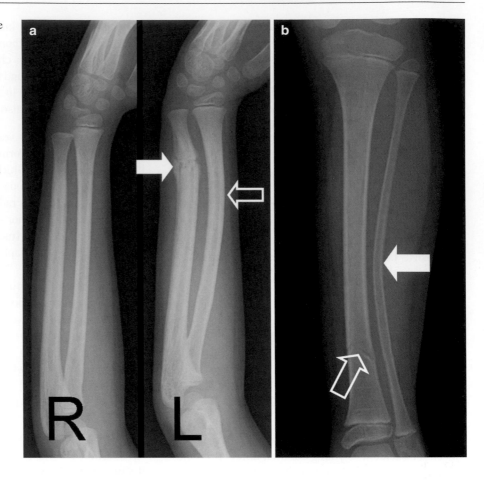

- Spiral: one could say that the fracture circles around the central axis, and the fracture line runs oblique in relation to the central axis.

With conventional radiology, it is not always possible to distinguish between an oblique and a spiral fracture.

1.3.2   The Healing and Remodelling of Fractures

After a fracture, the periosteum stays intact in children more often than in adults, because in children the periosteum is relatively thicker, stronger and more biologically active. When the periosteum stays intact, a continuity of tissue will grow over the location of the fracture. This results in a more stable fracture and reduces the chance of dislocation. Essentially, here the periosteum functions as a natural splint.

Moreover, a child's periosteum has greater potential to form bone than that of an adult. This adds extra stimulus to the healing process, resulting in faster remodelling of fractures in children than in adults. Low-grade deviations in alignment will be corrected faster, and even in gross deviations in alignment excellent remodelling can occur.

1.4   Fractures: Differential Diagnosis

During childhood, fractures are usually the result of accidents [17]. The differential diagnosis, apart from a witnessed fall or accident (as seen by an independent person) or periosteal reactions that resemble a healing fracture, is very comprehensive (Table 1.2). The table does not presume to be complete, but gives an overview of the most prevalent causes as described in the literature.

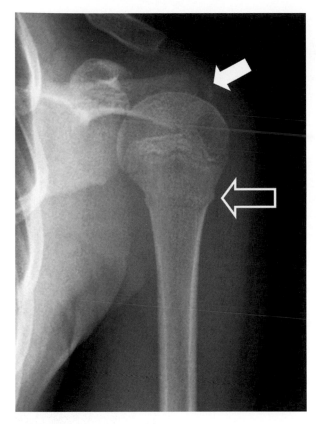

Fig. 1.4 Torus fracture of the proximal part of the left humerus (*open arrow*). Furthermore, in this patient an ossifying nucleus of the acromion can been seen (*arrow*), which is normal for the age of the patient

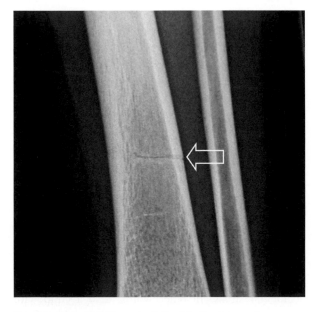

Fig. 1.5 Greenstick fracture of the tibia (*open arrow*)

Table 1.2 Differential diagnostics of fractures and periosteal reactions in childhood [51–53]

Fractures	
Trauma	Birth trauma
	Accidental
	Non-accidental – non-intentional (neglect)
	Non-accidental – intentional (abuse)
Anomalies in collagen forming	Osteogenesis imperfecta
	Copper deficiency
	Menkes syndrome
	Bruck syndrome
Congenital mineral-based defects	Prematurity: metabolic bone disease of prematurity
	Neuromuscular diseases
	Vitamin-D-resistant rickets (or hypophosphatemic rickets)
	X-linked hypophosphatemia
	Liver defects (e.g. Alagille syndrome)
	Malabsorption
	Familial osteoporosis
	Osteopetrosis
	Cole Carpenter syndrome
	Congenital CMV-infection
Acquired mineral-based defects	Vitamin-D-deficiency based on nutritional defects: rickets
	Use of diuretics, glucocorticoids and methotrexate
	Intoxications (e.g. lead)
	Cerebral paresis and spasticity
Other diseases with increased risks	Congenital insensitivity to pain, e.g.:
	• Spina bifida
	• Congenital pain insensitivity
	Stress fractures
Periosteal reactions	
Radiological differential diagnosis not related to fractures	Normal variants:
	• For example, the physiological periosteal thickening of the long bones (femur, tibia, humerus) in neonates and young infants
	Congenital syphilis
	Osteomyelitis
	Septic arthritis
	Osteoid osteoma en other tumours
	Leukaemia
	Vitamin-C-deficiency: scurvy
	Caffey's disease: infantile cortical hyperostosis
	Mucopolysaccharidosis
	Sickle-cell anaemia
	Anomalies related to the use of vitamins
	• Hypervitaminosis A
	• Vitamin-E therapy
	Treatment with prostaglandin E
	Metastases of a neuroblastoma
	Use of intra-osseous vascular access needles

When differentiating between fractures in children it is important to work in a structured manner. Central to the process is taking a detailed history. Furthermore, the age and level of development of the child should be taken into consideration (Chaps. 6 and 7): the younger the child, the more limited his/her mobility, and the more probable that the cause is non-accidental (Sects. 1.4.2 and 1.5). In the differentiation, biomechanical aspects should also be taken into consideration (Chaps. 2–5). Other factors that should be taken into account are the distribution of the fractures over the skeleton and the context in which the fractures were sustained. Table 1.3 provides an aid to make an evaluation and reach a differentiation between the various causes of the fractures.

1.4.1 Spontaneous Fractures: Pathological Fractures?

In the literature terms such as spontaneous and pathological fractures are frequently used (Fig. 1.6). In this context, Torwalt et al. describe a 4-year-old boy with cerebral paresis and palsy after a non-accidental brain injury [18]. The postmortem radiographs of this boy show fractures at various stages of healing in the left humerus and both femurs, tibiae and fibulae. Based on a comprehensive investigation, child abuse, accidents, metabolic diseases, other primary and secondary bone diseases and pathological fractures could be excluded. Torwalt et al. concluded that in this boy the conclusion was spontaneous fractures secondary to osteopenia. They define spontaneous fractures as 'fractures that occur without a clear demonstrable external (= traumatic) cause' [18]. One speaks of a pathological fracture in a clinical sense when, for whatever reason, the bone has been weakened by a disorder [19].

From a clinical point of view, the use of terms such as 'spontaneous' and 'pathological' in relation to the occurrence of fractures is understandable and acceptable. However, the use of these terms as an explanation for the occurrence of a fracture is from a biomechanical point of view an approach that is too limited, and as such incorrect. From a biomechanically point of view, fractures occur primarily when the stress on the bone exceeds its capacity to absorb stress. As a result it

Table 1.3 Evaluation of fractures in young children

Fractures	Type
	Location:
	• Axial of peripheral
	• Symmetric/asymmetric
	• Weight-bearing/non-weight-bearing parts the skeleton
	Number
	Age (known and unknown recent and old fractures)
	Other injuries
Skeleton	Configuration of the bones and the whole skeleton
	Bone density
	Other findings suggesting skeletal lesions, such as 'wormian bones'
Child	Age and level of development
	Underlying pathology
Anamnesis	Plausibility of the anamnesis:
	• Age and level of development
	• Accidental and non-accidental fractures
	• Disease-related fractures versus non-accidental fractures
	• Fracture biomechanics

bows, or even breaks. The type of fracture is determined by factors on the side on which stress is exerted as well as on the side that has the stress-absorbing capacity (see also Chap. 5). 'Spontaneous' and 'pathological' only pertain to the capacity of the bone to absorb stress. Based on its use, one implicitly concludes that even with minimal trauma or during normal care it is possible for weakened bone to sustain a fracture.

From a forensic point of view, the use of either term may lead to apparent certainties when based on these terms one has to differentiate between accidental and non-accidental causes. Hereby the context of the origin of the fracture is totally not taken into consideration. When a fracture is found in a child, the presence of the disorder that results in a decreased capacity to absorb stress (see, e.g. Table 1.2 and Chaps. 6 and 7) says nothing about the stress that can be exerted and the context in which the stress was exerted. The anamnesis and the clinical/radiological symptoms should determine the differentiation between accidental and non-accidental stress. In other words: also a child with proven bone defects can have fractures resulting from child abuse.

Fig. 1.6 (**a**) Five-year-old boy with a pathological fracture of the left radius (see inset) after a fall. (**b**) T2-weighted MRI of the radius shows a fluid-fluid level (*open arrow*), corresponding with an aneurysmal bone cyst. The diagnosis was histologically confirmed

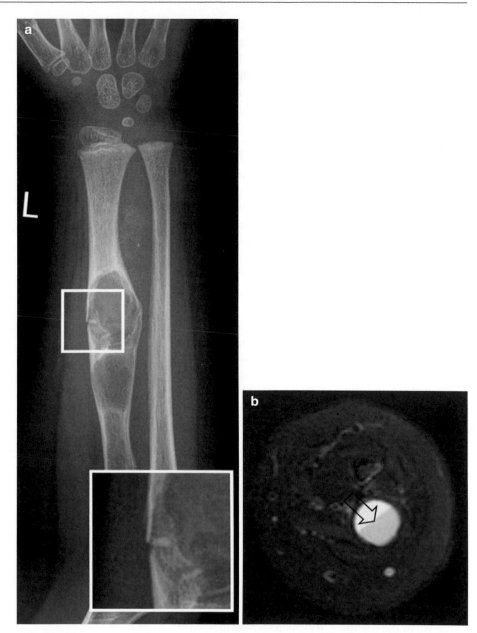

1.4.2 Cause of Fractures in Relation to Age and Level of Development

Between the ages of 1 and 4 years and in older children (>10 years), an accident is the most common cause of fractures [17]. In the group of children of 1–4 years, fractures of the upper extremities and the clavicle are most common, due to the reflex of the child to catch oneself on the stretched arm when falling. In children over 10 years of age, the number of traffic accidents will be higher than in younger children. Only rarely will one find fractures resulting from accidents in children of less than 1 year of age [20]. When a child grows up, it will become more mobile and enterprising, and the risk for accidental injury increases [21].

1.5 Fractures in Child Abuse

Rang poses that as many as 25% of fractures in children of less than 3 years of age will result from child abuse and/or neglect [17]. Fractures resulting from child abuse occur predominantly in children of less than 1 year of age [22]. Based on various studies, it is estimated that 50–69% of all fractures in children of less than 1 year old are the result of child abuse [23, 24]. It was also shown that children in this age group are at a high risk of being abused again, even after an intervention took place [25].

Unfortunately, it appears that in these young, often non-mobile, children fractures will often show hardly any clinically conspicuous symptoms such as swelling, redness of even a pseudoparesis, they may even have an occult course [26–28].

However, in young children child abuse remains not only unnoticed due to its occult course, but also because violence as a possible cause is not or inadequately considered, or is rejected on non-plausible grounds [29].

Between 1995 and 1999, Banaszkiewicz et al. carried out a retrospective study in all children under the age of 1 year which were brought into the emergency department of their hospital due to sustained fractures. The data of 74 children in total were re-evaluated. The average age of the children was 5 months (2 weeks to 1 year). Forty-six children had sustained a skull fracture. In 28 children there was a fracture of the long bones. After analysis, it appeared that the attending physician failed to assess possible child abuse correctly in nearly 30% of these children. In nearly 50% of children, the medical data did not show that child abuse had even been considered, whereas in retrospect child abuse would have been a plausible explanation in the differential diagnosis.

Oral et al. carried out a similar retrospective dossier study in 653 children of 3 years and younger who presented with a fracture over the period 1995–1999 [30]. The aim of their study was to establish whether in this group of children physicians inquired sufficiently into the cause of the fractures. Revision showed that, based on the data in the dossier, in 42% of children it had not been possible to exclude child abuse as the cause of the fracture. The missing data concerned:

- Information on the presence of (independent) eye witnesses at the moment the fracture was sustained.
- Information on previous injuries.
- Revision of previous medical data.
- Description of associated injuries.
- An evaluation to see whether the reason provided and the injury of the child could be explained when taking into account the level of development of the child.

Consequently, Oral distinguished four groups:

- Accidental injury (63%)
- Non-accidental injury ('inflicted injury') (13%)
- Missed non-accidental injury (23%)
- Missed accidental injury (0.6%)

Factors that had a positive influence on identifying child abuse were:

- The age of the child
- Multiple fractures
- Examination by a paediatrician

Fractures have been described in 55% of young children who had been victims of physical abuse [31, 32]. Non-accidental fractures in children indicate the use of severe violence, which emphasises the importance of identification. It is not always easy to differentiate between accidental and non-accidental fractures; however, it is crucial for a responsible intervention [33]. In a systematic review of the literature by Kemp et al., the predictive value of fractures as a sign of child abuse has been evaluated. Other indications, such the child's age or the injury that could lead to suspected child abuse were not taken into account. After a selection was made from 439 publications, 32 were analysed [34]. Based on this systematic analysis, they concluded amongst others that rib fractures had the strongest correlation with child abuse; in 71% of cases (95% CI 42–91%) with rib fractures it was a case of child abuse. They also found that none of the fractures were pathognomonic for child abuse.

As such, the skeletal lesions found in child abuse may be similar to lesions found after an accident. Whether a fracture results from child abuse is determined by a combination of:

- The type of fracture
- The age and level of development of the child (see Table 7.3)
- The manner in which the fracture was sustained (according to known data)
- The statement of the child, the parents or the care-givers regarding the origin of the fracture

When the above-mentioned combination shows discrepancies between the combined first three factors and the last one, the statement of the parents, child abuse is probable.

Radiological dating of fractures and performing the correct radiological examination are eminently important for an adequate diagnosis and protection at the moment that child abuse is suspected. Fractures as a result of violence can be found throughout the entire skeleton, are often present in multiple places, and may show various stages of healing on skeletal radiographs [20, 24, 35, 36]. Since in cases of child abuse it often happens that there is a delay in seeking medical help, dating may be complicated by further loading of the fracture by movement, additional injuries and renewed fractures. The more or less objective radiological dating (see Chap. 9) can spot inconsistencies regarding subjective anamnestic dating and the explanation of the injury [37].

1.5.1 Specificity of Fractures in Child Abuse

According to Kleinman, child abuse should always be considered in the following fractures or bone anomalies [38]:

- Periosteal reactions of the bone and newly formed bone
- Metaphyseal injuries
- Injuries to the growth plate
- Fractures of the diaphysis
- Dislocations

Hobbs mentions the following fractures as suspect [39]:

- Multiple and complicated skull fractures with a fracture width >3 mm
- Injuries to the epiphysis and metaphysis
- Fractures of ribs, scapulae and sternum
- Multiple fractures

In his opinion these fractures are more suspect than simple, uncomplicated fractures, shaft fractures of the long bones and fractures of the clavicle. Furthermore, Hobbs further maintains that fractures are more suspect when they occur together with other injuries; for example: a simple fracture (such as of the humerus) combined with multiple unexplained haematomas.

Child abuse should be considered in case of [40]:

- Multiple fractures in various stages of healing, even when no associated trauma is present, such as haematomas and (sub)cutaneous injuries.

Table 1.4 Specificity of skeletal injuries in child abuse, highest specificity applies in infants (Reprinted from [54]. With permission)

Specificity	Type of fracture/skeletal lesion
High specificity	Classic metaphyseal lesion
	Rib fractures, especially posterior
	Scapular fractures
	Spinous processes fractures
	Sternal fractures
Moderate specificity	Multiple fractures, specifically bilateral
	Fractures of different ages
	Epiphyseal separation
	Vertebral body fractures and subluxations
	Digital fractures
	Complex skull fractures
Common but low specificity	Subperiosteal new-bone formation
	Clavicular fractures
	Long bone shaft fractures
	Linear skull fractures

- Damage to the epiphysis and metaphysis, possibly multiple as in the inflicted traumatic brain injury formerly known as 'Shaken baby' syndrome.
- (A) single or multiple rib fracture(s).
- The presence of periosteal new-bone formation.
- A skull fracture, with or without signs of intracranial trauma.

Kleinman presents the following overview on the specificity of radiological findings regarding child abuse (see Table 1.4). He poses that it is likely for child abuse to be the cause when in lesions of average or low specificity there is no explanation for the cause of the trauma or when the explanation does not correspond with the nature of the trauma.

1.5.2 The Value of Haematomas in Differential Diagnosis

The little that is known about the presence of haematomas in relation to fractures in children has been learned through the fractures that resulted from child abuse. This leads to the perception that haematomas are sustained at the same time as fractures: the force required to cause a fracture will in all likelihood also result in haematomas. The reverse of this reasoning is that a lack of haematomas is proof that it took only very little force to break the bone and, as such, that the fracture results from a metabolic illness or from osteogenesis imperfecta [41–43]. Mathew et al. did a prospective study into the presence of haematomas around the location of the fracture in 88 children that showed no signs of bone pathology and found in total 93 fractures (49 boys, 39 girls; age 12 months to 13 years and 11 months) [44]. All children were seen within 24 h after the fracture had been sustained. Only in eight fractures haematomas were found in the initial phase. No haematomas were found in fractures that showed no dislocation or in fractures that were well covered by soft tissue. In 13 other fractures, haematomas appeared within 24 h after hospitalisation. Ultimately, 25 (28%) fractures were accompanied by haematomas 1 week after the fracture was sustained. According to Mathew et al., based on the lack of haematomas it is impossible to distinguish between fractures that are the result of bone disease and fractures resulting from child abuse. It appears that in acutely sustained fractures in children, local haematomas are less common than one would expect; however, based on the absence of haematomas, child abuse should not be excluded.

Starling et al. also did not find any relation between fractures and the presence of haematomas. After skull fractures had been excluded, it appeared that in less than 10% of children had fracture-related haematomas [45].

1.5.3 Characteristics of the Anamnesis

Most physicians will be able to identify children as victims of child abuse when they fall into the most severe clinical category of child abuse, such as young non-mobile children that sustained multiple fractures without identifiable cause. The problems arise mainly in children that sustained less severe trauma and have less obvious symptoms. To this category belong children that have just one fracture and no clear story of child abuse [46].

1.5.3.1 Anamnesis in Children

In child abuse the child is often not able to explain how the injuries were sustained. This applies in particular to children in a life-threatening situation. Such a situation makes conversation with the child (virtually) impossible. Besides, many children with serious

trauma resulting from child abuse are preverbal. When children are able to relate the situation, there is a fair chance that they will keep silent out of loyalty to the parents or out of fear for the perpetrator.

1.5.3.2 Patient History

When child abuse is suspected, it is important to pay attention to the patient history of the child and the other family members. In case of child abuse it is possible that the child has sustained (multiple) previous trauma and has prior hospitalisations. Various studies have shown that approximately 50% of all children in which child abuse was established had been seen by a physician for (in retrospect suspect) injuries [32]. Also, an abused child who returns to a non-safe home setting has a 30–50% chance to suffer additional trauma and an increased risk for lethal violence (up to10%) [47].

Very regularly earlier trauma and hospitalisation are seen in other members of the family, such as the other parent, other children or between siblings. This may proof that the violence is also directed at them. When compared to other men, it appears that men who maltreat their wife will frequently also maltreat their children. Women who were abused by their husband appeared to be twice as likely to maltreat their children compared to non-abused women. Seventy-six percent of the physically abused children allegedly used violence against a sibling [48].

1.5.3.3 The Origin of the Injuries

When a child makes a direct and spontaneous statement on how the injury was sustained, he or she will most likely tell the truth. This also applies to a witness that makes a statement regarding the origin of the injury. Yet, the statement of the witness should be closely examined, since the person will speak from his/her own set of values. On the one hand, the witness may play down what has been observed, on the other hand, it may be exaggerated. Also, the witness may serve his or her own self-interest by giving the statement.

The following items should be considered during the anamnesis:

- While the anamnesis is taken, there may be contradictions between the statements of: the child and the parent(s), between both the parents, or between parents and witness. Sometimes no explanation is given, since allegedly no witness was present.

- Also, the statements may constantly vary, when further prompted or when taken on consecutive days.
- Parents may give different statements to different people, or withdraw statements.
- Sometimes when the child is given a physical or radiological examination, previous injuries are found for which the parents are not able to give an adequate explanation.
- The statement may be in contradiction with the level of development of the child.
- The nature and/or location of the injury may be in contrast with the statement of the parents.
- The parents' statement only explains part of the injuries.
- According to the statement, the child himself/herself or one of the siblings is responsible for the injury.

1.5.3.4 Seeking Medical Help

In child abuse, one of the main characteristics of the anamnesis is that medical treatment was only sought at a late stage. The latency period can vary from hours to days after the injury was sustained. This is due to various reasons: shame, wrongly evaluated situation, hope for spontaneous recovery, and hope that the injury will no longer be recognisable as resulting from child abuse. Also, other persons besides the parent(s) may seek help, such as the grandparents or a teacher. Finally, help may be sought from others than their own general practitioner or paediatrician, without providing an plausible reason. Often this help is sought at odd times, such as during the evening.

1.5.3.5 Attitude and Reaction of the Parents

The contradiction between the severity of the injury and the reaction of the parent may have to the injury can be conspicuous. They may totally overreact to a minor injury. On the other hand, the caregiver may have hardly any or a very inadequate (remote, indifferent) reaction to (very severe) injuries. A parent who maltreats may completely overreact and sometimes react aggressively to innocent questions. For that matter, the non-maltreating parent may react in a similar manner. When child abuse is brought into the conversation, the parent may threaten to deny the child medical care.

When a physician wants to speak to the parents about a specific injury, he should be aware of a number of matters. It does not take long for parents to realise that the physician doubts their statement and may suspect child abuse. This applies to parents who maltreat as well as to parents who do not maltreat. This may cause the parents to take a defensive attitude directly at the start of the interview. The reactions may vary from denial and a tendency to isolation and then proceed via anger, bargaining and resignation to acceptance. Also, the physician will have to be aware that the parent to whom he speaks may be ignorant of the maltreating behaviour of the partner.

1.5.4 Perpetrators and Victims

Starling et al. were the first to initiate a study into the specific characteristics of perpetrators who cause fractures in children [45]. They evaluated the data of 194 children (age: 0–13.9 years; median 6 months) with in total 630 fractures. The median number of fractures per patient was 2 and the maximum was 31. In 153 children (79%) the perpetrator could be identified. Nearly 68% of perpetrators were male. Of all known perpetrators, 45% appeared to be the biological father.

Furthermore, there appeared to be a significant difference ($p=0.003$) between the median age of the children who had been abused by a male (4.5 months) and by a female perpetrator (10 months). In 44 of the 194 children, the primary injury was non-accidental skull-/brain trauma. Since it is not known whether the age of victims of non-accidental skull-/brain trauma differs from that of children with other non-accidental fractures, further study was done after the children with non-accidental skull/brain trauma were excluded. However, this analysis still showed a significant difference ($p=0.004$) between the median age of children abused by a male (5 months) or a female perpetrator (12 months).

1.6 The Role of the Radiologist When Child Abuse Is Suspected

It is essential that the radiologist who evaluates the characteristics of the fracture(s) has sufficient knowledge of the clinical history of the patient. Collaboration with other specialists (such as paediatricians or forensic physicians) has added value for the evaluation. In order to determine whether a fracture results from child abuse, the radiologist will need to reconstruct the reported trauma and evaluate the plausibility of the statement [49].

The radiologist will be expected to be able to [50]:

- Detect the radiological anomaly that suggests child abuse in suspect as well as in non-suspect cases.
- Distinguish between radiological abnormalities suspect for child abuse and other pathologies and normal variants.
- Evaluate whether the fracture and the underlying trauma mechanism are compatible with the statement of the child and/or parents regarding its origin.
- Date fractures within the limitations of scientific knowledge.

Finally, one could argue that the radiologist involved should support the Public Prosecutor in securing that justice takes its course.

1.7 Ethical Dilemmas in Suspicion of Child Abuse

In view of the potentially serious consequences of physical violence, it is important that child abuse is identified at an early stage. However, it is equally important to prevent that child abuse is diagnosed wrongly or on false grounds:

- Because an accident or disorder is seen as the most plausible or even only explanation for the found anomalies. This may lead to disruption of the family as a result of incorrectly applied measures of child protection or unjust legal prosecution of the parents.
- Because there is a coincidence of, on the one hand, the conclusion that an accident is the most plausible or even only cause of the injury that was found and, on the other hand, child abuse as the most plausible reason for other injuries or the behaviour of the child. In these cases, there is a risk that giving a plausible reason for the skeletal abnormalities may lead to the exclusion, on unjust grounds, of child abuse as plausible reason for the other abnormalities or the behaviour of the child. Consequently, the child will not be protected against a recurrence of the child abuse that is present.

References

1. World Health Organization. Child maltreatment. http://www.who.int/topics/child_abuse/en/
2. Laming H. The Victoria Climbié inquiry. http://www.victoria-climbie-inquiry.org.uk/
3. Coulter K (2000) Bruising and skin trauma. Pediatr Rev 21(1):34–5
4. Nobuyasu S. Cost and benefit simulation analysis of catastrophic maltreatment. In Franey K, Geffner R, Falconer R eds. The cost of child maltreatment: Who pays? We all do. Family Violence & Sexual Assault Institute, 2001
5. Stephenson T (1995) Bruising in children. Curr Paediatr 5:225–9
6. McCurdy, 1993 cited from Nobuyasu S. Cost and benefit simulation analysis of catastrophic maltreatment In Franey K, Geffner R, Falconer R eds. The cost of child maltreatment: Who pays? We all do. Family Violence & Sexual Assault Institute, 2001
7. McMahon P, Grossman W, Gaffney M et al (1995) Soft tissue injury as an indication of child abuse. J Bone Joint Surg 77(8):1179–83
8. Cramer KE (1996) Orthopedic aspects of child abuse. Pediatr Clin North Am 43(5):1035–51
9. Sinal SH, Stewart CD (1998) Physical abuse of children: a review for orthopedic surgeons. J South Orthop Assoc 7(4): 264–76
10. Holter JC, Friedman SB (1968) Child Abuse: early case finding in the emergency department. Pediatrics 42(1): 128–38
11. Hyden PW, Gallagher TA (1992) Child abuse intervention in the emergency room. Pediatr Clin North Am 39(5):1053–81
12. Lucas DR, Wezner KC, Milner JS et al (2002) Victim, perpetrator, family, and incident characteristics of infant and child homicide in the United States Air Force. Child Abuse Negl 26(2):167–86
13. Landin LA (1983) Fracture patterns in children. Analysis of 8, 682 fractures with special reference to incidence, etiology and secular changes in a Swedish urban population 1950–1979. Acta Orthop Scand Suppl 202:1–109
14. Landin LA (1997) Epidemiology of children's fractures. J Pediatr Orthop B 6(2):79–83
15. Worlock P, Stower M (1986) Fracture patterns in Nottingham children. J Pediatr Orthop 6(6):656–60
16. Wilkins KE, Aroojis AJ. The present status of children's fractures. In Beaty JH, Kasser JM eds. Rockwood and Wilkins' Fractures in children. Lippincott Williams & Wilkins, 5th ed, 2001, 3–20
17. Rang M, Willis RB (1977) Fractures and sprains. Pediatr Clin North Am 24(4):749–73
18. Torwalt CR, Balachandra AT, Youngson C et al (2002) Spontaneous fractures in the differential diagnosis of fractures in children. J Forensic Sci 47(6):1340–4
19. MacAusland WR. Sprains, fractures, dislocations. In Nardi GL, Zuidema GD eds. Surgery, a concise guide to clinical practice. Little Brown, 3rd ed, 1972, 945
20. Worlock P, Stower M, Barbor P (1986) Patterns of fractures in accidental and non-accidental injuries in children: a comparative study. Br Med J 12(6539):100–2
21. Lyons RA, Delahunty AM, Kraus D et al (1999) Children's fractures: a population based study. Inj Prev 5(2):129–32

22. Akbarnia B, Torg JS, Kirkpatrick J et al (1974) Manifestations of the battered child syndrome. J Bone Joint Surg 56(6): 1159–66

23. King J, Diefendorf D, Apthorp J et al (1988) Analysis of 429 fractures in 189 battered children. J Pediatr Orthop 8(5): 585–9

24. Leventhal JM, Thomas SA, Rosenfield NS et al (1993) Fractures in young children. Distinguishing child abuse from unintentional injuries. Am J Dis Child 147(1):87–92

25. Skellern CY, Wood DO, Murphy A et al (2000) Non-accidental fractures in infants: risk of further abuse. J Paediatr Child Health 36(6):590–2

26. Barsness KA, Cha ES, Bensard DD et al (2003) The positive predictive value of rib fractures as an indicator of nonacci-dental trauma in children. J Trauma 54(6):1107–10

27. Merten DF, Radlowski MA, Leonidas JC (1983) The abused child: a radiological reappraisal. Radiology 146(2):377–81

28. Cadzow SP, Armstrong KL (2000) Rib fractures in infants: Red alert! The clinical features, investigations and child pro-tection outcomes. J Paediatr Child Health 36(4):322–6

29. Banaszkiewicz PA, Scotland TR, Myerscough EJ (2002) Fractures in children younger than age 1 year: importance of collaboration with child protection services. J Pediatr Orthop 22(6):740–4

30. Oral R, Blum KL, Johnson C (2003) Fractures in young chil-dren: are physicians in the emergency department and ortho-pedic clinics adequately screening for possible abuse? Pediatr Emerg Care 19(3):148–53

31. Kogutt MS, Swischuk LE, Fagan CJ (1974) Patterns of injury and significance of uncommon fractures in the bat-tered child syndrome. Am J Roentgenol Radium Ther Nucl Med 121(1):143–9

32. Loder RT, Bookout C (1991) Fracture patterns in battered children. J Orthop Trauma 5(4):428–33

33. Taitz J, Moran K, O'Meara M (2004) Long bone fractures in children under 3 years of age: Is abuse being missed in Emergency Department presentations? J Pediatr Child Health 40(4):170–4

34. Kemp AM, Dustan F, Harrison S et al (2008) Patterns of skeletal fractures in child abuse: systematic review. Br Med J 337:a1518

35. Duhaime AC, Alario AJ, Lewander WJ et al (1992) Head injury in very young children: mechanisms, injury types, and ophthalmologic findings in 100 hospitalized patients younger than 2 years of age. Pediatrics 90(2 Pt 1):179–85

36. Jeerathanyasakun Y, Hiranyavanitch P, Bhummichitra D et al (2003) Causes of femoral shaft fracture in children under five years of age. J Med Assoc Thai 86(Suppl 3): S661–6

37. Kleinman P, Blackbourne B, Marks S et al (1989) Radiologic contributions to the investigation and prosecution of cases of fatal infant abuse. N Engl J Med 320(8):507–11

38. Kleinman PK. Diagnostic imaging of child abuse. Williams & Wilkins, 1987

39. Hobbs C. Fractures. In: Meadow R ed. ABC of child abuse. Br Med J, 3rd ed., 1997,9–13

40. Hobbs CJ, Hanks HGI, Wynne JM. Child abuse and neglect – a clinician's handbook. Churchill Livingstone, 1993, 57–65

41. Paterson CR (1987) Child abuse or copper deficiency? Br Med J 295:213

42. Taitz LS (1991) Child abuse and metabolic bone disease: are they often confused? Br Med J 302(6787):1244

43. Taitz LS. Child abuse: some myths and shibboleths. Hospital Update 1991:400–4

44. Mathew MO, Ramamohan N, Bennet GC (1998) Importance of bruising associated with paediatric fractures: prospective observational study. Br Med J 317(7166):1117–8

45. Starling SP, Sirotnak AP, Heisler KW et al (2007) Inflicted skeletal trauma: the relationship of perpetrators to their vic-tims. Child Abuse Negl 31(9):993–9

46. Kocher MS, Kasser JR (2000) Orthopaedic aspects of child abuse. J Am Acad Orthop Surg 8(1):10–20

47. McClain PW, Sacks JJ, Froehlke RG et al (1993) Estimates of fatal child abuse and neglect, United States, 1979 through 1988. Pediatrics 91(2):338–43

48. Baartman HEM. Opvoeden met alle geweld - hardnekkige gewoontes en hardhandige opvoeders. SWP uitgeverij, 1993, 28–9

49. Pierce MC, Bertocci GE (2006) Fractures resulting from inflicted trauma: assessing injury and history compatibility. Clin Ped Emerg Med 7(3):143–8

50. Van Rijn RR, Nijs HGT, Bilo RAC. Evidence based imaging in non-CNS non-accidental injury in Evidence-Based Imaging in Pediatrics Eds. Medina LS, Blackmore CC and Applegate KE Springer (In press)

51. Society for Pediatric Radiology. Critical review of 'tempo-rary brittle bone disease'. 2004

52. Altman DH, Smith RL. Unrecognized trauma in infants and children. J Bone Joint Surg Am 1960;42-A:407–13

53. O'Neill JA Jr, Meacham WF, Griffin PP et al (1973) Patterns of injury in the battered child syndrome. J Trauma 13(4):332–9

54. Kleinman PK. Skelet trauma: general considerations. In Kleinman PK. Diagnostic imaging of child abuse. Mosby, 2nd ed, 1998, 8–25

Head

2.1 Introduction

Young children regularly fall, and quite often they fall on their head. It is unknown how often this results in a skull fracture, since it is rarely indicated to perform a diagnostic examination, such as a radiograph or a CT scan. When there are no neurological symptoms, a radiograph of the skull is not clinically indicated (see Sect. 2.5). However, from a forensic point of view, a radiograph of the skull is indicated – especially when the child is less than 1 year old. This also applies when there are no neurological symptoms (see Sect. 2.6), even though a normal X-ray of the skull does not exclude intracranial injury.

A skull fracture seen during an operation or autopsy is not necessarily visible on a radiograph [1]. In 16 children with an epidural haemorrhage and a skull fracture, the skull fracture was radiologically visible in 10 children, in four children it was seen during operation and in two during autopsy [2].

2.2 Signs, Symptoms and Complications

Due to the lack of clinical symptoms or complications, the majority of skull fractures have little or no clinical consequences. A skull fracture is suspected based on the anamnesis or the physical examination. Older children may complain of a localised headache. Physical examination may reveal local swelling, a haematoma, a palpable fracture or indications for a basilar skull fracture.

Skull fractures do have indicative value: their presence implies that considerable force has been exerted on the skull [3]. However, it does not always mean that underlying structures such as dura, bridging veins or brain have been damaged (see Sect. 2.5).

The injury most often seen on skull radiographs of young children after a trauma is a fracture of the calvaria [4]. The incidence of skull fractures in children that present at the emergency department for a skull trauma ranges from 2% to 20% [5]. Most frequently it concerns a fracture of the parietal bone, followed by the occipital, frontal and temporal bones. Generally, it is a linear fracture without dislocation, followed by depressed fractures and basilar skull fractures. In principle, skull fractures of the calvaria do not cause any harm, unless they are accompanied by fragmentation causing bone-splinter damage to brain tissue. A possible complication of a skull fracture is a 'growing skull fracture'. This occurs when the dura is imbedded in the fracture and as such prevents healing (see Sect. 2.7).

2.3 Biomechanical Aspects of Fractures of the Cranium

Accidental and non-accidental craniocerebral trauma is the result of two kinds of impacting force: 'static' and 'dynamic' (or rapid) loading [6, 7]. In both types of fracture the skull changes shape, this applies to children as well as to adults. This book only discusses the effects of static and dynamic loading on the skull, and not the effects on the brain.

2.3.1 Static Loading

Static loading is a relatively slow impact of forces exerted on the skull over a protracted period of time

R. A. C. Bilo et al., *Forensic Aspects of Pediatric Fractures,*
DOI: 10.1007/978-3-540-78716-7_2, © Springer-Verlag Berlin Heidelberg 2010

(>200 ms). This occurs when the skull is squeezed and compressed, which may lead to multiple fractures. The results of static loading can be focal and diffuse. It may lead to a linear fracture restricted to one skull bone (focal), but often there are multiple fractures (diffuse). Static loading may occur during, for example, childbirth or traffic accidents, when the head is wedged for a period of time.

2.3.2 Dynamic Loading

Dynamic (or rapid) loading is the impact of forces over a shorter period (<200 ms, often even less than 50 ms). Dynamic loading can be subdivided into 'impulse' and 'impact' loading.

Impulse loading is the result of fast movements of the head, without impact (acceleration – deceleration). This does not lead to skull fractures.

When there are skull fractures in dynamic loading, they are always due to impact loading (= contact = cranial collision) [7]: blunt or penetrating trauma directly on the skull.

There are three possible situations:

- Head stationary – Object moves
- Head moves – Object stationary
- Head moves – Object moves

When head and object both move, there are again three options: both move in the same direction, they move in opposite directions, or the impact is oblique. The contact results in the head changing shape and there is (or may be) damage to the skull (including the scalp) and/or the object.

2.3.3 Possible Injuries from Dynamic Impact Loading

Dynamic impact loading may lead to the following injuries (in order of occurrence)

- Damage to the scalp
- Skull fractures
- Intracranial damage (contusions, epidural/subdural/subarachnoid haemorrhages, intracranial haemorrhages, axonal injuries).

2.3.3.1 Damage to the Scalp

In dynamic loading, damage to one or all layers of the scalp (epidermis, dermis, galea aponeurotica and periosteum of the skull) is always the result of impact loading. The skin may remain intact, in spite of damage to the deeper layers. Sometimes the deeper damage to the scalp is only found at autopsy of the deceased child [8].

Injuries that may be found are: haematomas, contusions, excoriations and lacerations of the (epi)dermis, subgaleal haemorrhages or a haematoma of the skull. Particularly in children, lacerations may be an important cause of blood loss. They are a potential point of entry for infection, especially with an associated skull fracture [9].

2.3.3.2 Skull Fractures

Compared to a child's skull, the adult skull is fairly rigid. The adult skull can cope with some deformation; however, when the deformation exceeds a certain point, no recovery is possible and a fracture will occur. Postmortem research has shown that the adult skull can be indented a few centimetres before it resumes its original shape with or without fracture [10, 11]. This may lead to considerable damage of the underlying tissue.

A child's skull is made of thin and malleable bone tissue and does not have the rigidity and strength of the adult skull. Moreover, the skull bones of a child are separated by sutures that have not been fused yet. According to Lancon et al., this makes the child's skull relatively resistant to fractures. In their opinion it takes a significant trauma [8]. However, the question is whether this position is correct. Weber maintains that a number of sites on the immature skull have increased susceptibility to fractures [12]; this applies in particular to the parietal bone in infants.

In relation to the adult skull, these specific properties of the infantile skull enable it to tolerate greater deformation before it breaks. This deformation may even lead to a depression of the cranium without incurring a fracture (the so-called ping-pong deformation of the skull = 'celluloid fracture', see Sect. 2.4.3.2).

The degree of deformation of the skull at the moment that the fracture is sustained and the nature and size of the fracture and the associated injury will depend on a number of factors (see [13]).

- Trauma-related
  - Location of contact
  - The force of the impact at the moment of contact
- Anatomy-related
  - The scalp
  - The age of the child
  - Shape, build, thickness and malleability of the skull at the point of impact and other sites

2.3.3.3 Trauma-Related Factors

The Location of the Contact Trauma

The location of the contact trauma determines only to a certain extent the location, nature and extent of the skull fracture.

Damage to the scalp is an important indicator for the primary site of impact. For this reason, a precise registration of external injuries is always required, in particular when physical violence is suspected. In 80% of children with a skull fracture external injury is found that indicates a skull trauma. In 84% of children fractures were found ipsilateral and in 16% contralateral from the point of impact [2]. However, the absence of external injuries does not exclude a skull fracture.

A study of adults that had sustained a skull fracture showed that, depending on the place of impact, different types of skull fracture can result from equal amounts of energy. It is not clear whether this can also be applied to children and, if so, whether this is the same for every age group.

A contact trauma on top of the cranium will usually lead to a cranial fracture that may carry on into the temporal region or the base of the skull. A blow to the occipital region will usually lead to a linear fracture in the posterior cranial fossa. A blow to the temporoparietal region may cause a fracture that runs through the temporal bone to the base of the skull. A blow to the forehead causes a fracture that may run into the orbit and even into the maxilla [14].

Force of Impact at the Moment of Contact

The amount of energy released at contact is determined by four elements (see also Sect. 2.6.3):

- The shape, weight and nature of the object. It may be a solid object that will not give way during contact (such as a hammer, concrete floor or stone) or a more or less soft object with a surface that gives way at contact (such as a mattress or a floor covered with thick soft carpet). In soft and yielding objects, the deformation of the surface will absorb a large part of the energy released at contact. Yet, the literature has shown that a child falling on a soft surface can also sustain a fracture [12]. In a solid non-giving surface hardly any energy is carried over to the object.
- The velocity resulting from the speed of the head and the object at the moment of impact.
- A fixed or free-moving head. When the head can move freely, it will move along in the same direction as the object. In this manner, part of the energy at impact is absorbed by the movement.
- The size of the contact surface. If contact takes place on a limited surface, all energy released at contact will be concentrated at this surface. If the site of impact is larger, the energy will spread itself over this surface.

2.3.3.4 Anatomy-Related Factors

The Scalp

The skull is covered by five layers: skin, subcutaneous fatty tissue, the epicranial muscles, subepicranial connective tissue and the pericranium. Tedeschi showed that when force is exerted on the skull, the skin will protect it against fractures. Compared to when the skin is present, the risk for a fracture increases tenfold when no skin is present [15].

The Age of the Child

In a short-distance fall, children with open sutures and a thinner albeit more malleable skull will generally sustain a fracture less often than older children with closed sutures and a more rigid skull. Yet, children up to 1 year old can sustain a skull fracture in a relatively small trauma, in spite of the substantial malleability of their skull (see Sect. 2.6.3). However, this will only rarely lead to serious intracranial injury. Life-threatening intracranial injury has even never been reported (see also Chap. 6).

Shape, Build and Thickness of the Skull

The cranium is constructed of two layers of bone with a sponge-like structure in between (diploid). The inner layer of compact bone is the most vulnerable. On impact this layer may be damaged, whereas the outer layer does not suffer any damage. When the impact generates enough energy, the outer layer will fracture too and this may result in loose bone fragments (Fig. 2.1). Young children do not have a diploid structure of the parietal bone, leading to an increased risk for sustaining a fracture in this bone in a short-distance fall [12].

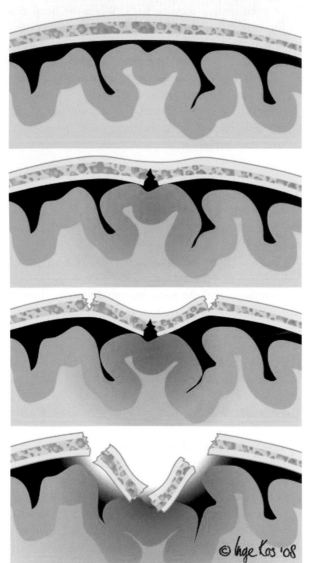

Fig. 2.1 Schematic representation of the various stages of skull fractures in contact injuries

2.4 Types of Skull Fracture

The type of fracture that the skull sustains depends mainly on the same trauma and anatomy-related factors that determine whether dynamic impact loading will result in a fracture [16]. Skull fractures can be categorised into: linear, complex and depression fractures.

The most prevalent type of fracture of the cranium is the linear fracture (Sect. 2.4.1). Here a single linear pattern can be seen. This type of fracture is usually restricted to one skull bone. Linear fractures may be present bilaterally and symmetrically.

Complex fractures show multiple fracture lines and inter-connecting fractures (Sect. 2.4.2).

In depression fractures, parts of the outer surface of the skull bone are displaced inwards over at least the thickness of the sponge-like bone layer (Sect. 2.4.3). A different kind of depression fracture is the ping-pong skull deformation in young children.

In all types, a comminuted skull fracture can be sustained when there is an associated laceration of the skin. In penetrating injuries there is not only a skull fracture, but also a laceration of the skin and injury to the dura. This results in a skull fracture that has an open connection between external and intracranial environment, presenting a considerable risk for infection.

Also, every type of fracture may potentially develop into a 'growing fracture' (see Sect. 2.7).

2.4.1 Linear Fractures

2.4.1.1 Simple Linear Fractures

Of all skull fractures in children, 74–90% are simple linear fractures (Fig. 2.2a and b) [17]. Such a fracture results from contact with a large flat object, in which the impact of a blunt trauma spreads over a large area. For example, the fall from the arm of a parent/carer that results in the head of the child banging into the floor [18]. This is a typical example of 'low velocity' impact [13].

When the head connects with an object with a large flat surface, the skull curvature flattens under the influence of the contact. The skull surface bows inwards, whereas the surrounding area bows outwards in a wave-like manner (Fig. 2.3) [14, 18]. The outward

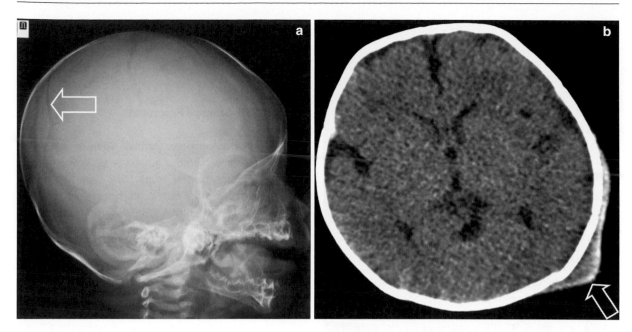

Fig. 2.2 (**a**) Two-month-old baby who, according to the anamnesis, had fallen from the arms of his 7-year-old sister. The fall had not been witnessed. The lateral view of the skull shows a parietal linear fracture (*open arrows*). (**b**) Additional CT in this patient shows post-traumatic soft-tissue swelling (*open arrow*) but no intracranial pathology

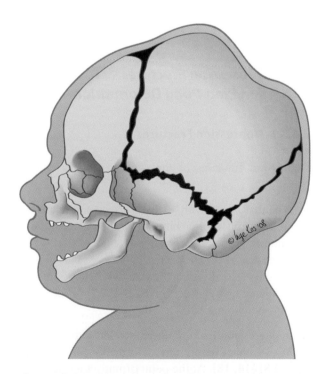

Fig. 2.3 Schematic representation of the wave pattern of skull deformation after contact with a relatively large surface. At the impact site there is inward deformation whereas peripherally the skull bows outwards

bowing of the skull may occur at a relatively large distance of the primary site of contact. Hence, the location of a linear fracture does not have to correspond with the place of contact [19]. After the skull has been deformed by the impact, it will try to resume its normal shape. At the moment that the inwardly bowed part resumes its normal shape, the fracture will spread from its original location into the direction of the place of impact as well as into the opposite direction. This may result in a fracture line that reaches the original place of contact or extents even further [13].

Although linear fractures are usually confined to one skull bone, it is possible that the fracture extents into the adjacent skull bone (Figs. 2.4 and 2.5a–d). In most linear fractures, external injuries are found, such as swelling of the overlying tissues or a haematoma. Sometimes a subgaleal haematoma is seen. The extent of the subgaleal haematoma may be such that it leads to anaemia [20].

In approximately 15–30% of linear fractures intracranial injury is found [5] (see Sect. 2.5). Linear fractures tend to show diastasis (see Sect. 2.7). However, in most patients linear fractures heal without any problems (also see Sect. 2.7).

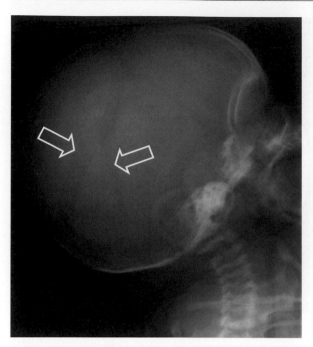

Fig. 2.4 Six-week-old neonate who presented at the emergency department for haematemesis. Since the laboratory values were not deviant, the patient was sent home. Four days later the infant was back at the emergency department, this time with multiple bruises. Radiological examination revealed a linear diastatic fracture that transgressed several sutures (*open arrows*)

2.4.1.2 Symmetrical Linear Fractures

In children, sometimes nearly symmetrical linear fractures are found resulting from bilateral compression of the skull between two surfaces [21]. This symmetry may also occur when the child hits the ground with the top of his/her head first [22] or is hit against the wall with great force and the energy released at contact spreads symmetrically over, for example, the parietal skull bones.

2.4.2 Complex Fractures

2.4.2.1 Circular (Concentric) Fractures

When the skull has a high velocity impact with a solid object, as happens in a high-energy trauma (concentric) complete or incomplete circular fractures may occur around the point of impact.

Concentric fractures are typical bowing fractures: the circles are formed in the outer surface of the skull

at the junction of the inward and outward bowing part of the skull, as the result of the extreme bowing at the point of impact [13, 23].

2.4.2.2 Star-Shaped Fractures

Star-shaped fractures are formed when a flat object comes into contact with a bowed bone at (very) high velocity. At the point of impact the bone suffers an impression that results into a number of fractures that all originate from the inward-bowing point of impact [18]. Star-shaped and circular fractures may both be present (Fig. 2.6).

2.4.2.3 Complex Fractures with Signs of Shattering

Complex fractures occur when there is a great deal of violence (Fig. 2.7). This type of fracture may also result from multiple blunt trauma to the head; for example, when the skull is hit repeatedly with a hammer. In this type of fracture the skin may or may not be intact.

2.4.3 Depression Fractures and Ping-Pong Deformation

2.4.3.1 Depression Fractures

Depression fractures of the skull can occur in two ways:

- When an object with a small surface and relatively high kinetic energy hits the skull, for example a hammer or the heel of a shoe.
- When an object (irrespective of the size of the object) hits only a small part of the skull with a large amount of kinetic energy (see also Sect. 2.4.2.2), such as a gun-shot wound.

In an depression fracture, there is besides the primary point of impact hardly any deformation of the skull (Fig. 2.8) [14, 18]. At the point of impact a fracture is sustained, possibly with fragmentation. The impression results from the inability of the inner layer of the skull bone to absorb the inward bowing adequately.

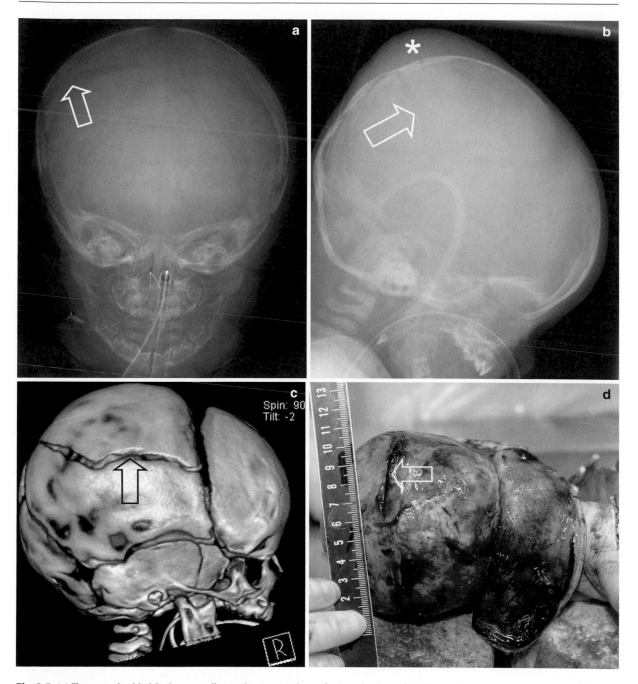

Fig. 2.5 (**a**) Two-month-old girl who, according to the anamnesis, had fallen from the changing table (85 cm high). When presented at the emergency department she was in deep coma. Five days later she died from the neurological trauma. The anterior-posterior skull view shows a bilateral linear fracture that transgressed multiple sutures (*open arrows*). (**b**) Lateral skull view shows besides the fracture in the parietal bone (*open arrow*) a clearly visible soft-tissue swelling corresponding to a post-traumatic haematoma (asterisk). (**c**) The fracture is visible on the three-dimensional CT reconstruction (*open arrow*); furthermore, conform the child's age, the sutures are still visible). (**d**) At autopsy the fracture in the parietal bone is clearly visible (*open arrow*)

The impression may reflect the shape of the object. Sometimes there is only an impression in the outer layer, whereas the inner layer remains intact [13].

Sometimes the skull is perforated. A number of these fractures have no complications. In one-third the dura is damaged, and in one in four children damage to the

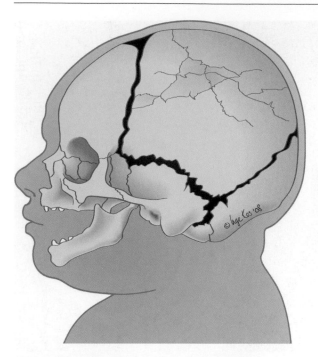

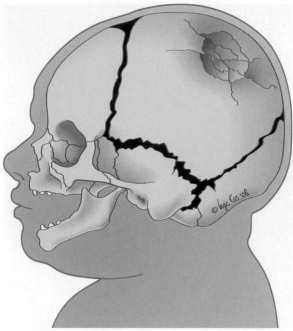

Fig. 2.6 Schematic representation of a burst fracture

Fig. 2.8 Schematic representation of a depression fracture

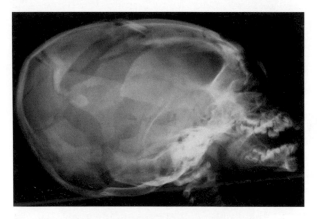

Fig. 2.7 The skull radiograph of a 1-year-old girl who was thrown from the fifth floor of an apartment building by her carer shows a crushed skull

2.4.3.2 Ping-Pong Deformation

In infants (generally <6 months old), when the impact site is small, instead of a depression fracture a ping-pong deformation of the skull may occur ('celluloid fracture') (Fig. 2.9a and b) [19]. This is due to the larger malleability and elasticity of the immature skull. In the differential diagnosis, one should be aware of congenital impressions of the skull (Figs. 2.10 and 2.11a and b).

2.5 Skull Fractures and Intracranial Injury

cerebral cortex is found [17]. A depression fracture increases the risk for posttraumatic seizures.

In approximately 30% of children with an depression fracture, intracranial injury is found [5, 24]. The deeper the fracture, the higher the chance that dura and brain tissue have been damaged. Besides intracranial haemorrhages, compression of the underlying brain tissue, laceration of the brain parenchyma and intraparenchymal bone fragments may occur [24, 25].

Skull fractures and intracranial injury are only correlated to a limited degree. Skull fractures may be present without intracranial injury. Dunning et al. mention that a skull fracture has a relative risk of 6.13 (95% CI 3.35–11.2) for intracranial haemorrhage [26]. On the other hand, there may be intracranial injury without a skull fracture. This applies to accidental as well as to non-accidental causes [13, 27].

According to Harwood-Nash, skull fractures are more often seen with associated subdural haemorrhages in older

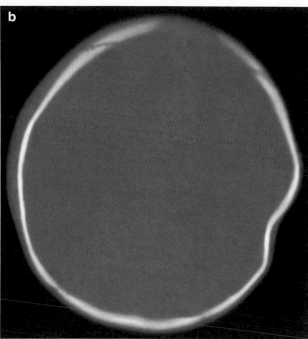

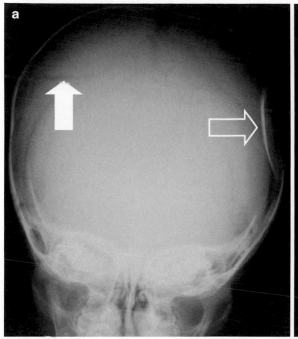

Fig. 2.9 (**a**) Eight-month-old infant, who had an obscure clinical history had allegedly fallen from a single bed on top of a drying rack (that lay on the floor). The skull view shows a ping-pong deforma-

tion (*open arrow*) and a linear fracture of the parietal bone (*arrow*). B Skull CT did not show any intracranial pathology. On the left-hand side, a cortical deformation without fracture can be seen

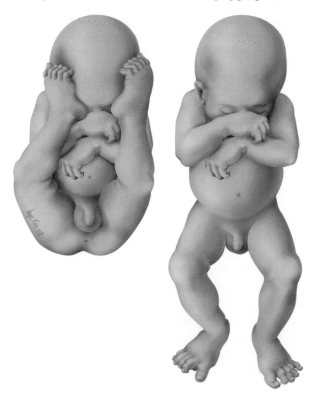

Fig. 2.10 Schematic representation of the origin of congenital impressions

children than in infants [2]. However, the location of the skull fracture is not a good indicator for the location of the subdural haemorrhage. The series of Harwood-Nash showed that subdural haemorrhages were predominantly found contralateral to the fracture [2].

It may happen that there is an epidural haematoma that results directly from the fracture. In a fracture of the temporal bone, the medial meningeal artery may be damaged, which can lead to an epidural haemorrhage in the temporoparietal area. Epidural haemorrhages are nearly always of arterial origin. In a fracture of the occipital bone, the venous sinus may be damaged, leading to a venous epidural haemorrhage in the posterior cranial fossa [20].

Mogby et al. carried out a retrospective study into the relation between skull fractures, visible on radiographs, and intracranial injury in 87 children under the age of 2 years old with a skull fracture [28]. In 67 children no neurological pathology was found. In 32 of those children, the researchers performed a CT scan to exclude intracranial injury. In six children (19%) small focal haemorrhages were found around the fracture. This did not result in an intervention or change in policy. Of the 32 children in the CT group, 29 were admitted as opposed to ten children

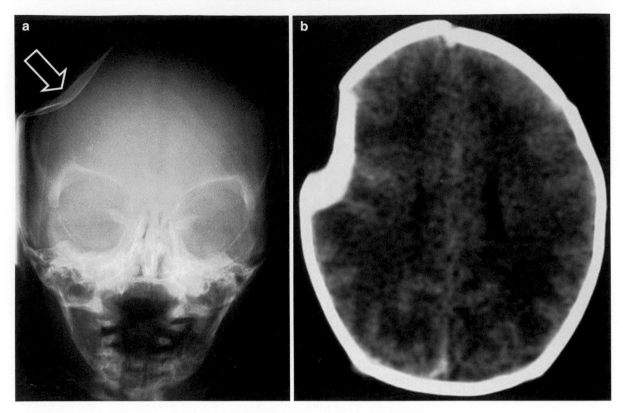

Fig. 2.11 (**a**) Three-day-old infant boy. Protracted breech presentation, no traumatic delivery. At physical examination a clearly visible impression of the skull was seen. Skull view shows an impression of the right parietal bone (*open arrow*). (**b**) Follow-up CT did not show any signs of trauma. In view of the anamnesis and the clinical findings, this image is due to a congenital impression

who did not have a CT. The children in the CT group were hospitalised longer. None of the children without neurological symptoms developed neurological complication at a later stage. In 20 of 87 children, acute neurological pathology was found. They all had a CT scan, and in 16 of 20 children pathology was found. Three children had minor pathology, 13 children showed serious pathology. In 15 children with acute neurological pathology further examination was performed within the scope of possible care proceedings. Based on these findings, 13 of them where placed into care. Mogby et al. concluded that detection of a skull fracture is more reliable using conventional radiology. Furthermore, no direct correlation was found between skull fractures and intracranial injury. According to Mogby et al., there is no indication for a CT scan based solely on the presence of a skull fracture. A CT scan is indicated when there are neurological symptoms. Finally, they concluded that a CT scan has added value when child abuse is seriously suspected, even when there are no neurological symptoms and conventional radiology shows no fractures.

Demaerel et al. found that 45% of infants under the age of 2 years with intracranial injury did not have a skull fracture. It was also found that 56% of children with a skull fracture did not have any intracranial injuries. Finally, Demaerel et al. concluded that it is impossible to differentiate between accidental and non-accidental causes based on radiological examination [29].

Gruskin and Schutzman performed a retrospect study into the predictors of complications in skull-/brain trauma in 278 infants under the age of 2 years, presenting at the emergency department of an academic hospital [30]. They concluded that clinical signs and symptoms were not suitable as predictors for skull fractures and/or intracranial injury. Also, they found three characteristics to identify children that are at low risk for complications:

- A fall of less than 1 m
- No neurological symptoms in the anamnesis
- No abnormalities of the scalp at physical examination

2.6 Skull Fractures: Differential Diagnosis

In children, skull fractures due to dynamic impact loading are regularly seen. There are three types of cause: accidental (accident of fall, in traffic, playing sports, around the home, etc.), non-accidental (physical violence) or medical (birth, bone diseases, etc.). Per age group, differences are seen when categorising for cause.

Children of less than 1 year old are six times more likely to sustain a skull fracture than older children [31–33]. In children of this age the skull fracture is often the result of child abuse, although one should not dismiss accidental falls or birth trauma out of hand (see Sects. 2.6.1. and 2.6.3). In children from approximately 1 year (if sufficiently mobile) to the age of 4, accidental falls during play seem to be the most prevalent cause. In children between 4 and 14 years of age, it is mostly traffic accidents and violence [34, 35].

2.6.1 Skull Fractures and Child Abuse

In physical violence, the fracture is the result of the direct impact of considerable external force, such as contact with a flat surface or a punch with a fist. Physical violence seems to be involved in only a relatively small part of skull fractures in childhood. Johnstone et al. evaluated 409 children under the age of 13 years; only 3% of skull fractures were due to child abuse [36]. However, this percentage increases dramatically as the studied population gets younger. Hobbs came to the conclusion that 33% (29 of 89 children) of skull fractures in children of less than 2 years of age result from child abuse [37]. Leventhal et al. studied 93 children under the age of 3 years with skull fractures; 80% was less than 1 year old. In the group of infants of less than 1 year old, 27% of fractures resulted from child abuse [38]. Meservy et al. evaluated 134 children of less than 2 years old; in 39 infants (29%) child abuse was the cause of the skull fracture [39].

According to Kleinman et al., 10–13% of all cases of physical violence concern skull fractures [27]. Merten et al. found a comparable percentage, slightly less than 10% (67 children with a skull fracture in a total of 712 abused children) [40]. Neither Kleinman nor Merten differentiated for age.

Loder and Bookout carried out research in abused children of less than 16 months of age that had sustained fractures as a consequence. In 35% of children a skull fracture was found [41].

Reece maintains that 80% of skull fractures sustained through child abuse occur in infants of less than 1 year old [42].

Of all fractures sustained by children as the result of child abuse 7–30% are skull fractures [27]. According to some authors, skull fractures are even the one but most frequently occurring fracture in child abuse [31, 43, 44].

In 41% of children that die as a result of physical violence, skull fractures are found [33].

2.6.2 Type of Skull Fracture and Child Abuse

The most prevalent skull fracture in physical violence is the unilaterally localised, simple linear fracture of the parietal bone without depression. However, this is also happens to be the most prevalent skull fracture in accidents [19].

When the fracture is bilaterally present or when there are multiple fractures with depression and diastasis >3 mm, one should consider child abuse as the main cause, especially with a ambiguous patient history. Also, in depression fractures, fractures with diastasis of the fracture lines and occipital fractures, one should consider physical violence as a possible cause [8, 39, 40, 45–47].

Kleinman even considers depression fractures of the occipital bone as very suspect for child abuse [48]. However, the presence of the earlier-mentioned fractures, taken out of context, is never evidence of physical violence [49, 50].

Finally, the literature reports regularly that fractures that transgress the sutures (carry from one skull bone into the other) are highly suspect for child abuse (see, e.g. Fig. 8.46). However, this appears to be incorrect: fractures that continue into the adjacent bone are also found in accidental causes [51, 52].

2.6.3 Differential Diagnosis Between Non-accidental and Accidental Fractures

In the differential diagnosis of non-accidental skull fractures, one should be aware of accidental fractures that result from either static or dynamic impact loading.

fracture. Some mention a distance of less than 1 m, and emphasise at the same time that it is very rare [69]. Also, one often refers to complicating factors that are associated with the fall at the moment the skull fractures occur, such as a fall from the arms of a parent or carer [69].

Johnson et al. carried out a study in 72 consecutive children of <5 years old (4 months to 4 years and 9 months), who presented at the emergency department due to skull injuries after a fall [70]. They collected data on distance of fall in a free fall or falling down the stairs, the surface area of the landing and the length of the child. Distance of fall ranged from 50 cm to 3 m. Most children fell less than 1 m. Of the 72 children, 49 fell on a hard surface and 23 on a soft surface (covered in carpet). In 52 children the fall resulted in a visible injury to the head (35 on hard surface, 17 on soft surface – there was no significant difference). There were visible skull injuries in all children that had fallen over >1.5 m, and in 95% of children that had fallen over a distance of >1 m. In 32 children (44%), a skull radiograph was made. In four cases a skull fracture was visible, of which three were linear. Two of the children with a linear fracture had fallen >1 m. One child sustained the fracture in a fall of 80–90 cm against the stone edge around a fireplace. The 4th child sustained a basilar fracture in a fall of over 3 m from a window on the first floor. Johnson et al. concluded that children seldom sustain serious injuries in accidents in and around the home. They maintain that skull fractures are rare and occur only in <5% of all accidents. In their opinion, it takes a fall of at least 1 m or, in lesser distances, on a limited surface area to cause a skull fracture.

Thomas et al. carried out a study in 112 children of <1 year old that had experienced a skull trauma [71]. In 96 children a skull radiograph was made. According to the parents, 32 children fell over a distance of >1 m. Thomas et al. found six children with a skull fracture that belonged to the group of 80 children that had fallen over a distance of <1 m. According to the parents, two children with a skull fracture had fallen from a height of <30 cm. In four of the six children that had sustained a fracture the physicians were sufficiently concerned to report the incident to the child protection service. When additional examinations were performed, two of the children were found to have further fractures. Based on the statements of the parents, it appeared to be impossible to predict which children had skull fractures. The presence of external injuries or neurological symptoms appeared to be an unreliable indicator for skull fractures. The reported distance of the fall was also not indicative. Hence, Thomas et al. are of the opinion that in children of <1 year of age that present with head trauma, a skull radiograph should routinely be made. In their study it led to the identification of four children with a skull fracture as the result of child abuse.

2.6.3.5 Skull Fractures in an Uncomplicated Fall

An uncomplicated fall is a short-distance free fall on a flat surface. The fall originates from a position in which the child stands still or lies still and is the result of the child's own movement patron, in accordance with its level of development. Hereby one may think of a situation in which the child falls from a changing table because it turns over, or when a child falls over while standing because it loses balance.

Data on how a child sustains a skull fracture after an uncomplicated fall have been derived from fall studies as performed by Weber [12, 51, 72]. They can also be derived from data of accidental falls in children as observed by independent bystanders.

Fall Studies in Deceased Children

Nearly every young child has fallen on his/her head from a standing position or from limited height; for example, from a changing table or from a stroller. Since there is a difference of opinion between several physicians and researchers on whether children that fall from such a height can sustain a skull fracture, Weber did experimental research with deceased children of <8.2 months old. In his first article he describes three test series each with five children who he dropped in free fall from a height of 0.82 m on several surfaces (stone-tile surface, carpeted floor, foam-supported linoleum floor) [51]. Hereby, the horizontally positioned body and the parieto-occipital part of the skull hit the surface simultaneously. In all cases autopsy showed linear skull fractures of the parietal bone. One child sustained bilateral fractures. In three children the fractures run across the sutures. Based on this study, Weber concluded that skull fractures can be sustained in a fall from a changing table. He also concluded that when child abuse is suspected, differentiation with an accidental fall is only possible when the whole picture is taken into consideration. In a second article Weber describes a follow-up study in another 35 children who he dropped on a soft surface [72]. In 10 children a 2 cm thick foam rubber mat was used and for the other 25 a once folded, 8 cm thick blanket. Weber found a skull fracture in one child in the rubber-mat group (two linear fractures in the left parietal bone). In the other group, he found bowing fractures in four children (linear fractures or ping-pong fractures).

In interpreting Weber's data, one must be aware of the fact that a living child will fall differently to a deceased child, due to active muscle tension and, when old enough, a fall reflex. Yet, Weber's studies show that it is possible to sustain a skull fracture in an uncomplicated fall from a height of <1 m.

Uncomplicated Fall over a Short Distance (Maximal 1–1.5 m)

The medical literature contains many articles and case notes on the nature of skull fractures after a short-distance fall (<1–1.5 m). Based on the earlier-mentioned data one may conclude that skull fractures resulting from such a fall can occur in living children. In the literature one sometimes comes across case notes on severe to life-threatening injuries sustained in a short-distance fall. In such cases, there are often complicating factors associated with the fall (see below and Chap. 6).

Helfer et al. described injuries in 246 children of <5 years of age [73]. The group consisted of 161 children whose parents filled out a questionnaire when they saw a physician for a fall over a distance of <90 cm (bed or settee) and 85 children who had fallen from their crib/cot or from the examination table during their stay in hospital. Two children in the group that had fallen outside the hospital had sustained a skull fracture (age < 6 months). In the children who had fallen while hospitalised, one skull fracture was found. The majority of children did not have any externally visible injuries.

Nimityongskul and Anderson did research into the origin of injuries in 76 children (age ranged from neonate to 16 years), who had fallen out of bed, crib/cot or chair while hospitalised [74]; 57 children were <5 years of age and 23 children <1 year of age. Fall distance was between 30 and 100 cm. Most children had superficial injuries (haematomas of the scalp and

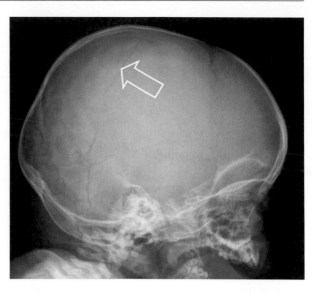

Fig. 2.12 Eight-month-old boy infant with cutaneous swelling after a fall from a bed. Radiological examination shows a linear fracture of the skull (*open arrow*)

lacerations of the face). One 12-month-old child had an uncomplicated occipital skull fracture.

Lyons and Oates described 207 children of <6 years of age who had fallen from their crib/cot (n=124) or bed (n=83) [75]. The distance of the fall ranged from 65 cm (lowered side rail) to 110 cm (side rail up) in a fall from a crib or cot, and from 50 to 85 cm (including side rails) in a fall from a bed. In 31 children there were visible injuries, in 26 to the skull. In one child (age 10 months), an uncomplicated linear skull fracture was found after a fall from a cot (Fig. 2.12).

Tarantino et al. studied 167 children of <10 months old (average age 5.2 months, 56% male), who fell over a distance of less than 1.25 m and for that reason presented at the emergency department [76]. They excluded all falls from baby walkers and car seats, falls down the stairs and all accidents resulting from walking, running or climbing. They also excluded children that had fallen on objects or on whom a carer had fallen. Fifty-fife percent of children fell out of bed, 20% fell from the arms of a parent/carer (being dropped), 16% fell from a settee and 10% fell in a different manner. Eighty-five percent of children had no or minimal injuries. The remaining children (n=25) had severe skull trauma: 16 a closed-head injury, of whom 12 had sustained a skull fracture, two had intracranial haemorrhaging and seven had fracture of one of the long bones. Additional examination revealed that the children who had sustained intracranial haemorrhages were victims of child abuse. After these two children had been excluded, it appeared that the only risk to sustain a severe injury in a fall was from the arms of a carer.

Tarantino et al. concluded that the biomechanics of a fall from the arms of a carer may be different from other kinds of short-distance fall, such as a fall from a bed, settee or changing table.

The research of Warrington and Wright also confirmed the findings in studies from before 1995, which are largely based on the data of fall incidents while hospitalised. Warrington and Wright studied accidents in non-mobile children in the home setting [69]. By using questionnaires that had to be filled out they requested parents of 6-month-old children to describe every accident since birth. They asked the parents to describe the type of fall, the distance of the fall, the injury and the medical help given (in case this was sought). The number of forms returned was 11,466. In 2,554 children, 3,357 fall incidents were reported. Fifty-three percent of children fell out of bed or from the settee, and 12% fell from an arm while being carried or when the person who carried the child fell down while holding the child. In the remaining children a large diversity of falls was seen: from a table, chair or changing table, from a baby bouncer, etc. In <1% cause of the fall was not reported. Seventy-six percent of children fell only once, and in 5% it was thrice or more. The number of falls increased with the age of the child. Less than 25% occurred before the age of 4 months. Only 14% of children sustained visible injuries, of which 56% were haematomas. In 97% the injury was visible on the head. Less than 1% (21 children) sustained a concussion or fracture. One-hundred and sixty-two children were taken to hospital after their fall, and 18 children were hospitalised. In the hospital, a skull fracture was diagnosed in three children; however, this was no reason for hospitalisation. Skull fractures were never seen after a fall from a bed or settee. None of the children suffered intracranial injuries such as subdural or epidural haemorrhages.

2.6.3.6 Skull Fractures in a Complicated Fall

In a complicated fall, the child does not have a short-distance free fall, landing on a flat surface. There may be complications during:

- The initial moments of a fall: for example, the arms of a carer, a fall from a swinging swing or a fall with a baby walker.
- The fall itself: for example, a fall of the carer who holds the child on his/her arm, and in which the carer falls fully or partly on the child; a fall from a bunk bed in which the child comes into contact with parts of the bed while falling; or a fall with a baby walker from the stairs.
- The landing: for example, a fall on a non-flat surface or a fall on objects.

One also speaks of a complicated fall when the child falls from great height and the complications, such as sustaining a complex skull fracture and intracranial injury, are mainly the result of the higher velocity at landing.

Fall from the Arms of Parent/Carer

Warrington and Wright studied the incidence of falling in non-mobile children in a home setting (see paragraph 2.6.3.5) [69]. The study of Tarantino et al. also looked into the consequences of a fall from the arms of a parent/carer (see paragraph 2.6.3.5) [76].

Minns reports the possibility that infants, as early as 5 weeks old and when held with one hand against the shoulder of the carer, are able to lean back in such a manner that they fall. This usually involves a fall of approximately 1.5 m [77]. As a result of such a fall, they may sustain a focal haematoma and even extensive skull fractures and focal contusion of the brain (Fig. 2.13). Minns maintains that in these children there will be no other signs of encephalopathy or any delay in seeking medical help. A good anamnesis and careful scrutiny of the circumstances will provide ample information to differentiate between accidental and non-accidental skull/brain trauma.

In 2004, Pediatrics published an article of Bechtel et al. called 'Characteristics that distinguish accidental from abusive injury in hospitalised young children with head trauma' [78]. In 2005, a letter of Lueder was published in response, regarding retinal haemorrhages in a number of accidental falls [79]. In their answer to Lueder's letter, Bechtel et al. described a number of situations in which children had fallen, for example, from the hands of parents/carers and consequently sustained skull fractures and other injuries (see Table 2.2) [80].

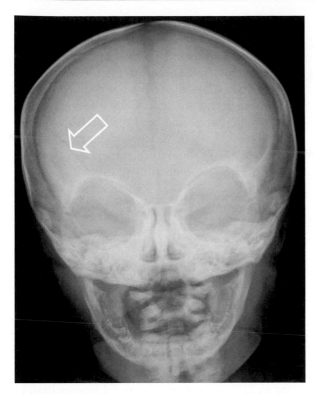

Fig. 2.13 Six-week-old infant girl who had fallen from the arms of her mother on a tile floor. Radiological examination shows a linear fracture of the skull (*open arrow*)

Fall on an Object

Wheeler and Shope described a 7-month-old infant who fell out of bed and sustained a ping-pong fracture of the skull (2 × 4 × 0.5 cm in the right parietal bone) [81]. The child appeared to have fallen over a distance of approximately 60 cm on top of a metal toy car.

Nobody saw the fall. There were no signs of underlying brain damage, retinal haemorrhages or other fractures.

Fall from a Perambulator or Stroller

A fall from a perambulator, in particular in children of <1 year old, is not rare. Injuries are mainly found in the head/neck area (including intracranial injuries and skull fractures) [82, 83]. According to Watson and Ozanne, the risk for serious injuries is considerable, since by far the majority of children (96% of children in their study) that had fallen from a perambulator fell on their head [84].

Serious cranial injury has only been described in case reports. It concerns typical injuries that originate from contact; for example, epidural haemorrhages [85]. This does not have to lead to a skull fracture [85]. Permanent injuries as well as death are extremely rare [82–85]. In their review of the literature, Lee and Fong found three children that died after their parents reported a fall from a perambulator. In the end, two of the children appeared to be victims of child abuse [85].

Arnholz et al. describe the origin of bilateral skull fractures in a 6-week-old baby who had fallen from a perambulator from a height of approximately 90 cm on top of his/her head on concrete steps [22]. As associated injuries 'two separate and symmetrical areas of scalp haemorrhage' were found. Arnholz et al. point out that bilateral fractures are rarely the result of an accident and for that reason should be seen as extremely suspect for child abuse. Their findings correspond with Weber's experiments with deceased children (see Sect. 2.6.3.5).

Table 2.2 Injuries in children who fell from the arms of a carer [78–80]

Age	Distance	Context	Witnesses?	Findings at examination
1 month	1 meter	Fell from the father's arms, who was lying on the bed	+	Skull fracture right side of the skull Epidural haemorrhage Retina bleed (one eye) in right eye
4 month	1 meter	Fell from the arms of an older child	?	Skull fracture on the lift side Intraretinal bleeds at the back of the left eye
4 month	1.25 meter	Fell from mother's arms and hit its head against the edge of the table	+	Skull fracture on the right side Intracranial haemorrhage Intraretinal bleeds around the optical disc and arcs
8 month	60 cm	Fell from mother's arms, who was lying on the settee	?	Skull fracture on the left side Epidural haemorrhage One intraretinal bleed in the left eye

Fall from Shopping Trolley

Smith et al. evaluated retrospectively the emergency department data of over 75,000 shopping trolley-related injuries in children <15 years of age [86]. Eighty-four percent of children was <5 years. The most prevalent injuries were head and neck injuries (74%).

In a prospective study, Smith et al. evaluated 62 children ranging in age from 4 months to 10 years (average 2.8 years) that had presented at the emergency department for shopping-trolley-related injuries over a period of 15 months [87]. The majority of children had sustained the injury by falling out of the trolley (58%), followed by toppling over of the trolley (26%). Injury resulting from falling out of the trolley occurred at all ages, whereas toppling over of the trolley was mainly responsible for injuries in children <1 year old. Forty-nine children (79%) appeared to have sustained head injuries, of which five had skull fractures. Smith et al. concluded that accidents with shopping trolleys can lead to serious and potentially life-threatening injuries, although there were no cases of (intra)cranial injury – in spite of falling on a solid (often concrete) surface. No intracranial haemorrhages were found.

Fall from Bouncy Chairs, Baby Bouncers and Car Seats

Wickham and Abrahamson studied the risk of the use bouncy chairs (Fig. 2.14) and car seats [88]. Seventeen of the 131 children (average age: 6.9 months) with head injury they examined appeared to have fallen from bouncy chairs or car seats. All falls with bouncy chairs took place while the child was seated in his/her chair which was placed on a high surface (such as a table). This also seemed to be the case in two of the six children in the car-seat group. Fourteen of 17 children fell on a solid surface. One child had sustained a skull fracture as a result of the fall. There were no serious or life-threatening injuries.

A baby bouncer is a playing device (Fig. 2.15) made for children that are well able to keep their head upright, but are yet unable to walk (see Chap. 6). The literature only has few case reports that point at the risks of the use of baby bouncers [89–91]. Unfortunately, the literature is not quite clear on the definition of a baby bouncer, which makes it difficult to compare the results.

Clayton describes a case of a fatal fall from a baby bouncer [89]. A 5-month-old child had fallen after two other children had rocked the child in the bouncer. At the time of the fall, the head was no more than 60 cm from the floor. Clayton is correct in pointing out that one does not necessarily have to fall from great height to sustain life-threatening head trauma. After the fall the child cried loudly at the top of its lungs; 7 h later it died. Examination showed a large epidural haemorrhage at the left side, without skull fracture.

Fall from a High Chair

In particular children of less than 1 year of age seem to fall regularly with or from high chairs. The study of Watson and Ozanne showed that 75% of children who fell out of a high chair landed on their head [84]. The majority of those children sustained head injuries [92, 93]. In 103 children, Mayr et al. found haematomas or lacerations of the scalp or face (68.9%), skull fractures (15.5) and concussion (13.6%) [93]. Powell et al. found in 21% of children intracranial injuries [93]. In the (albeit limited) literature, serious or even life-threatening injuries have rarely been described. Only

Fig. 2.14 Bouncy chair

Fig. 2.15 Baby bouncer

Watson and Ozanne mention 1 child that died from a fall from a high chair [84].

Fall from Stairs

Many parents have experienced at some time that their young child fell downstairs. This means that annually the number of falls down the stairs must be very high. Usually it results in little or no injuries. This is probably why the paediatric literature contains but a few publications on this type of accident and the occurrence of skull fractures in these accidents.

In a prospective study, Joffe and Ludwig describe 363 children, ranging in age from 1 month to nearly 19 years, with injuries resulting from a fall downstairs

(average age 55 months) [94]. Fifty-four children were <1 year old. Ten children were carried by their parent/carer. Twenty-four children were in a baby walker when they fell downstairs. Children who had been abused were excluded from the study. The majority of children sustained light superficial injuries, 73% had injuries to head and neck. Head trauma was more often seen in children that were less than 4 years of age. Six children had sustained a skull fracture (all <3 years old). Four of the six skull fractures were sustained in the ten children that fell from their parents/carers hands while going downstairs. None of the children was in a life-threatening situation. According to Joffe and Ludwig, a fall downstairs is really a series of much smaller falls. The first fall is the longest by height: the height of the child itself plus the number of steps of the stair.

Chiavello et al. studied the effects of a fall downstairs in 69 children of less than 5 years of age (average age 2 years), including three children that had taken a fall with their parent/carer [95]. They excluded accidents with baby walkers and children suspected of being abused. The majority of injuries were not serious. Fifteen children had sustained serious injuries such as concussion (11 children – 16%), skull fractures (five children – 7%), cerebral contusion (two children – 3%), subdural haemorrhages (one child – 1%) and fracture of the second cervical vertebra (one child – 1%). The three children who had been carried by their parent/carer who had fallen on the child against the stairs, had sustained the most serious injuries: two children had skull fractures. One of them also had a small subdural haemorrhage and cerebral contusion. This was also the child that had sustained a fracture of the second cervical vertebra. These injuries occurred in a fall while being carried downstairs by an adult. Chaviello et al. concluded that head and neck injuries are the most prevalent injuries, and that it is rare to have injuries on more than one body part.

Chaviello as well as Joffe concluded that a free fall causes more damage than a fall from the same height downstairs.

Fall with a Baby Walker

Accidents with baby walkers occur regularly in young children up to 1 year old. Injuries are caused by various mechanisms: going head over heels, falling down the stairs or from an elevation, or by crushing of fingers. The most prevalent location for injuries is the head and neck area, including the face [96]. The majority of the injuries concern the head or face and are relatively innocent. The majority and most serious injuries occur when falling downstairs with a baby walker [97–101]. In this context skull fractures have been mentioned frequently [99, 100, 102–104]; the fractures may be linear but also complex fractures are seen [105]. Mayr et al. found basilar fractures in 19 of the 172 children they evaluated [103]; 15 had suffered a fracture of the cranium and 4 a basilar fracture.

Smith et al. studied 271 children that had been treated for baby walker-related trauma [106]. In the 26 children in Smith's study, a skull fracture was established (17 parietal, eight frontal and one occipital). They saw three children with a depressed fracture of the skull of whom two had a second skull fracture without depression. Three children with a skull fracture also had intracranial haemorrhages, of which two were subdural haemorrhages. The skull fractures all occurred in the group of children that had fallen downstairs. Chaviello et al. found intracranial haemorrhages in 5 of the 65 children they evaluated [104]. Death is rarely reported. The study of Chaviello et al. reported one deceased child (skull fracture, subdural haemorrhage and fracture of the cervical spine) [104].

In an advice on the use of baby walkers, the American Academy of Pediatrics (AAP, 2001) reports that between 1973 and 1998 they received reports on 34 children who had died from a fall with a baby walker [107]. Due to the considerable risk for light to very serious injuries and death, the AAP issues a negative advice regarding the use of baby walkers.

Fall from a Bunk Bed

Although one may think that a fall from a bunk bed, besides the larger distance of the fall, is comparable to a fall from a lower bed, it appears that, based on data from the literature, the risk for serious injury is considerably higher for a fall from a bunk bed [108]. Injuries may be sustained by falling from the top bed or the bottom bed and from the ladder. The fall may occur during sleep, when getting out of bed or while playing.

The majority of children suffers head trauma, including facial injuries, in particular in a fall from the top bed [109, 110]. A fall from the top bed also often causes more serious injuries [109]. Skull fractures are not often reported. Mayr et al. found seven skull fractures in a total of 218 children [111]. MacGregor did not find any skull fractures at all, in spite of the fact that a number of children showed notable neurological symptoms: unconsciousness, drowsiness or vomiting [110].

In spite of the high number, the severity and diversity of the injuries that occur when children fall from a bunk bed, hardly any mention of intracranial injury can be found in the medical literature. Selbst mentions a child with a skull fracture and a subdural haemorrhage [109]. In none of the children MacGregor found intracranial haemorrhages, not even in complex falls; for example, when during the fall a child hits another piece of furniture before hitting the ground [110]. Mayr et al. too did not find any intracranial haemorrhages [111].

In conclusion, it is remarkable that none of the earlier-mentioned studies reported the death of a child after a fall from a bunk bed.

Fall from a Great Height

The fall distance necessary to cause damage in young children in a free fall has been a continuous subject of discussion [112]. Williams evaluated the data of 398 consecutive victims of a fall. In the end, 106 children were selected for further evaluation [112]. In this group the fall had been witnessed by another person than the carer, and the context of the fall had been documented. In Table 2.2 Williams' findings are specified. Williams also evaluated the data of 53 children with an anamnesis that indicated a fall as the cause of the sustained injuries, without an independent eye witness to confirm this cause. In this group 2 children had died after a fall of less than 3 m (both fell over a distance of even less than 1.5 m). In the group with the independent eye witness, there were 44 children that had fallen over less than 3 m. In this group, three children had sustained a small depressed fracture; however, none of the children in this group died. It appeared that the children that sustained a depressed fracture had fallen against a sharp edge. In the group of children whose fall had been witnessed by an independent observer, one child died after a fall of over 20 m (Table 2.3).

Williams concluded that 'infants and small children are relatively resistant to injuries from free falls, and falls of less than 10 ft are unlikely to produce serious or life-threatening injury'.

Table 2.3 Injuries in falls witnessed by others than the carer (distance fall: 0.5–20 m) [112]

Severity of injury	N		<3 m	>3 m
None	15		8	7
Mild	77	Haematomas, abrasions, simple fractures	24	43
Serious	14	Intracranial haemorrhages, brain oedema Depression fractures, compound skull fracture	3	11

The majority of injuries sustained by a child who falls from a great height are injuries in the head-neck area [113, 114]. The most prevalent injury, besides visible injuries, is the skull fracture, which may be accompanied by intracranial symptoms (subdural, subarachnoidal and epidural) and cerebral contusions [113, 115–117]. There may be fractures of the cranium as well as of the base of the skull [117]. The risk for a fatal course increases with distance of fall, for example a fall from a balcony, roof, stairs, diving board or from an open window or tree [115]. Hereby intracranial injuries are the main cause of death [117].

The majority of children who fall from a great height is less than 5 or 6 years old and fall over a distance of 3–7 m (one or two floors) in or in the direct vicinity of the home, mostly during the warm seasons [113–115, 118]. On the whole parents do not witness the fall, unless they are directly involved in the fall. Mayr et al. describe three cases in which a parent is directly involved (a mother who jumped with the child, and two mothers threw their child out of the window) [118].

2.6.3.7 Dynamic Impact Loading: Crush Injuries Caused by Toppling Televisions and Other Heavy Objects

Various publications warn for the risk that a child runs with toppling televisions. In particular wide-screen televisions on unstable cupboards or cupboards that the child can climb on are notorious [119–124]. Although Duhaime et al. call the cause of the skull/brain trauma static loading [67], this type of accident has more in common with dynamic loading, as found in accidental falls. It is not rare for a double impact to occur: first the moment that the child falls on top of its head of the cupboard and then the moment that the television and/or the cupboard topple(s) over on the child. Both contact forms lead to dynamic impact loading.

Injuries by toppling televisions are predominantly found in children between 1 and 3 years of age (see Table 2.4). The most common cause of death in these children is severe skull-/brain trauma [122]. Bernard et al. report in a retrospective study of in total 73 incidents (average age 36 months) the death of 28 children (average age 31 months). In their study population the head was the most prevalent anatomical location for injuries (externally visible injury, skull fractures and intracranial injuries) (72%) [119]. In the end, they evaluated 14 deceased children in their study. Thirteen of the children died from skull/brain trauma, while the remaining child died from generalised crush injuries (injuries in which several body parts and organs are seriously damaged and/or crushed). In their article they do not specify why only 14 deceased children were chosen for further evaluation.

DiScala et al. also carried out a retrospective study in 183 children under the age of 7 [120]. In their study 68.7% had a skull-/brain trauma, and 43.7% had injuries to one or more body parts or organs (see Table 2.4). More than a quarter of children had injuries with an injury-severity score of 10–75 (Table 2.4).

Approximately one third of the children had to be admitted to an intensive care unit; five children died due to massive intracranial haemorrhages.

Table 2.4 Anatomical location of injuries and 'injury severity score' in toppling televisions [120]

Anatomical location of the injury	N	%
Skull/brain	58	31.7
Arms or legs	28	15.3
Face, abdomen, skin	17	9.3
Combination of more than two injuries: skull/brain, face, chest, abdomen, arms, legs, skin	80	43.7
Total head/neck area	125	68.3
Injury severity score	N	%
1–9 (mild)	127	69.4
10–15 (moderate)	32	17.5
16–24 (severe)	13	7.1
25–75 (life-threatening)	7	3.8
Unknown	4	2.2

Based on their study, Scheidler et al. maintain that the most prevalent injuries are to the head, abdomen and arms/legs (fractures) [121]. Their study mentions five deceased children in a total of 43, all resulting from skull/brain trauma. Four children sustained an abdominal trauma, and in three children surgical intervention was indicated. None of the children with an abdominal trauma died.

Ota et al. pose that the injuries sustained from toppling televisions are usually not serious or life-threatening [124]. However, the earlier cited medical literature shows that life-threatening injuries occur regularly (3–>35%).

Yahya et al. indicate that when televisions topple on children, skull/brain trauma is the most prevalent cause of death [123]. Only the article of Bernard gives another cause of death, namely generalised crush injury [119]. Furthermore, earlier-mentioned literature shows that children that die as the result of toppling televisions instantly show clinical symptoms and are in near immediate need of intensive care.

2.6.3.8 Dynamic Impact Loading: Skull Fractures in Utero

In utero skull fractures due to maternal trauma have been mentioned in the medical literature for over a century [125]. These fractures may be accompanied by serious injury that is sometimes incompatible with life. Intracranial (subdural/subarachnoidal, intraventricular) haemorrhages, cerebral oedema, hypoxic ischaemic damage and parenchymal injuries have been reported [126–128].

Although it is possible for fractures to occur in every all bone of the unborn child, skull fractures appear to be the most prevalent in in utero trauma [129, 130]. In utero skull fractures may be found in all skull bones [127]. Multiple depressed skull fractures may also occur [131].

With the increase in the number of traffic accidents, the majority of skull fractures in utero are related to severe maternal injuries (fractures of the pelvis). As a result of the fracture and dislocation of the pelvic bones, the skull is pressed with a great deal of force against the sacrum [125]. The highest risk is during the third trimester, when the skull has descended into the pelvis. This is often accompanied by severe maternal trauma, although this is not always the case. Härtle and

Ko describe the case of a 19-year-old pregnant woman without significant injuries who had been involved in a traffic accident. Due to foetal distress it was decided to perform a Caesarean section. The child was found to have a linear fracture in the left parietal bone plus a skull haematoma on the left side at the location of the fracture. The authors assumed that the fracture was caused by blunt trauma directly through the abdominal wall during the accident [125].

Staffort et al. describe eight cases of in utero foetal trauma (two children had sustained skull fractures with cortical lacerations and focal contusion) that were fatal secondary to traffic accidents [128]. In all cases, the mother survived, usually with only limited injuries.

The incidence of trauma during pregnancy was earlier estimated to be 6–7% [129–132]. The majority of these trauma appeared to be the result of traffic accidents, followed by falling and physical violence.

2.6.3.9 Anatomic Variants and Other Findings in Differential Diagnostics

In radiological differential diagnostics one should be aware of so-called pseudo-fractures, such as impressions of blood vessels, but also different aspects of sutures and connective tissue fissures [133]. Also, super-positioned externally localised objects may cause confusion. For example, this may the case with plaids or hair bows.

2.7 Growing Fractures of the Skull

Most skull fractures sustained during childhood heal without any complications. A growing fracture of the skull is a relatively rare complication of a skull fracture and is usually found in children up to the age of toddler/ small child. In a growing fracture there is progressive diastasis of the fracture line (Fig. 2.16a and b). In 1816, John Hopkins was the first to describe a growing fracture in a child as a complication of head trauma (from 137).

A growing fracture is also called a leptomeningeal cyst for the frequently present relation with a cyst-like mass filled with cerebrospinal fluid. Other terms in use are a.o.: cerebrocranial erosion, traumatic meningocele, growing skull fracture, diastatic fracture, cranial-burst fracture and cephalhydrocele [134, 135].

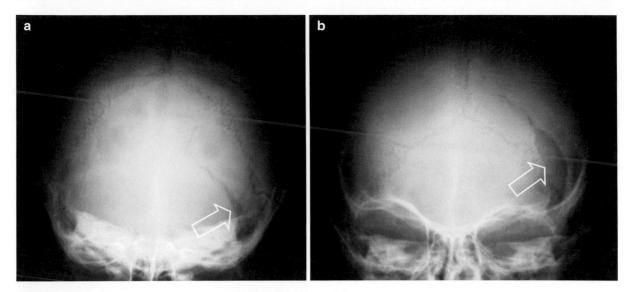

Fig. 2.16 (**a**) Two-year-old girl who presented at the emergency department after a fall on the head. The skull view showed a diastatic fracture on the left side (*open arrow*). (**b**) Follow-up view after 3 months, clearly shows the growing skull fracture (*open arrow*)

2.7.1 Epidemiology

The literature reports an incidence that ranges from 0.05% to 1.6% for all skull fractures. Usually, it concerns children in the first 3 years of their life, with a notable preference for the first year. A growing fracture is hardly ever seen in children >8 years [136–140]. There may be a considerable period of time between the moment the clinical pathology is inflicted and the moment the diagnosis is made [141, 142]. Sometimes the diagnosis is not made until the patient is >60 years old [143, 144]. Consequently, in certain cases it is impossible to relate to the initial trauma.

2.7.2 Etiology

Growing fractures usually occur after serious head trauma, most frequently after a fall, a traffic accident or in child abuse. There are case reports on the origin of growing fractures following the occurrence of skull fractures in utero (this concerned a child with bilateral parietal fractures and a one-sided leptomeningeal cyst at birth) [145], or from a difficult delivery with vacuum extraction [60, 61, 146, 147].

A growing fracture can also occur as complication after neurosurgery for corrective cranial vault reshaping [148].

2.7.3 Growing Skull Fractures and Child Abuse

Hobbs evaluated 89 children under the age of 2 with skull fractures [37]. In 60 cases he found an accidental cause. In the remaining children, child abuse was the cause of the fractures. In the group children with accidental causes, he did not find but one growing fracture, whereas the six abused children did have a growing fracture (see Table 2.1).

Hobbs's results seem to contradict the results of the study of Donahue. He evaluated 13 children with a growing fracture, ranging in age from 1 to 17 months with an average age of 5.7 months. Seven children had suffered serious injuries in traffic accidents, and five were victims of child abuse. In one child the physicians were not clear about the cause [135]. The children in Donahue's study were all seen when acute. They showed a conspicuous haematoma of the scalp and a Glasgow Coma Score of 10 points or less, indicating recent serious trauma.

When the data of Hobbs and Donahue are combined [37, 135], they show that in young children head trauma with herniation of intracranial tissue (either in the acute phase or at a later stage) is the result of severe trauma. It must be possible to objectify the circumstances of the trauma in order to accept an accidental cause. In other circumstances, child abuse is the most likely cause in this group of young children.

2.7.4 Pathogenesis

The exact pathophysiology of growing fractures is still under discussion. It appears that skull fractures are not inclined to show diastasis when the underlying dura is intact. The origin of growing fractures seems to depend on many factors. The factors involved are: head trauma with a large fracture, the presence of a dura laceration (Fig. 2.17a and b), damage to the parenchyma at the location of the skull fracture and the dura laceration, and damage sustained at the time of maximal brain growth [134, 149].

Muhonen et al. maintain that herniation of brain tissue/leptomeningeal cyst, without indications for increased intracranial pressure, points to physiological growth and to pulsations of the cerebrospinal fluid as the cause of diastasis/growth of the fracture [142]. The force of the pulsations widens the skull fracture. The pulsations also push intracranial tissue into the fracture line. This makes it impossible for the osteoblasts to migrate to the fracture; hence, there is no new-bone formation and consequently no healing. Finally, there is resorption of the adjacent bone as a result of the continuous pressure of the tissue herniation through the defect in the bone [149].

It seems that insufficiently closed dura lacerations during craniotomy can also lead to growing fractures of the skull. These findings support the idea that traumatic damage to the dura is the most important risk factor in the development of a growing fracture [149].

2.7.5 Clinical Symptoms

Most growing fractures can be found in the calvaria, in particular in the parietal bone (50%) [150]. Sometimes they can be found at the base of the skull or in the roof of the orbit. It is very rare for a growing fracture to be present in the posttraumatic diastasis of a suture [149]. Generally, it concerns linear fractures. Normally, a depressed fracture will not develop into a growing fracture [151]; however, a linear fracture that originates from a depressed fracture can develop into a growing fracture [152]. In a fracture with a diastasis >4 mm, there is an increased risk for the development of a growing fracture [153, 154].

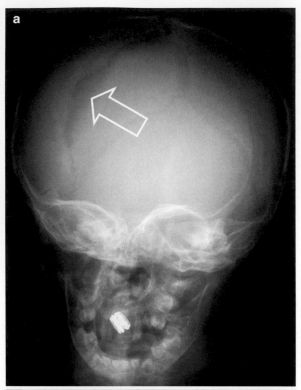

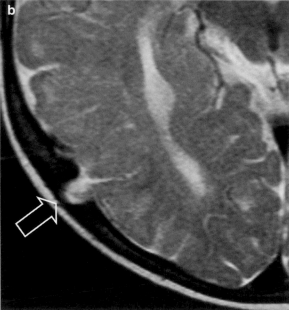

Fig. 2.17 (a) One-year-old girl with a growing skull fracture. The skull view shows a diastatic fracture on the right dorsal parietal side. (b) Pre-operative MRI shows a dura defect and prolapsed meninges and brain tissue in the diastatic fracture (*open arrow*)

3.1 Introduction

Due to the malleability of the thorax in (young) children, rib fractures are seen less frequent than in adults. The most prevalent causes in young children are child abuse, direct severe thoracic trauma and congenital bone disorders. In this group of children it is possibly the most overlooked fracture, since often there are no conspicuous clinical symptoms. Rib fractures in older children and adults are mainly the result of accidents.

Williams and Connolly analysed ten articles from the medical literature to arrive at a number of general conclusions on rib fractures in young children [1]. They summarise their conclusion in a clinical bottom line:

- The likelihood that child abuse is the cause of rib fractures decreases as the child grows older.
- Rib fractures in children <3 years old are very suspect for child abuse.

- The absence of fractures on a radiograph does not exclude their presence. In particular, fresh paravertebral-localised fractures are not always (clearly) visible on radiographs, unless there is dislocation of the fracture (Fig. 3.1).

3.2 Signs, Symptoms and Complications

Rib fractures rarely show symptoms or complications and are in young children hardly ever a reason for hospital referral. It is assumed that approximately 80% of fractures do not give any complaints [2]. This means, as mentioned earlier, that in an unknown number of young children rib fractures are not diagnosed. When they are found, it is an accidental finding in a child that is examined for other reasons (Fig. 3.2), or a finding within the scope of a full radiological examination in a

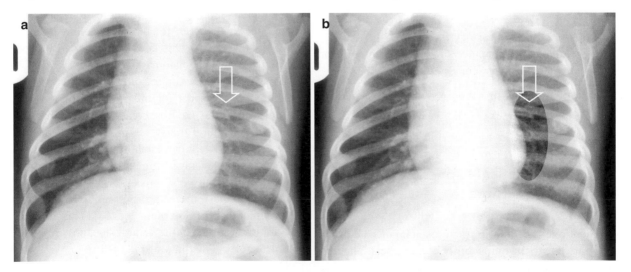

Fig. 3.1 (a) Fresh rib fractures on the left posterior side with mutual dislocation of the fracture ends. (b) (a) has been enhanced with a photo-enhancement programme to improve the visibility of the fractures

R. A. C. Bilo et al., *Forensic Aspects of Pediatric Fractures*,
DOI: 10.1007/978-3-540-78716-7_3, © Springer-Verlag Berlin Heidelberg 2010

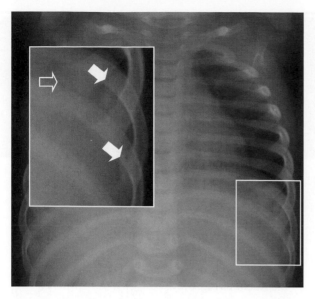

Fig. 3.2 The mother of an 8-month-old child lodged a complaint for domestic violence. Shortly before, the boy had presented at the emergency department because the father had supposedly fallen down the stairs while carrying the child on his arm. The combination of complaint and earlier accident resulted in a full skeletal survey. The chest radiograph showed healing anterior (*open arrow*) and anterolateral rib fractures (*arrow*) on the left side

young child that is suspected of being abused. It has been established that when rib fractures are found, they are seldom the only anomaly (Fig. 3.3a–f) [3].

Complaints are only seen with pleura irritation or when there are other injuries. This may cause pain and lead to noticeable crying.

As a result of rib fractures the following – albeit very rare – complications may occur:

- Rupture of intercostal vessels
- Development of a haemothorax, a pneumothorax or subcutaneous emphysema

In case of fractures of the lower ribs, one should be aware of simultaneous damage to the spleen, stomach and/or bowels [4].

3.3 Biomechanical Aspects of Rib Fractures

As mentioned before, rib fractures in infants are probably rare due to the malleability of their chest. The ribs will rather deform than break, unless a certain level is exceeded.

Older children and adults sustain rib fractures as a result of accidents, such as a fall or a traffic accident. In children below the age of 2, without congenital metabolic bone disease, it is rare to find another cause for rib fractures than child abuse [5–7]. In these infants, accidental rib fractures are rare and nearly always the result of severe thoracic trauma in an accident [8]. Rib fractures are seldom seen as a result of deliveries, resuscitations and physiotherapy (see further on). Due to the malleability of the chest, one can exclude the possibility of rib fractures resulting from picking the child up in normal daily interactions and care.

Rib fractures result from two different kinds of impacting force: static loading (compression) and dynamic impact loading (direct external forces on the ribs).

3.3.1 Static Loading: Compression

In young children rib fractures are usually caused by static loading resulting from compression and/or deformation of the chest, as happens when the chest is circled by both hands and compressed [4, 9]. Here, the forces released during compression may have various effects and lead to fractures at different locations (Figs. 3.4 and 3.5 and Table 3.1). These fractures may be single of multiple, and are often found bilateral. The fractures will first be sustained at the posterior side, at the place where the mechanical forces are highest and where there is leverage. When compression increases, lateral and then anterior fractures will follow the posterior fractures [10]. This does not necessarily leave externally visible haematomas.

In particular posterior fractures (posterior or posterolateral) are suspect for this mechanism, since at the posterior side the ribs break when compressed against the vertebral transverse processes. By means of experiments, Kleinman established that there had to be considerable leverage from the posterior end of the rib against the transverse processes [11]. This effect occurs when the transverse processes is compressed in the direction of the sternum [12, 13]. This causes a fracture in the cortex at the ventral side, possibly with complete cortical disruption [11, 14–16].

During accidents (mostly fractures due to dynamic impact loading) and in medical proceedings

Fig. 3.3 (**a**) Three-month-old boy admitted to the intensive care unit with a Glasgow coma score of 3. At physical examination skin lesions are found corresponding with burns, possibly a cigarette (*open arrow*) and a haematoma suspect for a bite injury (*arrow*). (**b**) Spinal view of the skeletal survey shows healing rib fractures (*open arrow*) on the left posterior side. (**c**) Skull shows a comminuted bilateral skull fracture (besides the physiologically open sutures). (**d**) Doppler ultrasound of the skull made at the paediatric intensive care unit shows a retrograde flow during diastole in the pericallosal artery. This is congruous with intracranial pressure in cerebral oedema. (**e**) CT at admittance shows an oedematous swollen brain with signs of infarction. (**f**) CT made 7 months after the first day of hospitalisation shows sever focal and diffuse tissue loss

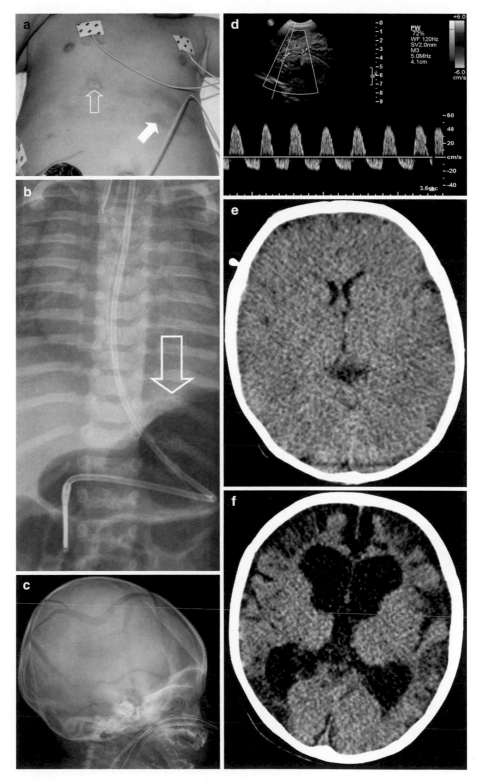

(compression during, for example, resuscitation – static loading) this leverage is seldom seen. During accidents, this kind of fracture only occurs when the joint is subject to great force. A comprehensive anamnesis in which detailed attention is paid to the events and actions enables differentiation.

In front-to-back compression the sternum is pushed inwards, this is also the case when the vertebrae are not pushed in the direction of the sternum. Hereby the costochondral junctions are pushed inwards, which may result in fractures [16].

Lateral compression may lead to fractures on the posterior side of the costochondral junction.

In summary, compression results in two kinds of fracture:

- Resulting from stress in the rib (costochondral, anterior, lateral, and posterior)
- Resulting from leverage (around the vertebra)

It was found that compression fractures are seldom accompanied by bruising [8], although in the shape of thumb and finger prints (thumb print at the anterior/upper part of the chest and fingerprints at the posterior side, possibly paravertebral) they may be the only clinical signs for compression fractures of the ribs (Fig. 3.6a and b) [17].

3.3.2 Dynamic Impact Loading: Direct Impact of External Force

In only a minority of cases, rib fractures will result from directly exerted force on the chest. This is true for accidental violence (e.g. a fall on an object or an accident) as non-accidental violence (e.g. a blow/punch or kick). Rib fractures can also be sustained by sudden deceleration, when a child hits a blunt object or wall at high speed. Independent of the nature of the force applied, the fracture is sustained at either the place of impact or the place where as a result of the impact the greatest stress is exerted on the rib (Figs. 3.7 and 3.8). Often haematomas can be found at the place of impact [18].

Rib fractures due to contact (dynamic impact loading) are found mostly in mobile children of >2 years old, whereas fractures due to compression (static loading) are predominantly found in younger children [4].

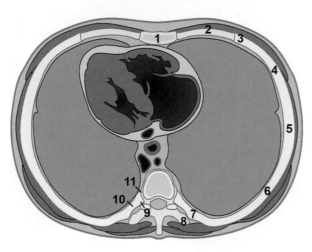

Fig. 3.4 Anatomy of the costal arch and possible locations for rib fractures in anterior-posterior and sideways compression. 1. Sternum. 2. Rib cartilage. 3. Sternal end of the rib. 4. Anterior costal arch. 5. Lateral costal arch. 6. Posterior costal arch. 7. Costal tubercle. 8. Tubercle of the transverse process of the vertebra. 9. Rib head. 10. Rib neck. 11. Costovertebral joint

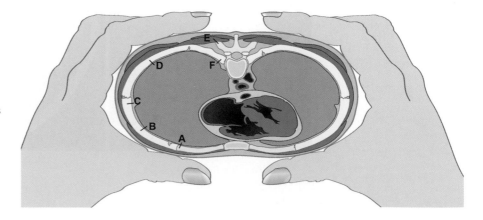

Fig. 3.5 Schematic representation of bimanual chest compression. Fractures locations at the:
(**a**) costochondral junction.
(**b**) Anterior costal arch.
(**c**) Lateral costal arch.
(**d**) Posterior costal arch.
(**e**) Transverse processes.
(**f**) Head of the rib

Table 3.1 Biomechanics of rib fractures [9]

Compression	Mechanism	Fractures located at:
Symmetrical		
Anterior-posterior	Force exerted from the front (back on surface) – sternum moved towards spine – compression on the inside of the ribs and tension on the outside of the ribs	• Anterior, lateral and posterior costal arch • Costochondral junction (possibly)
Anterior-posterior/posterior-anterior	Force exerted from the front as well as the back – sternum and spine moved towards each other – leverage of rib on transverse process	• Transverse process (leverage) • Head of the rib (costovertebral joint)
Posterior-anterior	Force exerted from back (front on surface) – spine moved towards sternum – leverage of rib on transverse process	• Transverse process (leverage) • Rib head (costovertebral joint)
From the side	Force exerted from the side – lateral costal arches moved toward each other In the presence of leverage: (depends on the manner of holding and compressing)	• Anterior, lateral and posterior costal arch • Costochondral junction (possibly) • Transverse process (leverage) • Rib head (costovertebral joint)
Asymmetrical		
Combinations of anterior-posterior and sideways compression	Forces exerted to different degrees from the front, back and side– oblique – asymmetrical deformation of the ribcage in which the right or left anterior side is pushed in the direction of, respectively, the left or right posterior side	• Fractures possible at all anatomical locations

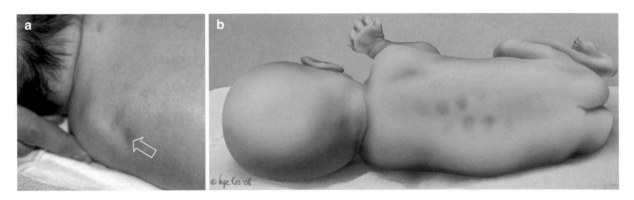

Fig. 3.6 A Haematomas at the location of the finger prints (*open arrow*) on the back of the patient in Fig. 3.3. (**b**) Graphic representation of haematomas in the shape of finger prints on the back, resulting from compression of the chest

3.4 Rib Fractures and Child Abuse

Rib fractures are probably the most common fracture resulting from physical violence (3.6). Of all rib fractures sustained in of child abuse, 90% are found in children <2 years of age [2, 12]. Five to 27% of all fractures sustained by child abuse are rib fractures [13, 19]. It is probable that rib fractures may be found even more frequently in abused children; however, since these fractures usually do not cause any complaints, an unknown number will not be diagnosed. In children that have died from physical violence, one regularly finds fresh and healed/healing rib fractures. In autopsy cases, Kleinman et al. found radiographic evidence of 84 rib fractures (51%) in a total number of 164 fractures in 31 abused children [16].

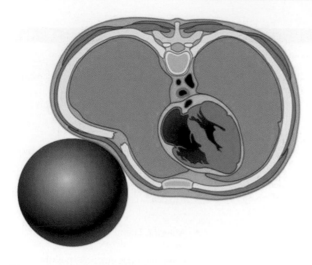

Fig. 3.7 Graphic representation of a rib fracture at the contact site after blunt chest trauma

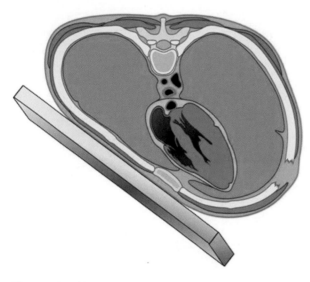

Fig. 3.8 Graphic representation of a rib fracture at the site of the highest stress after blunt chest trauma

In a retrospective study, Barsness et al. researched the positive predictive values (PPV) of rib fractures regarding child abuse in young children [20]. Over a 6-year period, they identified 62 children <3 years old with in total 316 rib fractures. They established that in 51 children (82%) the fractures were the result of physical violence. Their study showed that in children <3 years of age the PPV of a rib fracture as indicator of child abuse is 95%. The PPV increased to 100% at the moment that, based on the anamnesis and clinical data, all other causes of rib fractures, such as illness or accident, could be excluded. Furthermore, their study showed that:

- In child abuse, multiple fractures are more prevalent than single fractures.
- Child abuse was likely when the fractures were located predominantly posterior and lateral (in 78% of children).
- Rib fractures (single or multiple) were the only skeletal signs of child abuse in 29% of their study population.

This corresponded with the data found by Cadzow and Armstrong [8]. It was also found that rib fractures are often found in abused children who sustained fractures of (one of) the extremities or had intracranial pathology (Figs. 3.9a–c and 3.10a–e) [8].

Child abuse should be considered as the cause of the rib fractures when [7, 21, 22]:

- Rib fractures are found after the perinatal period (although rib fractures have been reported sporadically in complicated deliveries).
- There are no indications for bone disease.
- There is no adequate explanation for a trauma that caused the injuries, or when parents/carers provide no explanation at all.
- Multiple bilateral fractures are found particularly in the lower ribs on the posterior and lateral side (combinations of fractures on the posterior and anterior sides are feasible).
- Multiple fractures are found, and based on new-bone formation it can be established that the fractures differ in age (Fig. 3.11a and b).

Posterior-located rib fractures seem to be most prevalent between the 4th and 9th rib. Lateral rib fractures are most prevalent in the lower part of the chest. Damage to the anterior costochondral junction is usually found between the 2nd and 9th rib [23].

One rib can sustain fractures at different locations. When this happens to several ribs it can lead to a 'flail' chest. Hereby the chest wall of the child moves in the opposite direction when breathing: at inspiration the chest wall moves inwards and at expiration outwards. At physical examination it will be found that the chest is no longer firm and feels less malleable. Gibson and Tobias report a 21-day-old infant with a flail chest resulting from non-accidental trauma [24]. They state that child abuse is the most likely explanation for a flail chest in infants when there are no clear indications for serious chest trauma or a metabolic disorder.

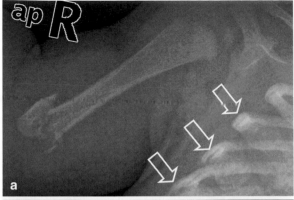

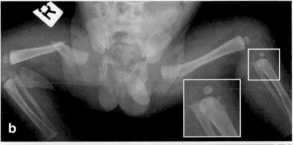

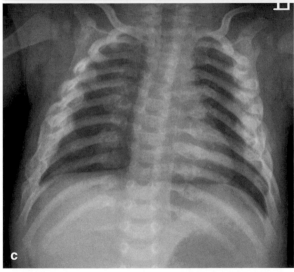

The reliability of the detection of rib fractures depends on the technique used. It seems justified to use detailed radiographs to establish these injuries in living and deceased children (see also Chap. 8) [16].

3.4.1 Posterior Rib Fractures

Eighty percent of all non-accidental rib fractures are posterior fractures. Often, the location of the fracture is not visible until there is callus formation (Figs. 3.12 and 3.13a–c) [13]. Since in the acute phase the fracture can easily be overlooked, it is recommended to make a chest radiograph when non-accidental chest compression is suspected, at the first exanimation as well as at 2-week follow-up [4, 25]. In case of enduring doubt regarding the presence of rib fractures in the acute phase, one may consider to perform a bone scintigraphy (see Chap. 8).

3.4.2 Fractures of the First Rib

Strouse and Owings evaluated 35 children of <2 years of age with rib fractures. Only in four children a fracture of the first rib was found. One child had osteogenesis imperfecta (OI) and three children were victims of child abuse. Strouse and Owings concluded that fractures of the 1st rib (uni- or bilateral) are very suspect for child abuse, since it takes a good deal of force to fracture these ribs. Hereby one should think along the line of direct-impact violence, compression, shaking or acute axial loading [26].

Fig. 3.9 (**a**) Right distal metaphyseal humerus fracture in a 3-month-old boy. The healing mid-axillar rib fractures are clearly visible on this view (*open arrows*), but were missed when reporting the humerus fracture. At the age of 3–4 weeks he had already been seen for a fracture of the left humerus. The physicians deemed the parent's statement that the child had been picked up awkwardly plausible. (**b**) Six days after the visit for the distal metaphyseal humerus fracture, the child presented again at the emergency department, this time for a suspected femur fracture on the right. The radiograph shows a transverse mid-shaft femur fracture and a metaphyseal corner fracture of the proximal part of the left (see inset). These findings resulted in a full skeletal survey. (**c**) The chest radiograph showed more than 30 rib fractures originating from different points in time and showing different stages of healing.

3.4.3 Injuries to the Costochondral Junction

In the literature there are only a limited number of articles in which the authors draw attention to injuries to the costochondral junction that result from child abuse (Fig. 3.14).

Smeets et al. reported a physically battered child with fractures of skull, ribs and long bones. An

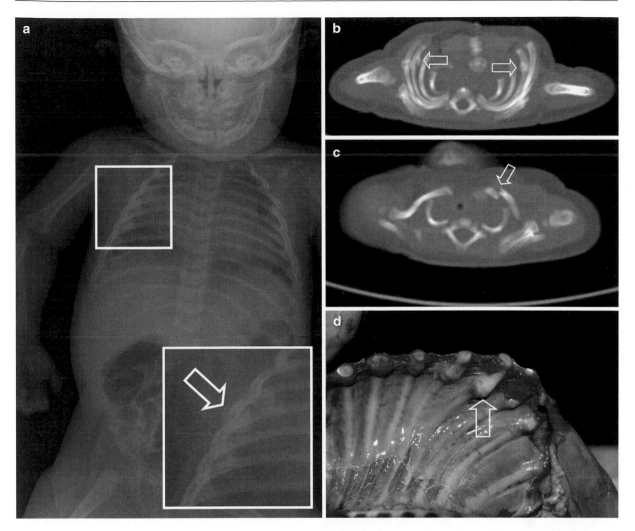

Fig. 3.15 (**a**) Postmortem radiograph of a 2-month-old girl found dead in her crib. In compliance with the Dutch SIDS protocol a skeletal survey was done. The chest radiograph showed bilaterally localised lateral rib fractures which were, when considering the callus formation, not recently sustained (see inset, *open arrow*). (**b**) Bilateral-localised lateral rib fractures of an older date, visible on the total-body CT scan (MIP images, *open arrow*). (**c**) Left clavicle fracture (*open arrow*). This fracture was only visible on the CT scan and not on the radiograph, not even retrospectively. (**d**) Photograph at autopsy shows callus formation on the anterior side of the left chest wall (*open arrow*)

one a skull fracture [38]. In another retrospective study of over 20,000 births, no rib fractures were found [39]. Neither did Bhat et al. find any rib fractures in their study of 34,946 live-born infants [40]. The literature only counts a limited number of case reports on rib fractures in new-born infants (see Table 3.3).

Rib fractures resulting from birth seem to be unlikely in normal term birth and a normal postpartum physical examination. All children described up to the present day had, as far as one can evaluate from case reports, various symptoms that pointed to a traumatic birth: cephalic haematoma, haematomas, swelling and

subcutaneous crepitus. The rib fractures were multiple, and located unilateral and posterior.

3.5.2 Rib Fractures and Resuscitation

Hoke and Chamberlain mentioned that in the medical literature the incidence of rib fractures in adults resulting from conventional cardiopulmonary resuscitation ranges from 13% to 97% [41]. They also mention that it is rare for any rib fractures to occur during

Table 3.2 Differences between accidental and non-accidental rib fractures [74]

	Accidental	Non-accidental
Primary complaint	Severe trauma with adequate anamnesis: traffic accidents, fall from a height, shot wounds	Unexplained respiratory problems (usually no complaints)
Age child		
Average	8 years and 7 months	3 months
Range	2–15 years	0.5–7 months
Number of fractures		
Average	3.3	11.8
Range	1–8	3–23

cardiopulmonary resuscitation in otherwise healthy children, irrespective of whether well-trained or untrained personnel perform the massage. Various other studies confirm this proposition [7, 42, 43]. The reported incidence in children ranges from 0% to 2%. Hoke and Chamberlain maintain that child abuse should always be considered when rib fractures are present after resuscitation, in view of the low incidence of rib fractures after resuscitation and that:

- The reasons for resuscitation (cardiac arrest) should be carefully examined.
- The child should be screened for further abnormalities that could indicate child abuse [41].

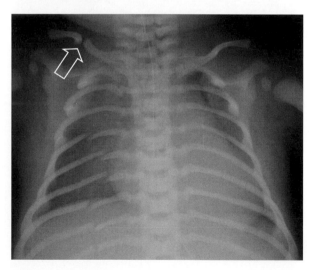

Fig. 3.16 Macrosomal neonate born at 41 weeks, birth weight 5,656 g. Vaginal delivery was complicated by shoulder dystocia. Clinically, a fracture of the right clavicle was seen immediately after birth. A chest radiograph at admittance shows besides the clavicle fracture (*open arrow*), multiple ipsilateral posterior rib fractures (ribs 4–9)

Feldman and Brewer examined 113 children who had to be resuscitated [7]. This group included 41 abused children. Twenty-nine children had rib fractures (14 of those were caused by child abuse). Other causes for fractures were: a traffic accident (four children), rickets/osteoporosis (five children), surgical interventions (five children) and osteogenesis imperfecta (one child). In spite of lengthy resuscitation, no fractures could be attributed to this procedure. Resuscitations were performed by persons with completely different levels of expertise in this field (parents, emergency department personnel, other hospital personnel and combinations of the aforementioned. Fractures that were the result of child abuse were often present in multiples, were of different ages and spread over multiple adjacent ribs. Moreover, frequently these children also showed other physical and radiological signs of mistreatment and neglect.

Spevak et al. performed a retrospective study of autopsy data and postmortem radiographs of 91 infants <1 year of old, resuscitated for other reasons than child abuse (56 boys, 35 girls; average 2.4 months – ranging from 26 h to 8.5 months) [42]. In none of the infants rib fractures were found. The conclusion of Spevak et al. was: 'when rib fractures are encountered in an otherwise normal child, child abuse must be considered'.

Bush et al. did a retrospective study into type, number and severity of unexpected complications in resuscitations in children [44]. They evaluated in total 211 children under the age of 12 years (average age 19 months). Children with anamnestic or physical signs of prior trauma were excluded from the study. Cause of death was: cod death (56%), drowning (8%), congenital cardiac defects (7%) and pneumonia (4%). Average time of resuscitation was 45 min (ranging from 5 to 80 min) Fifteen children (7%) sustained injuries that were

Table 3.3 Rib fractures resulting from delivery (Reprinted from [82]. With permission)

Author	Sex	Birth weight (g)	Dystocia	Delivery	Fracture location
Thomas [5]	Nk	5896	Nk	Forceps	Right posterior ribs 5–7
Rizzolo [75]	Nk	3300	+	Vacuum	5 Ribs posterolateral[a]
Barry [76]	Nk	5020	+	Normal	5 Ribs posterior[a]
Hartmann [77]	F	3912	–	Vacuum	Right posterior ribs 4–8
	M	4205		Vacuum	Right posterior ribs 6–8
Bulloch [78]	Nk	3946	+	Vacuum	Right posterior ribs 4–6 + right clavicle
Durani [79]	M	4309	–	Normal	Left posterior rib 7 + left clavicle
Ibanez [80]	M	3800	+	Vacuum	Right posterior ribs 7 and 8
Landman [81]	F	4400	–	Normal	Left posterior ribs 5–7 + left clavicle
	M	4500	–	Normal	Left posterior ribs 5–7
Van Rijn [82]	F	5070	+	McRoberts	Right posterior ribs 6 and 7 + right clavicle
	M	5020	+	Forceps	Left posterior ribs 4–6 + left clavicle
	M	4300	+	Normal	Left posterior ribs 5–8 + left clavicle
	F	5656	+	Normal	Right posterior ribs 4–9 + right clavicle

Nk not known

[a]Number known, exact location unknown

significant from a medical point of view and that could be considered as resulting from the resuscitation: retroperitoneal haemorrhages (two children), pneumothorax (one child), pulmonary haemorrhage (one child), epicardial haematoma (one child) and perforation of the stomach (one child). Although some children had been resuscitated for a protracted period of time by various persons with different levels of expertise, rib fractures at the costochondral junction were found in only one child. Bush et al. concluded that notable injury inflicted by medical procedures is rare and is only seen in 3% of children. According to Bush et al. one should, irrespective of the resuscitation, always consider child abuse as a cause when traumatic injury is found after resuscitation. Furthermore, they mention that the case reports found, only discuss rib fractures after prolonged and strenuous resuscitation. Gunther et al. confirm the earlier-mentioned data [31].

Betz and Liebhardt evaluated the cause of death of 233 children between the ages of 5 days and 7 years [43]. In 190 children death from natural causes was proclaimed, the others died after a trauma. Ninety-four of the children who died a natural death had been resuscitated. Two of them had bilateral fractures in the midclavicular line. In 15 of the 43 trauma-related deaths, rib fractures were found, predominantly on the posterior side. In this study it is remarkable that the physicians caused more frequently or nearly exclusively notable

injuries during resuscitation. This makes the regularly provided explanation for rib fractures in deceased children – e.g. that they are the result of resuscitation by an inexperienced person in panic – quite improbable.

In 2006, Maguire et al. published a comprehensive study of the literature into the prevalence of rib fractures in cardiopulmonary resuscitation (427 articles in various languages, published between 1950 and 1 October 2005) [45]. In the end they included six studies with the data of in total 923 children. Three resuscitated children had sustained an anterior-located rib fracture. Two fractures were mid-clavicular and one was located at the costochondral junction. The presence of multiple fractures has also been described [45]. Resuscitation was carried out for different periods of time by trained medical personnel and by non-trained non-medical personnel. Maguire et al. could not find one well-documented posterior-localised rib fracture that resulted from resuscitation. They remarked that in the study they evaluated, the most modern and sensitive techniques for the detection of rib fractures in young children had not been applied.

The study of Dolinak underlines the conclusion of Maguire et al. regarding the diagnostics of rib fractures [46]. Dolinak evaluated the data of 70 consecutive autopsies in infants between 2 weeks and 8 months old that had been resuscitated. Children with injuries (either anamnestic or from examination) were excluded. After carefully removing the pleura from the ribs of eight children, he found subtle anterolateral-located rib fractures. Seven of the infants had more than one fracture (up to ten fractures in total). Five children had bilateral rib fractures. There was little or no associated blood loss around the fracture line, and as such the fracture could easily have been overlooked were it not for the removal of the pleura. Dolinak maintains that the rib fractures he found were the equivalent of rib fractures regularly found after resuscitation in adults.

3.5.2.1 Posterior Rib Fractures in Resuscitation?

From previous data it can be concluded that rib fractures in resuscitation happen rarely and that, when they occur, they are localised at the anterior and anterolateral side and (seldom or) never at the posterior side. From a biomechanical point of view this seems correct when the resuscitation took place in the traditional way, 'two-finger' cardiac massage ('two-finger' infant cardiopulmonary resuscitation). Hereby anterior-posterior compression is applied, with the child supine on a flat solid surface, and the sternum is pressed towards the spine during cardiac massage. Pressure is exerted exclusively on the front of the chest. In relation to the ribs and the costochondral junction, the sternum is moved inwards. At the same time, the spine and the ribs are more or less stationary on the flat solid surface (Section 3.3.1). According to Chapman, this makes it impossible for leverage of the ribs on the vertebral processes to take place [17]. Even if the infant lies on a soft surface, such as a bed, it is unlikely that there will

be posterior rib fractures, since the chest as a whole and the ribs and spine on the posterior side are pressed simultaneously into the soft surface below. Moreover, according to Worm and Jones, the forces exerted in two-finger cardiac massage are below the level of force required to cause rib fractures [9].

In the international guidelines of 2000 for the resuscitation of neonates and infants and in the revised version of these guidelines of 2006, the 'two-thumb-encircling hands chest compression' is considered to be an effective form of cardiac massage [47, 48]. In this manner of resuscitation, anterior-posterior compression is exerted while the ribcage of the infant is encircled by both hands (thumbs on the sternum and fingers on the back) and sternum and spine are compressed towards each other (bimanual anterior-posterior compressions) (Fig. 3.17). This manner of encircling the chest is similar to the earlier described manner in non-accidental compression(Section 3.3.1).

In 'two-thumbs resuscitation', there are more risk factors for sustaining rib fractures [9]. There is a risk that the compressions during resuscitation are too deep (more than the recommended depth of one third of the anterior-posterior diameter of the chest) [47, 48], that the compressions are too firm and/or that there is too much deformation of the ribs. This increases the risk for fractures and, due to the posterior leverage, also the risk for posterior rib fractures. This has been confirmed by Clouse and Lantz [49]. They described four infants (1 day to 3 months old), who had been admitted to hospital and had died of natural causes. At autopsy, posterior rib fractures were found in these infants. Child abuse was considered to be ruled out.

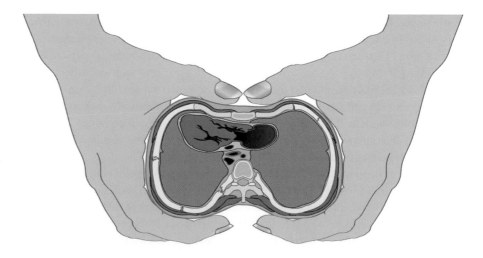

Fig. 3.17 Graphic representation of the 'two thumbs encircling hands chest compression), as advised in 2006 by the International Liaison Committee on Resuscitation (ILCOR)

All children had been resuscitated by two-thumb-encircling hands compressions. Three children showed recent rib fractures related to the resuscitation attempts shortly before they died. One child showed older rib fractures with callus formation; however, this finding could be explained by repeated resuscitation attempts.

The earlier-mentioned data show that two-thumbs resuscitation may cause posterior rib fractures and that in cases in which rib fractures are seen in resuscitated infants, it is important to inquire in great detail how and by whom the resuscitation was performed (possibly more than one person).

3.5.3 Rib Fractures and Physiotherapy

Over the past few years a number of articles have been published in which authors report rib fractures resulting from chest physiotherapy (CPT).

Chalumet et al. describe five children (all boys, average age 3 months) over a period of 4 years who appeared to have sustained a rib fracture after CPT for bronchiolitis (four children) or pneumonia (one child) [50]. The average number of fractures was 4 (range 1–5). The fractures were located between the 3rd and the 8th rib, in four children lateral and in one child posterior. The authors estimate that the prevalence of rib fractures due to CPT is 1:1,000 in children admitted for bronchiolitis or pneumonia. They consider CPT to be a rare cause of rib fractures.

Gorincour et al. did a prospective study into rib fractures in children treated for bronchiolitis [51]. They found in total six children of less than 2 years old with lateral rib fractures and possible remnants of rib fractures. The authors believe that in these children no plausible grounds for child abuse were present. The only possibility left was CPT. Twelve of the 14 defects found were localised in the lateral part of the chest from the 4th to the 7th rib. No defects were found at the costochondral junctions. In 12 of 14 defects, reaction of the periosteum was seen without a clearly visible fracture. According to the authors this was feasible since repeated CPT causes subperiosteal haemorrhages rather than real fractures. Finally, Chanelière et al. describe two children that had sustained lateral rib fractures after physiotherapy for bronchiolitis [52]. The authors posed that, although rib fractures resulting from physiotherapy are rare, physicians should be aware of the possibility when confronted with rib fractures.

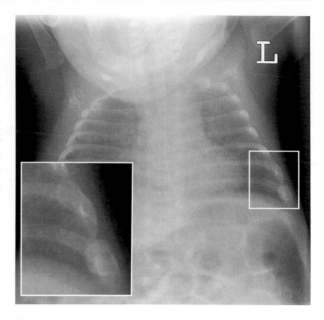

Fig. 3.18 Premature infant born after a pregnancy of 26 weeks, and 10 weeks old at the time of the chest radiograph. As accidental finding, left lateral rib fractures were seen (see inset). Laboratory test did not show any indications for metabolic defects

3.5.4 Rib Fractures in Premature Infants

Compared to term neonates, premature infants are at higher risk for fractures in day-to-day handling. Most often these are fractures of the long bones and ribs (Fig. 3.18). Skeletal lesions in premature infants usually cause no clinical symptoms. According to Helfer et al., even during passive exercising a parent may cause a fracture in a premature infant [53].

Prematurely born children and critically ill neonates also run a high risk for sustaining rib fractures during resuscitation. These are nearly always located anterolateral (front and side) [13]. These premature children also run an increased risk for rickets, which may include rib fractures [54–56].

3.5.5 Rib Fractures in Serious Coughing Fits

Various publications draw attention to rib fractures that result from the forces released during prolonged and forceful coughing in general and in severe coughing fits

Fig. 4.10 (**a**) Nine-year-old girl with Langerhans cell histiocytosis. The conventional radiograph of the cervical spine shows a collapsed vertebral body at the level C4 & C6 (*open arrow*). (**b**) Sagittal CT reconstruction shows a vertebra plana at the C4 level (*open arrow*) and a less severe vertebral collapse at level C6. (**c**) T2-weighted sagittal MRI view of the earlier found (CT and conventional radiograph) cervical collapse at the C4 level (*open arrow*) and C6. Collapsed vertebrae seen at the thoracic level (*arrows*). All fractures are consistent with Langerhans cell histiocytosis

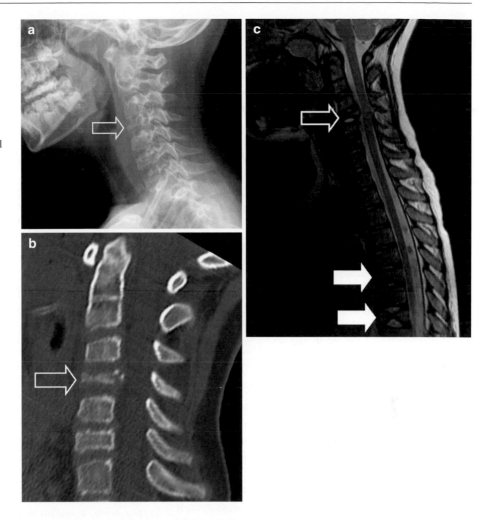

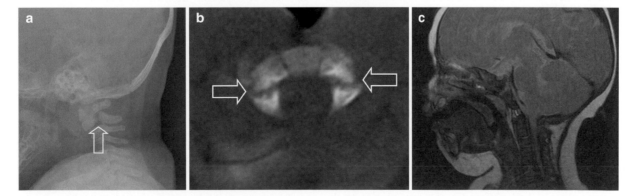

Fig. 4.11 (**a**) Radiological examination for suspected child abuse. The cervical spine view shows anterolisthesis (>3 mm) and a defect in the arch of C2 (*open arrow*) (Reprinted from [76]. With permission). (**b**) CT of the cervical spine shows a sclerotic margin of the arch defects (*open arrow*). (c) MRI of the cervical spine shows no signs of haematoma or bone oedema (sub-optimal quality due to movement artefacts)

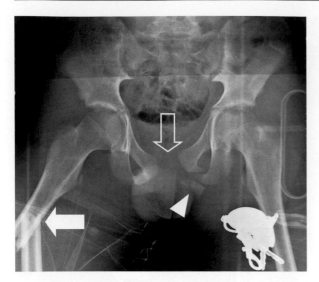

Fig. 4.12 After high-energy trauma, the pelvic view of a young patient shows diastasis of the symphysis pubis (*open arrow*) a fracture of the inferior pubic ramus and the left pubic bone (*arrow point*), and a transverse fracture of the right femur (*arrow*)

In the medical literature, pelvic fractures resulting from child abuse are rarely found [98–100]. Fractures of the pubic bone and ischium have been reported [18]. Sometimes, the only sign of child abuse may be a periosteal reaction [8]. Since it takes a great deal of force to cause a pelvic fracture, child abuse should be considered when the anamnesis does not mention severe trauma [101]. Moreover, it is not rare to find other injuries resulting from child abuse, such as severe intracranial injuries or other fractures [102].

In violence-induced femur fractures it is essential that the pelvis is meticulously examined for the presence of fractures on the side of the femur fracture [44].

Extensive haematomas from physical or sexual abuse in the area of the perineum, buttocks and thighs may result in heterotopic calcifications in the muscles and fatty tissue of the pelvic area and thighs [98].

Johnson et al. describe two children that sustained pelvic fractures and one child with a fracture of the femoral shaft related to sexual abuse [103]. A 3-year-old girl had suffered extensive injuries to the soft tissue of the arms, legs and perineum. Moreover, she showed fractures of both pubic arches and the sacral side of the right sacroiliac joint. A 5-year-old girl had presented with acute abdominal complaints and pneumoperitoneum due to a rectum rupture from sexual abuse; she also had an old healed fracture of the pubic arch with damage to the pubic symphysis. The last girl, 5 months old, had sustained a tear of the hymen and a fracture of the femoral shaft without dislocation.

References

1. England SP, Sundberg S. Management of common pediatric fractures. Ped Clin North Am 1996;43(5):991–1012
2. Kogutt MS, Swischuk LE, Fagan CJ. Patterns of injury and significance of uncommon fractures in the battered child syndrome. Am J Roentg 1974; 121(1):143–9
3. Miller DS, Boswick JA Jr. Lesions of the brachial plexus associated with fractures of the clavicle. Clin Orthop Relat Res 1969;64:144–9
4. Nordqvist A, Petersson C. The incidence of fractures of the clavicle. Clin Orthop Relat Res 1994;300:127–32
5. Pyper JB. Non-union of fractures of the clavicle. Injury 1978;9(4):268–70
6. Rowe CR. An atlas of anatomy and treatment of midclavicular fractures. Clin Orthop Relat Res 1968;58:29–42
7. Goddard NJ, Stabler J, Albert JS. Atlanto-axial rotatory fixation and fracture of the clavicle: an association and classification. J Bone Joint Surg [Br] 1990;72(1):72–5
8. Kleinman PK. Diagnostic imaging of child abuse. Williams and Wilkins, 1987
9. Merten DF, Radkowski MA, Leonidar JC. The abused child: a radiologic reappraisal. Radiology 1983;146(2):377–81
10. Herndon WA. Child abuse in a military population. J Pediatr Orthop 1983;3(1):73–6
11. Joseph PR, Rosenfeld W. Clavicular fractures in neonates. Am J Dis Child 1990;144(2):165–7
12. Cohen AW, Otto SR. Obstetric clavicular fractures: a three year analysis. J Reprod Med 1980;25(3):119–22
13. Farkas R, Levine S. X-ray incidence of fractured clavicle in vertex presentation. Am J Obstet Gynecol 1950;59:204–6
14. Rubin A. Birth injuries: incidence, mechanisms, and end results. Obstet Gynecol 1964;23:218–21
15. Camus M, Lefevre G, Veron P et al Traumatismes obstétricaux du nouveau-né. Enquete retrospective à propos de 20409 naissances. J Gynecol Obstet Biol Reprod 1985;14: 1033–44
16. Bhat BV, Kumar A, Oumachigui A. Bone injuries during delivery. Indian J Pediatr 1994;61(4):401–5
17. Jones E. Skeletal growth and development as related to trauma. In Green NE, Swiontkowski MF. Skeletal trauma in children. Saunders, 1998, 2
18. Merten DF, Cooperman DR, Thompson GH. Skeletal manifestations of child abuse. In Reece RM. Child abuse – medical diagnosis and management. Lea & Febiger 1992, 23–53
19. Merten DF, Carpenter BC. Radiologic imaging of inflicted injury in the child abuse syndrome. Ped Clin North Am 1990;37(4):815–37

20. Johnson CF. Inflicted injury vs. accidental injury. Peds Clin North Am 1990;379(4):791–811

21. Launius GD, Silberstein MJ, Luisini A et al Radiology of child abuse. In Monteleone JA, Brodeur AE. Child maltreatment – a clinical guide and reference. GW Medical 2nd edition 1998, 31–58

22. Landin LA. Fracture patterns in children. Analysis of 8,682 fractures with special reference to incidence, etiology and secular changes in a Swedish urban population 1950–1979. Acta Orthop Scand Suppl 1983;202:1–109

23. Lichtenberg RP. A study of 2532 fractures in children. Am J Surg 1954;87:330–8

24. Kreisinger V. Sur le traitement des fractures de la clavicule. Rev Chir 1927;65:396–407

25. Stanley D, Trowbridge EA, Norris SH. The mechanism of clavicular fractures. A clinical and biomechanical analysis. J Bone Joint Surg [Br] 1988;70(3):461–4

26. Kleinman PK. Skelet trauma: general considerations. In Kleinman PK. Diagnostic imaging of child abuse. Mosby, 2nd ed, 1998, 8–25

27. Hobbs CJ,Hanks HGI, Wynne JM. Child abuse and neglect – a clinician's handbook. Churchill Livingstone, 1993, 57–65

28. Hechter S, Huyer D, Manson D. Sternal fractures as a manifestation of abusive injury in children. Pediatr Radiol 2002;32(12):902–6

29. Wada A, Fujii T, Takamura K et al Sternal segment dislocation in children. J Pediatr Orthop 2002;22(6):729–31

30. Hoke RS, Chamberlain D. Skeletal chest injuries secondary to cardiopulmonary resuscitation. Resuscitation 2004;63(3): 327–38

31. Nijs S, Broos PL. Sterno-manubrial dislocation in a 9-year-old gymnast. Acta Chir Belg 2005;105(4):422–4

32. DeFriend DE, Franklin K. Isolated sternal fracture--a swing-related injury in two children. Pediatr Radiol 2001;31(3): 200–2

33. Imitani R. Fractures of the scapula: a review of 53 fractures. J Trauma 1975;15(6):473–8

34. Wilber MC, Evans EB. Fractures of the scapula: an analysis of forty cases and a review of the literature. J Bone Joint Surg 1977;59(3):358–62

35. McGinnis M, Denton JR. Fractures of the scapula: a retrospective study of 40 fractured scapulae. J Trauma 1989;29 (11):1488–93

36. Ada JR, Miller ME. Scapular fractures. Analysis of 113 cases. Clin Orthop Relat Res 1991;(269):174–80

37. McGahan JP, Rab GT, Dublin A. Fractures of the scapula. J Trauma 1980;20(10):880–3

38. Thompson DA, Flynn TC, Miller PW et al The significance of scapular fractures. J Trauma 1985;25(10):974–7

39. Swischuk LE. Radiographic signs of skeletal trauma. In Ludwig S, Kornberg AE. Child Abuse - a medical reference. Churchill Livingstone, 1992, 151–74

40. Kleinman PK, Spevak MR. Variations in acromial ossification simulating infant abuse in victims of sudden infant death syndrome. Radiology 1991;180(1):185–7

41. Keats TE, Anderson MW. Atlas of normal roentgen variants which may simulate disease. Mosby Elsevier, 2006

42. Cirak B, Ziegfeld S, Knight VM et al Spinal injuries in children. J Pediatr Surg 2004;39(4):607–12

43. Gabos PG, Tuten HR, Leet A, Stanton RP. Fracture-dislocation of the lumbar spine in an abused child. Pediatrics 1998;101(3 Pt 1):473–7

44. Brodeur AE, Monteleone JA. Child Maltreatment. A Clinical Guide and Reference. GW Medical, 1994, 32

45. Vialle R, Mary P, Schmider L et al Spinal fracture through the neurocentral synchondrosis in battered children: a report of three cases. Spine 2006;31(11):e345–9

46. Ghatan S, Ellenbogen RG. Pediatric spine and spinal cord injury after inflicted trauma. Neurosurg Clin N Am 2002; 13(2):227–33

47. Akbarnia BA, Torg JS, Kirkpatrick J et al Manifestations of the battered-child syndrome. J Bone Joint Surg Am 1974; 56(6):1159–66

48. Galleno H, Oppenheim WL. The battered-child syndrome revisited. Clin Orthop Relat Res 1982;(162):11–9

49. Bode KS, Newton PO. Pediatric nonaccidental trauma thoracolumbar fracture-dislocation: posterior spinal fusion with pedicle screw fixation in an 8-month-old boy. Spine 2007;32 (14):E388–93

50. Swischuk LE. Spine and spinal cord trauma in the battered child syndrome. Radiology 1969;92(4):733–8

51. Cullen JC. Spinal lesions in battered babies. J Bone Joint Surg Br 1975;57(3):364–6

52. Dickson RA, Leatherman KD. Spinal injuries in child abuse: case report. J Trauma 1078;18(12):811–2

53. Gosnold JK, Sivaloganathan S. Spinal cord damage in a case of nonaccidental injury in children. Med Sci Law 1980; 20(1):54–7

54. Kleinman PK, Zito JL. Avulsion of the spinous processes caused by infant abuse. Radiology 1984;151(2):389–91

55. Piatt JH, Steinberg M. Isolated spinal cord injury as a presentation of child abuse. Pediatrics 1995;96(4 Pt 1):780–2

56. King J, Diefendorf D, Apthorp J et al Analysis of 429 fractures in 189 battered children. J Ped Ortho 1988;8(5):585–9

57. Akbarnia BA, Campbell RM. The role of the orthopedic surgeon in child abuse. In Morrissy RT, Winter RB. Lovell and Winter's Pediatric Orthopaedics. Lippincott, Williams and Wilkins Publ, 3rd ed, 1990

58. Kleinman PK, Marks SC. Vertebral body fractures in child abuse: radiologic-histopathologic correlates. Invest Radiol 1992;27(9):715–22

59. Diamond P, Hansen CM, Christofersen MR. Child abuse presenting as a thoracolumbar spinal fracture dislocation: a case report. Pediatr Emerg Care 1994;10(2):83–6

60. American College of Radiology. ACR Appropriateness Criteria Suspected Physical Abuse – Child. ACR, 2005 http://www.acr.org/

61. Ogden JA. Skeletal injury in the child. Saunders, 2nd ed, 1990

62. Conry BG, Hall CM. Cervical spine fractures and rear car seat restraints. Arch Dis Child 1987;62(12):1267–8

63. McGrory BJ, Klassen RA, Chao EY et al Acute fracture and dislocations of the cervical spine in children and adolescents. J Bone Joint Surg 1993;75(7):988–95

64. Schwartz GR, Wright SW, Fein JA et al Pediatric cervical spine injury sustained in falls from low heights. Ann Emerg Med 1997;30(3):249–52

65. Shulman ST, Madden JD, Esterly JR et al Transection of the spinal cord. A rare obstetrical complication of cephalic delivery. Arch Dis Child 1971;46(247):291–4

66. Torg B, Das M. Trampoline and minitrampoline injuries to the cervical spine. Clin Sports Med 1985;4(1):45–60

67. Caffey J. The whiplash shaken infant syndrome: manual shaking by the extremities with whiplash-induced intracranial

and intraocular bleedings, linked with residual permanent brain damage and mental retardation. Pediatrics 1974; 54(4): 396–403

68. Rooks J, Sisler C, Burton B. Cervical spine injury in child abuse: report of two cases. Pediatr Radiol 1998;28(3): 193–5

69. Oral R, Rahhal R, Elshershari H et al Intentional avulsion fracture of the second cervical vertebra in a hypotonic child. Pediatr Emerg Care 2006;22(5):352–4

70. Thomas NH, Robinson L, Evans A et al The floppy infant: a new manifestation of nonaccidental injury. Pediatr Neurosurg 1995;23(4):188–91

71. Shannon P, Smith CR, Deck J et al Axonal injury and the neuropathology of shaken baby syndrome. Acta Neuropathol 1998;95(6):625–31

72. Brown RL, Brunn MA, Garcia VF. Cervical spine injuries in children: a review of 103 patients treated consecutively at a level 1 pediatric trauma center. J Pediatr Surg 2001;36(8): 1107–14

73. http://www.chirurgenwerk.eu/Afwijking_trauma_wervelkolom_C2_Hangman.html

74. Wood-Jo shows fractures of the vertebral nes F. The ideal lesion produced by judicial hangings. Lancet 1913;1:53–4

75. Weiss MH, Kaufman B. Hangman's fracture in an infant. Am J Dis Child 1964;126(2):268–9

76. van Rijn RR, Kool DR, 2005. de Witt Hamer PC et al. CB. An abused five-month-old girl: Hangman's fracture or congenital arch defect?. J Emerg Med 29(1), 61–5

77. Pizzutillo PD, Rocha EF, D'Astous J et al Bilateral fractures of the pedicle of the second cervical vertebra in the young child. J Bone Joint Surg 1986;68(6):892–6

78. Ruff SJ, Taylor TKF. Hangman's fracture in an infant. J Bone Joint Surg 1986;68(5):702–3

79. McGrory BE, Fenichel GM. Hangmans fracture subsequent to shaking an infant. Ann Neurol 1977;2(1):82

80. Kleinman PK, Shelton YA. Hangman's fracture in an abused infant: imaging features. Pediatr Radiol 1997;27(9):776–7

81. Ranjith RK, Mullett JH, Burke TE. Hangman's fracture caused by suspected child abuse. A case report. J Pediatr Orthop 2002;11(4):329–32

82. Gille P, Bonneville JF, François JY et al [Fractures of axis pedicles in battered infant] [Article in French] Chir Pediatr 1980;21(5):343–4

83. Campbell J, Bonnett C. Spinal cord injury in children. Clin Orthop Rel Res 1975;(112):114–23

84. Hadley MN, Zabramski JM, Browner CM et al Pediatric spinal trauma. Review of 122 cases of spinal cord and vertebral column injuries. J Neurosurg 1988;68(1):18–24

85. Hegenbarth R, Ebel KD. Roentgen findings in fractures of the vertebral column in childhood: examination of 35 patients and its results. Pediatr Radiol 1976;5(1):34–9

86. Horal J, Nachemson A, Scheller S. Clinical and radiological long term follow-up of vertebral fractures in children. Acta Orthop Scand 1972;43(6):491–503

87. Kewalramani LS, Krause JF, Sterling HM. Acute spinal-cord lesions in a pediatric population: epidemiological and clinical features. Paraplegia 1980;18(3):206–19

88. Kewalramani LS, Tori JA. Spinal cord trauma in children. Neurologic patterns, radiologic features, and pathomechanics of injury. Spine 1980;5(1):11–8

89. Paulson JA. The epidemiology of injuries in adolescents. Pediatr Ann 1988;17(2):84–96

90. Sneed RC, Stover SL, Fine PR. Spinal cord injury associated with all-terrain vehicle accidents. Pediatrics 1986;77(3): 271–4

91. Hubbard DD. Injuries of the spine in children and adolescents. Clin Orthop Rel Res 1974;(100):56–65

92. Aufdermaur M. Spinal injuries in juveniles. Necropsy findings in twelve cases. J Bone Joint Surg Br 1974;56B(3): 513–9

93. Renard M, Tridon P, Kuhnast M et al Three unusual cases of spinal cord injury in childhood. Paraplegia 1979;16(1): 130–4

94. Sieradzki JP, Sarwark JF. Thoracolumbar fracture-dislocation in child abuse: case report, closed reduction technique and review of the literature. Pediatr Neurosurg 2008;44(3): 253–7

95. Carrion WV, Dormans JP, Drummond DS et al Circumferential growth plate fracture of the thoracolumbar spine from child abuse. J Pediatr Orthop 1996;16(2):210–4

96. Levin TL, Berdon WE, Cassell I et al Thoracolumbar fracture with listhesis – an uncommon manifestation of child abuse. Pediatr Radiol 2003;33(5):305–10

97. Aronica-Pollak PA, Stefan VH, McLemore J. Coronal cleft vertebra initially suspected as an abusive fracture in an infant. J Forensic Sci 2003;48(4):836–8

98. Ablin DS, Greenspan A, Reinhart MA. Pelvic injuries in child abuse. Pediatr Radiol. 1992;22(6):454–7

99. Prendergast NC, deRoux SJ, Adsay NV. Non-accidental pediatric pelvic fracture: a case report. Pediatr Radiol 1998; 28(5):344–6

100. Tan TX, Gelfand MJ. Battered child syndrome. Uncommon pelvic fractures detected by bone scintigraphy. Clin Nucl Med 1997;22(5):321–2

101. Starling SP, Heller RM, Jenny C. Pelvic fractures in infants as a sign of physical abuse. Child Abuse Negl. 2002;26(5): 475–80

102. Nazer H, Daradkeh T, Mohamed S et al A diagnostic dilemma in Jordan: two child abuse case studies. Child Abuse Negl 1988;12(4):593–9

103. Johnson K, Chapman S, Hall CM. Skeletal injuries associated with sexual abuse. Pediatr Radiol 2004;34(8):620–3

The Extremities

5

5.1 Introduction

In his original publication from 1962 on 'The battered child syndrome', Kempe calls the child's arms and legs the handles used to inflict trauma [1]. This may lead to fractures, in particular of the long bones. However, in mobile children fractures of arms and legs are also frequently caused by accidents. Depending on the force of the impact, specific fractures will occur in specific parts of the long bones. Sometimes their location is an indicator for child abuse. In other cases, the anamnesis and the level of development of the child will make it possible to differentiate between accidental and non-accidental injuries.

5.2 Anatomy and Physiology

The bones of the human skeleton can be categorised according to their shape:

- Long and short long bones
  - Long: Femur, tibia, humerus, radius and ulna
  - Short: Phalanges of hands and feet, such as the metacarpals and metatarsals
- Short and irregular bones, such as the carpals and tarsals

Irrespective of their anatomical location, the long as well as the short long bones are all constructed in the same manner (Figs. 5.1 and 5.2a–c), i.e.:

- Diaphysis: the medulla-containing middle part (the shaft) of a long bone.
- Epiphysis: the end part of a long bone.

- Metaphysis: the area of the long bone between the diaphysis and the epiphysis. This part contains the growth plate.

Longitudinal growth of the long bones takes place in the growth plate, whereas growth in width originates in the periosteum. The epiphyses determine the size and form of the joint ends.

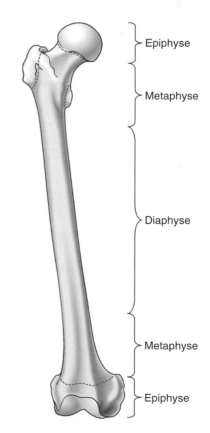

Fig. 5.1 Schematic representation of the anatomy of the long bones

R. A. C. Bilo et al., *Forensic Aspects of Pediatric Fractures,*
DOI: 10.1007/978-3-540-78716-7_5, © Springer-Verlag Berlin Heidelberg 2010

Fig. 5.2 (**a**) Histological section of the distal femur of a 3-month-old neonate, which shows ossification of the distal epiphysis of the femur (asterisk). (**b**) Corresponding specimen photo of the distal femur, showing ossification of the epiphysis of the distal femur. (**c**) Corresponding radiograph of the distal femur, showing ossification of the epiphysis of the distal femur

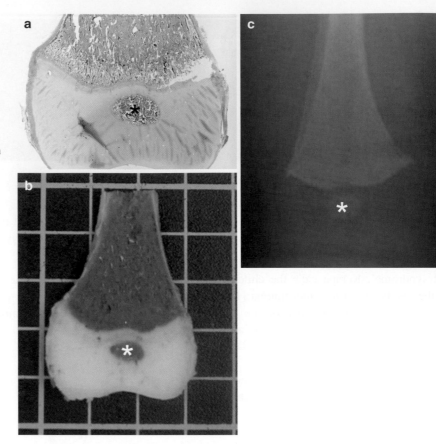

5.3 Shaft Fractures

5.3.1 General Aspects of Shaft Fractures

Many authors maintain that a spiral fracture of the shaft of one of the long bones, in particular of the femur, is proof for physical violence; however, this is incorrect. The only conclusion one can make with any certainty when confronted with such a fracture is that this fracture is based on torque, a rotating motion along the long axis of the bone. Torque is often seen in accidents, for example, slipping while running [2–4]. The fracture may also occur in a fall in which knee and hip remain stationary and the patient rotates in relation to the stationary joints. This happens regularly, not just in the femur, but also in the tibia. Consequently, such a fracture can only be evaluated when the context of its origin is also taken into consideration. However, when such a fracture is encountered in a child that does not yet walk, child abuse is very likely.

5.3.2 Biomechanical Aspects

In the analysis of what bone is exposed to in either daily life or under the impact of force, a number of aspects should be considered, such as [5]:

- The force or combination of forces exerted on the bone in day-to-day use and when under the impact of force: the load bearing of the bone ('load').
- The force of the bone to resist this load: tension ('stress').
- The changes in shape or size of tissue in reaction to this stress: stretch ('strain'). In strain, three pure forms can be distinguished: compression, tension and shearing. Furthermore, various combinations may be seen, such as bowing and torque.

When a fracture is sustained, the three pure forms (load, stress, strain) seldom occur just by themselves, but nearly always a combination of the three is seen (Table 5.1).

Table 5.1 Biomechanical aspects of shaft fractures (a.o. 6)

Force/combination of forces	Fracture type	

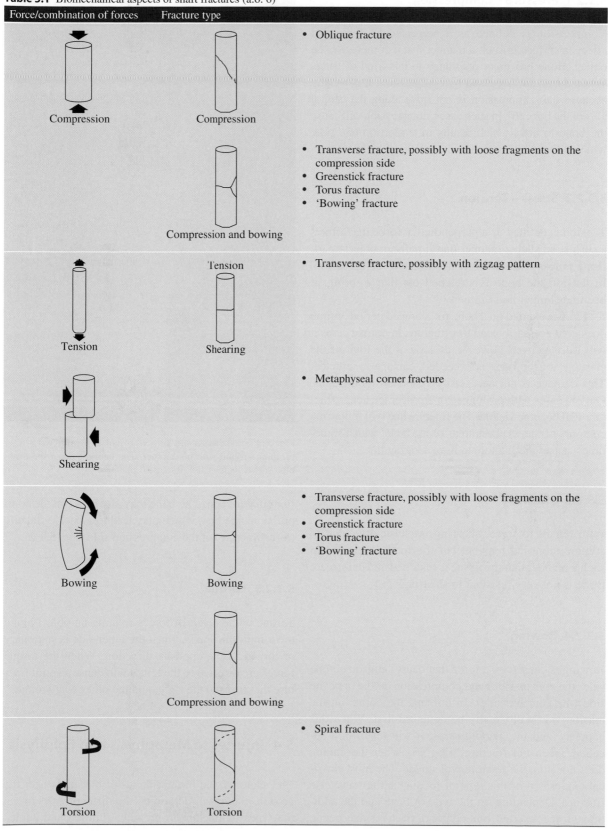

- Oblique fracture

- Transverse fracture, possibly with loose fragments on the compression side
- Greenstick fracture
- Torus fracture
- 'Bowing' fracture

- Transverse fracture, possibly with zigzag pattern

- Metaphyseal corner fracture

- Transverse fracture, possibly with loose fragments on the compression side
- Greenstick fracture
- Torus fracture
- 'Bowing' fracture

- Spiral fracture

Compression — Compression — Compression and bowing

Tension — Tension — Shearing

Shearing

Bowing — Bowing — Compression and bowing

Torsion — Torsion

5.3.2.1 Pressure – Compression

Compression is defined as a perpendicular force that affects a surface in such a manner that it compresses the object. Bone has great resistance to this kind of force. When a fracture is caused by compression, it is usually because the compression is not quite along the central axis of the bone [6]. In such cases, compression will cause the bone to bow, which results in tension on one side, which ultimately determines the nature of the fracture.

5.3.2.2 Stress – Tension

Tension is defined as a perpendicular force that affects a surface in such a manner that it pulls an object apart. Bone is less resistant to tension than to compression. In tension the bone is stretched out like a spring: it becomes longer and thinner.

Tension exerted on a bone for a limited period of time does not necessarily lead to a fracture. In normal cases it will fully recover; however, as soon as the limit of the elasticity of the bone is exceeded, damage is inflicted. This damage is not necessarily visible on radiographs. Only in cases with prolonged or stronger tension, a fracture will become visible. The fracture line will follow the contours of the weakest areas of the bone, which sometimes causes the fracture to have a zigzag line.

5.3.2.3 Shearing

With regard to force, shearing is physically equal to compression and tension, but the force is exerted in such a manner that the tissue is distorted and deformed. Bone is not very resistant to shearing.

5.3.2.4 Bowing

Bowing is caused by a force that causes tension on one side (the convex side) and compression on the opposite side (the concave side). In bowing, the cortex on the tension side will usually be damaged first. When this happens, and the loading stops, it will result in a so-called 'greenstick fracture' (Fig. 5.3). When the loading does not stop, the fracture will spread. The most classical expression of this type of loading is the transverse fracture. Depending on the type of bone and the additional forces exerted, other types of fractures may occur.

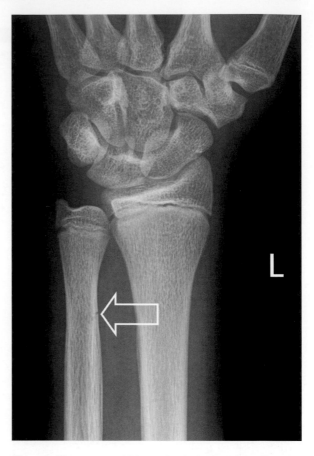

Fig. 5.3 Sixteen-year-old boy who had a painful wrist after romping around with his brother. The lateral side of the distal ulna shows a greenstick fracture (*open arrow*)

In immature bone, the bone may also yield on the compression side first, which may lead to a buckle fracture (torus fracture) of the compression side (Fig. 5.4).

5.3.2.5 Torque

Torque is the result of forces rotating an object along the longitudinal axis, when the other side is stationary or turned in the opposite direction. When the torque forces are directed to the left, it will cause a spiral fracture that turns to the right, and the other way around.

5.4 Injuries to Metaphysis and Epiphysis

The anatomy and biomechanics of the joints near the growth plates will determine the differences between the types of fracture in growing children and adults.

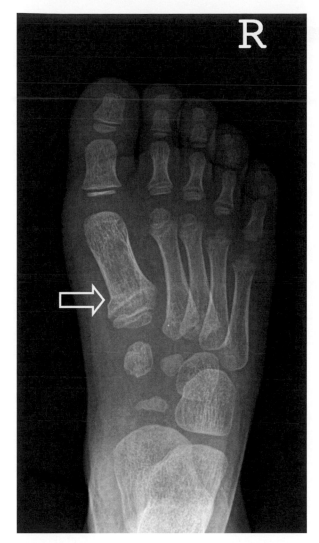

Fig. 5.4 Three-year-old boy with a torus fracture of metatarsal I of the right foot after taking a jump (*open arrow*)

Growth plates are the weakest areas in the growing skeleton. In trauma, they do not have the same resistance to injury as do tendons and ligaments.

5.4.1 Salter-Harris Classification

Trauma during childhood may result in typical fractures around the growth plates, the so-called Salter-Harris fractures (Table 5.2). These fractures often result from accidental trauma in childhood (they are seen in 30% of all trauma-related fractures) and in mobile children are primarily not suspect for child

abuse [7]. The Salter-Harris type II fractures are the most prevalent (Fig. 5.5 and Table 5.2) [8].

5.4.2 The Metaphyseal Corner Fracture

The classical metaphyseal corner fracture (classical metaphyseal lesion – CML) is, besides rib fractures, the most specific fracture seen in child abuse. Caffey was the first to describe this lesion [9]. Kleinman introduced the term 'classical metaphyseal lesion' [10]. When no plausible reason is offered, this type of fracture is seen by many as highly specific for inflicted injury [9, 11].

CMLs can be found in 39–50% of children under the age of 18 months of whom a skeletal survey was made because of suspected child abuse. They are almost exclusively seen in children of less than 2 years of age, bilateral as well as unilateral. The lesion may also be seen in just one bone or around one joint. Hereby should be mentioned that in a CML of the proximal tibial metaphysis there is often an associated avulsion fracture of the femur (distal metaphysis). CMLs are most frequently found in the distal femur, the proximal and distal tibia (Fig. 5.6a) and the proximal humerus (Fig. 5.6b), the tibial metaphysis being the most prevalent location for avulsion fractures in young abused children [12]. However, lesions to the elbow and wrist have also been reported (Fig. 5.6c) [10, 13–18]. The long-term consequences of CMLs appear to be minimal or even absent [19].

Hymel and Spivak maintain that the violent shaking of a child may lead to simultaneous avulsion fractures of the distal femur and the proximal and distal tibia accompanied by fractures of the posterior ribs and inflicted skull/brain injuries ('abusive head trauma', Fig. 5.7a–g) [18].

5.4.2.1 Radiological Aspects

A CML is composed of a series of micro-fractures right through the metaphysis. The lesion runs parallel to the growth plate, but does not necessarily extent over the full circumference of the bone [10]. When the micro-fractures are present over the full circumference of the bone, the radiographs will show a growth plate that is disconnected from the shaft, with a broad and flat centre and a wider edge (a so-called 'bucket-handle fracture', Fig. 5.8a).

Sometimes the radiographs only show the wider edge (a so-called 'corner fracture'; Fig. 5.8b). This

Table 5.2 Classification of meta-epiphyseal fractures according to Salter-Harris

Type		
		Metaphysis Growth plate Epiphysis
I		In type I the fracture line 'follows' the growth plate, separating epiphysis and metaphysis. The growth plate is still attached to the epiphysis. Usually there is no damage to the growth plate. Type I is seen in particular in young children The mechanism involved is shearing (see Sect. 5.3.2). Dislocation is only seen when the periosteum has been damaged. The healing process is quick (usually within 2–3 weeks) An uncommon type I is a fracture of the proximal femur called slipped capital femoral epiphysis (SCFE)
II		Type II is the most common, generally in children >10 years old. The fracture runs through the metaphysis and the growth plate As seen in type I, the mechanism involved is a shearing force or avulsion due to an angular force. This type of fracture usually heals quickly
III		Type III is rarely seen, and then mostly to the lower legs. The fracture runs through the epiphysis and the growth plate. Although the growth zone has been damaged, hardly any growth disturbance is seen after a type III fracture
IV		In type IV the fracture runs across the epiphysis, growth plate and metaphysis. In the long run this fracture may lead to deformation of the joint as a result of the bony bridging of the growth plate which may impede local growth
V		Type V is a compression fracture of the growth plate due to axial loading. This type is commonly seen in the knee and ankle

type of fracture usually shows no periosteal reaction. Callus formation is limited or lacking. The lesions ('corner fracture' and 'bucket-handle fracture') are different radiographic projections of the same lesion.

5.4.2.2 Biomechanical Aspects

The direction of the lesion is perpendicular to the axis of the bone. This shows clearly that a shearing force has been exerted on the end of the bone. The calcium-

Fig. 5.25 (**a**) Five-month-old girl who had sustained a greenstick fracture of the distal femur (*open arrow*, A-P view). (**b**) Lateral view of the femur shows a cortical defect (*open arrow*)

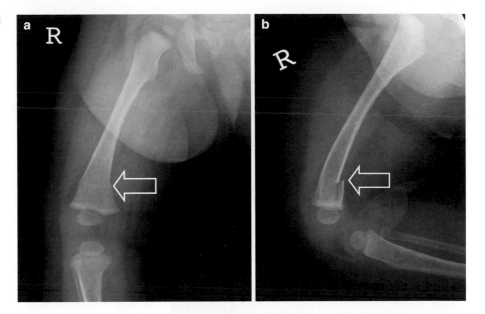

abuse in mobile children is highly unlikely when there are no additional signs such as an inconsistent story, haematomas or other fractures. When a non-mobile child presents with a fracture of the femur, it is an important indication for child abuse.

Blake et al. evaluated 42 children in the age of 1–5 years that presented with a shaft fracture. Thirty-four of them had fallen [79]. In 14 children the anamnesis led to suspected child abuse, but only in one child there was proof. Yet, Blakemore et al. maintain that when a young child presents with a femoral-shaft fracture, child abuse should always be considered when the patient history mentions a fall and there are no eye-witnesses to confirm either the fall or its context. The distance of the fall may also provide an indication towards the cause. In case the anamnesis shows that the fracture is caused by a fall of less than 1 m in height, this is an unlikely statement [80]. The force required to cause a mid-shaft fracture is considerable and requires a substantial acceleration-deceleration trauma.

In children of 5 years and older and adolescents, a shaft fracture is hardly ever the result of child abuse. The most likely cause is a high-energy trauma, such as a traffic accident. In this age group, in 90% of cases the cause is a traffic accident [69, 81, 82]. In the United States, shot wounds are increasingly a cause for shaft fractures [68].

Only occasionally fractures are caused by sexual abuse. In 5% of a group of sexually abused children, Johnson et al. found fractures as a sign of child abuse.

According to the authors, these fractures are seldom or never the result of sexual acts. In three children they did find fractures resulting from sexual acts. A 5-month-old girl sustained a femoral fracture without dislocation as the result of abuse [83].

5.7.3.1 Birth Trauma-Related Femoral-Shaft Fractures

A birth trauma may lead to femoral fractures (Fig. 5.26a and b). However, this happens rarely (see Chap. 6). Morris et al. recorded an incidence of 0.13 in 1,000 live births (seven neonates with in total eight fractures in 55,296 live births) [84]. Spiral fractures of the proximal part of the femur were most commonly seen and have been reported in breech birth, forceps births, twin births, premature births and Caesarean sections.

Not all fractures are immediately identified after birth. A study by Morris et al. even showed that in the majority of children there was a delay in diagnosis. In only two children the fracture was established immediately post partum. In the other children there was a delay of 2–21 days, even when hospitalised [84]. Such a delay may unjustly lead to suspected child abuse. Up to a certain extent it is possible to differentiate between birth and other trauma by evaluating the formation of callus. Cumming mentions that callus can be found as early as 7 days post partum [85]. When a fracture is found in an unusual location, or when there is no callus

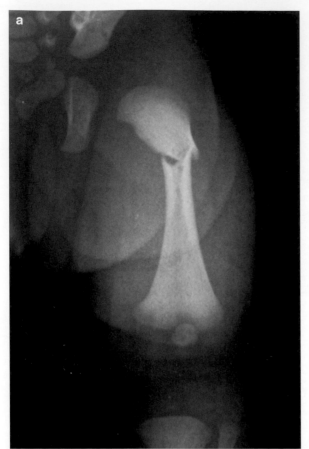

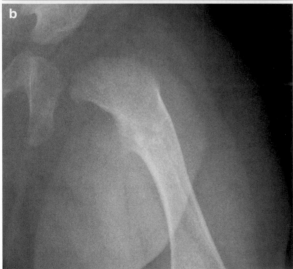

Fig. 5.26 (**a**) One-day-old neonate (birth weight 2,215 g) with a femur fracture after a complicated delivery with transverse presentation. (**b**) After 4 months the fracture has healed practically seamless

visible 11 days after birth, child abuse must be considered as possible cause.

5.7.3.2 Disease-Related Fractures

In differential diagnoses one should be aware of disease-related fractures, in particular when there is a 'blank' anamnesis. In children, pathological fractures are relatively rare, but may be seen in children with generalised osteopenia, such as osteoporosis imperfecta (OI). When a femur-shaft fracture is found in a child, and there are no signs of violence or significant trauma, OI must be considered [3]. Other causes of generalised osteopenia in which a minor trauma may cause a fracture of the femoral shaft are neurological diseases such as cerebral palsy or meningomyocele [86–89]. Pathological fractures may be seen in patients with neoplasms. Usually these are benign lesions such as eosinophylic granuloma and bone cysts. Pathological femur fractures are seldom seen in patients suffering from osteosarcoma or a Ewing sarcoma (see Chap. 7) [68].

5.8 Tibia and Fibula

5.8.1 General Aspects of Fractures of the Lower Leg

In young children, fractures of the tibial shaft are very suspect for child abuse. Direct-impact force on the shaft may lead to transverse or oblique fractures. Grabbing hold of the leg and turning with great force may lead to spiral and oblique fractures. The fracture lines are not always visible; however, a reaction of the periosteum with callus formation is regularly found.

Metaphyseal corner fractures of the tibia are a regular occurring phenomenon [33, 90]. In these cases the proximal growth plate is affected more often than the distal growth plate (see Sect. 5.4.2) [16]. Accidental spiral fractures or oblique fractures are often seen in mobile children of 3–4 years old [91, 92].

Fibula fractures are rarely seen in child abuse. When they do occur, they result from direct- impact

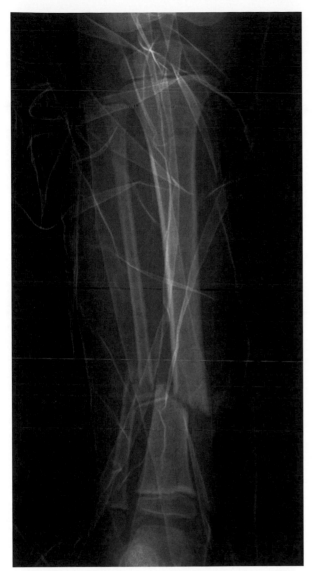

Fig. 5.27 Distal fracture of tibia and fibula in a 4-year-old boy after high-energy trauma, car vs pedestrian (radiograph was taken in a vacuum splint)

Fig. 5.28 Graphic representation of a spoke injury

These easily avoidable injuries are known as 'spokes' injuries and unfortunately, at least in the Netherlands with many cycling parents, these are seen on a regular basis.

5.8.2 Isolated (Spiral) Fracture of the Tibia

force to the shaft. Usually a simultaneous fracture of the tibia is seen.

Simultaneous fractures of the tibia and fibula are often seen in accidents (Fig. 5.27). Fractures of tibia and fibula may also occur when the child is seated on the backseat of a bike (usually a bike of one of the parents) and the foot gets caught between the frame and the spokes of the wheel (Figs. 5.28 and 5.29) [93, 94].

Mellick at al. pose that isolated spiral fractures of the tibia are often seen in children <8 years old, usually as the result of an accident. In their study, they found that 95% of all fractures were seen in the lower two thirds of the tibia. They seldom noticed alignment abnormalities based on the mutual dislocation of the ends of the fracture. They suggested that when these fractures are caused by an accident, they should no longer be called 'toddler's fracture', but accidental spiral fractures of the tibia (CAST – Childhood Accidental Spiral Tibia fractures, Fig. 5.30) [95].

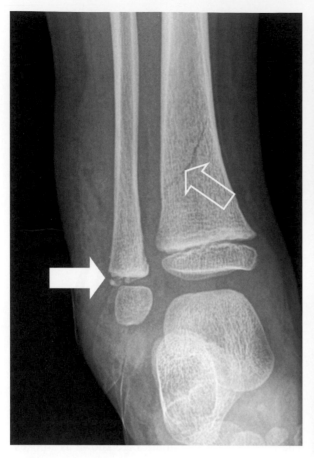

Fig. 5.29 Spoke injury in a 4-month-old girl who was seated at the back of her mother's bike. The trauma resulted in an oblique fracture of the tibia (*open arrow*) and a Salter-Harris type II fracture of the fibula (*arrow*)

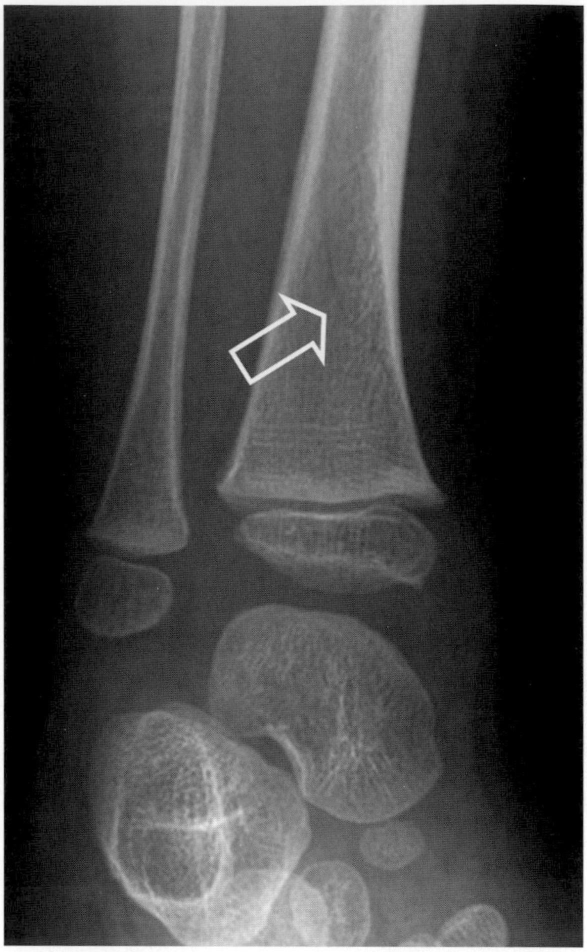

Fig. 5.30 Childhood accidental spiral tibia fracture in a 22-month-old boy

5.9 Shaft Fractures of the Lower Extremities

In 2005, Coffey et al. published an article that supports the earlier-mentioned data on shaft fractures in the upper and lower leg [96]. In this study, fractures of the lower extremities and their possible relation to child abuse were retrospectively evaluated. The study comprised data of 5,497 trauma patients. Of this population, 4,942 children were >18 months old. One hundred and four (2%) children appeared to have been abused. In the group of 555 children of ≤18 months old, 175 children (32%) were found to have fallen victim to child abuse.

Looking at fractures in all extremities, it appeared that in children of >18 months old, injuries to the extremities ($n = 1186$) were in 1% ($n = 16$) of cases due to child abuse, whereas this was 67% ($n = 44$) in children of <18 months old ($n = 66$). When only the injuries of the lower extremities were considered, 41 (75%) of the 55 fractures in the younger group were the result of child abuse. In this group, 134 (27%) of 500 other injuries were also found to be the result of physical violence. In 22 cases a femur fracture was seen and in 14 cases a tibia fracture. Coffey et al. concluded:

- In children of >18 months old, child abuse is an unusual cause for injuries to the legs.
- In children of ≤18 months old, injuries to the legs, and in particular fractures, are an evident indication for child abuse: 'Clinicians must thoroughly

investigate lower extremity injuries in this age group'.

5.10 Hands and Feet

In child abuse, fractures of the hands and feet are unusual. In older children they are usually the result of accidents (Figs. 5.31 and 5.32a–c) [21]. When fractures due to child abuse are found in older children, they may be metaphyseal/epiphyseal and diaphyseal fractures, mostly located in the metacarpals (Fig. 5.33) or metatarsals. It often concerns multiple fingers and/or toes [61].

In children <1 year old, fractures of the hands and feet are suspect for child abuse (Fig. 5.34a and b). Nimkin et al. evaluated 11 fractures of hands and feet in infants of <10 months old. They found predominantly torus fractures, either of the metacarpals or the proximal phalanges of the hands, and comparable fractures of the first metatarsals of the feet. Only one child showed clinical symptoms [97].

The lesions are the result of direct-impact force, either by being hit with an object or by punching [61]. Fractures may also be caused by hyperflexion or hyperextension.

5.11 Subperiosteal Haemorrhages/ Calcifications

Subperiosteal haemorrhages may be caused by friction trauma, in which the perpetrator makes a rotating movement while holding on to the upper arms, or from a blunt trauma. These haemorrhages are not immediately visible on a radiograph. A 2-week follow-up of the radiograph is indicated. When a subperiosteal haemorrhage is present, a double contour is seen due to 'lifting' of the periosteum.

Subperiosteal haemorrhages/calcifications must be distinguished from physiological periosteal thickening of the long bones (femur, tibia, humerus) in neonates and infants, and from skeletal lesions seen in vitamin-C deficiency, vitamin-A intoxication, infantile cortical hyperostosis, osteomyelitis, malignancies (such as leukaemia) and congenital syphilis (see Chap. 7).

5.12 Growth-Retardation Lines

5.12.1 General Aspects of Growth-Retardation Lines

Metaphyseal growth-retardation lines are formed in periods when growth is delayed or has ceased and may remain visible for months [98]. They are evidence of a disturbance in longitudinal growth, which takes place in the metaphyses. These lines have been reported in a multitude of childhood diseases in which a disturbance (a delay or even a temporary cessation) in growth is seen; causes of 'organic failure to thrive'. This phenomenon may occur in every disease with a severe course of illness.

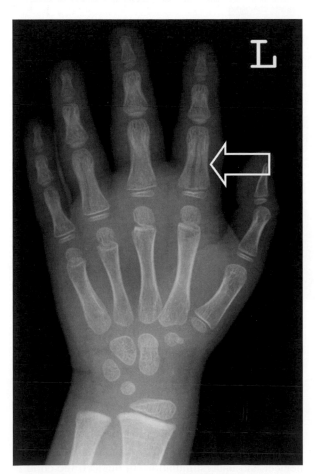

Fig. 5.31 Fracture of the proximal phalanx (*open arrow*) of a 4-year-old girl who had a television topple on her hand

Fig. 5.32 (**a**) Two-year-old girl who had a drawer fall on her hand while playing. Radiological examination revealed a fracture of the capitate bone (Reprinted from Obdeijn MC, van Vliet C, van Rijn RR. Capitate and hamate fracture in a child: the value of MRI imaging Emerg Radiol. 2009 May 26. [Epub ahead of print] DOI 10.1007/s10140-009-0815-9. With permission.) (**b**) Postero-anterior view of the hand shows the fracture of the capitate bone. (**c**) Coronal STIR-weighted MRI shows bone oedema at the location of earlier-mentioned capitate fracture (*open arrow*); however, also of the hamate bone (*arrow*)

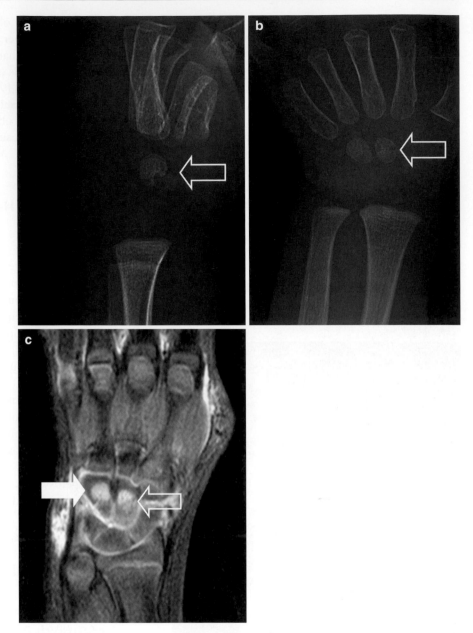

The documented causes include: malnourishment [99], infections [99], hypothyroidism [100], parahypothyroidism [101], Cushing's syndrome [102], chronic diseases, chronic juvenile arthritis [103], and chemotherapy in children with malignancies and other medications (Fig. 5.35) [104–106]. The lines were also found in children that had been immobilised after orthopaedic surgery [107].

5.12.2 *Growth-Retardation Lines and Non-organic Failure to Thrive*

Growth disturbances are not just caused by diseases. In the Western world, the most common cause of growth and development retardation – in other words, the most common cause for 'failure to thrive' – is neglect and understimulation. In neglect, the child is

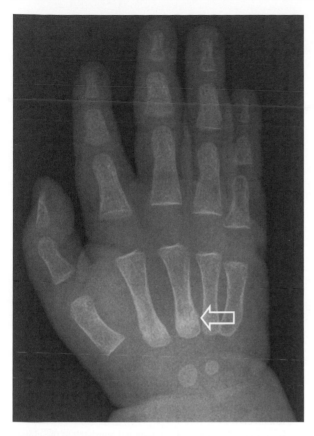

Fig. 5.33 Sclerotic aspect of the base of metacarpal 3 of the right hand (*open arrow*), suspect for a healed fracture

offered insufficient calories (malnourishment) and/or insufficient affective stimulation. As early as 1967, Patton and Gardner mentioned metaphyseal growth-retardation lines in their book on maternal deprivation [108]. Maternal deprivation stands for a serious disturbance in the relation between parent (mother) and child, and a lack of bonding between parent (mother) and child. The deprivation consists of neglect, rejection and isolation of the child. Maternal deprivation syndrome leads to serious growth retardation, delayed skeletal maturation and retarded motor and intellectual development [109]. This multitude of physical symptoms is nowadays summarised in the term 'non-organic failure to thrive'. Khadilkar et al. confirm the observation of Patton and Gardner that the origin of these lines may involve psychological factors [110].

Animal tests suggest that the lines are formed after an initial retardation or cessation in growth, followed by resumed growth [99, 107]. According to Khadilkar et al., in children they seem to occur in similar circumstances [110]. In case the process is cyclic (repeated periods of delayed growth interspersed with periods of resumed growth) a large number of lines may be found. These lines will always remain visible, up to and including puberty.

When multiple growth-retardation lines are found in a child, non-organic failure to thrive will be, after

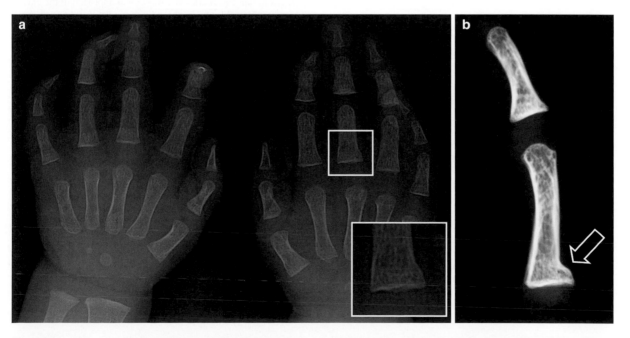

Fig. 5.34 (**a**) One and a half-month-old girl found dead in her crib. Radiological examination of the hands revealed a torus fracture at the base of the proximal phalanx of the third finger of the right hand (see inset). (**b**) Radiograph of the finger, sampled at autopsy. The radiograph has been taken with a mammography system, because of its high resolution

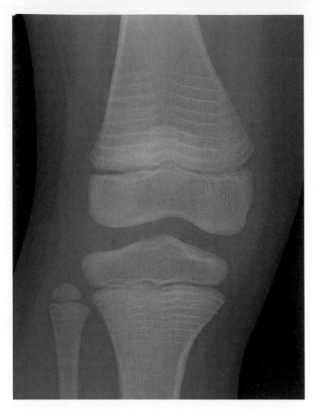

Fig. 5.35 Growth retardation lines in a 5-year-old girl after treatment with intravenous bisphosphates, due to fibrous dysplasia in the left maxillary sinus

exclusion of other (organic) causes, the most probable cause [110].

References

1. Kempe CH, Silverman FN, Steele BF et al The battered child syndrome. JAMA 1962;181(1):17–24
2. Beals RK, Tufts E. Fractured femur in infancy: the role of child abuse. J Pediatr Orthop 1983;3(5):583–6
3. Leventhal JM, Thomas SA, Rosenfeld NS et al Fractures in young children. Distinguishing child abuse from unintentional injuries. Am J Dis Child 1993;147(1):87–92
4. Thomas SA, Rosenfeld NS, Leventhal JM et al Long-bone fractures in young children: distinguishing accidental injuries from child abuse. Pediatrics 1991;88(3):471–6
5. Nordin M, Frankel VH. Biomechanica van botten en botweefsel. In Snijders CJ, Nordin M, Frankel VH. Biomechanica van het skeletstelsel. Elsevier Gezondheidszorg, 4e druk, 2004, 49–150
6. Carter D. The biomechanics of bone. In Nahum AM, Melvin J. The biomechanics of trauma. Appleton and Lange, 1984, 15–90
7. Mann DC, Rajmaira S. Distribution of physeal and nonphyseal fractures in 2,650 long bone fractures in children aged 0–16 years. J Pediatr Orthop 1990;10(6):713–6
8. Kawamoto K, Kim W-C, Tsuchida Y, et al Incidence of physeal injuries in Japanese children. J Pediatr Orthop B 2006;15(2):126–130
9. Caffey J. Some traumatic lesions in growing bones other than fractures and dislocations: clinical and radiological features: The Mackenzie Davidson Memorial Lecture. Br J Radiol 1957;30(353):225–38
10. Kleinman PK, Marks SC, Blackbourne B. The metaphyseal lesion in abused infants: a radiologic-histopathologic study. Am J Roentgenol 1986;146(5):895–905
11. Kleinman PK. Skeletal trauma: general considerations. In Kleinman PK. Diagnostic imaging of child abuse. Mosby, 2 nd ed, 1998, 8–25
12. Kleinman PK. The lower extremity. In Kleinman PK. Diagnostic imaging of child abuse. Mosby, 2nd ed, 1998, 26–71
13. Osier LK, Marks SC Jr, Kleinman PK. Metaphyseal extensions of hypertrophied chondrocytes in abused infants indicate healing fractures. J Pediatr Orthop 1993;13(2):249–54
14. Kleinman PK, Marks SC. A regional approach to the classic metaphyseal lesion in abused infants: the proximal humerus. Am J Roentgenol 1996;167(6):1399–1403
15. Kleinman PK, Marks SC. A regional approach to the classic metaphyseal lesion in abused infants: the distal tibia. Am J Roentgenol 1996;166(5):1207–12
16. Kleinman PK, Marks SC. A regional approach to the classic metaphyseal lesion in abused infants: the proximal tibia. Am J Roentgenol 1996;166(2):421–6
17. Kleinman PK, Marks SC. A regional approach to the classic metaphyseal lesion in abused infants: the distal femur. Am J Roentgenol 1998;170(1):43–7
18. Hymel KP, Spivack BS. The biomechanics of physical injury. In Reece RM, Ludwig S. Child abuse – medical diagnosis and management. Lippincott Williams en Wilkins, 2nd ed. 2001, 1–22
19. DeLee JC, Wilkins KE, Rogers LF, Rockwood CA. Fracture-separation of the distal humeral epiphysis. J Bone Joint Surg Am 1980;62(1):46–51
20. Alexander CJ. Effect of growth rate on the strength of the growth plate shaft junction. Skeletal Radiol 1976;1:67–76
21. Merten DF, Radkowski MA, Leonidas JC. The abused child: a radiological reappraisal. Radiology 1983;146(2):377–81
22. Loder RT, Bookout C. Fracture patterns in battered children. J Orthop Trauma 1991;5(4):428–33
23. Grayev AM, Boal DK, Wallach DM, Segal LS. Metaphyseal fractures mimicking abuse during treatment for clubfoot. Pediatr Radiol 2001;31(8):559–63
24. Lysack JT, Soboleski D. Classic metaphyseal lesion following external cephalic version and cesarean section. Pediatr Radiol 2003;33(6):422–4
25. O'Connell A, Donoghue VB. Can classic metaphyseal lesions follow uncomplicated ceasarian section? Pediatr Radiol 2007;37(5):488–491

26. Buonuomo PS, Ruggiero A, Zampino G et al A newborn with multiple fractures as first presentation of infantile myofibromatosis. J Perinatol 2006;26(10):653–5

27. Hohl JC. Fractures of the humerus in children. Orthop Clin North Am 1976;7(3):557–71

28. Landin LA. Fracture patterns in children. Analysis of 8,682 fractures with special reference to incidence, etiology and secular changes in a Swedish urban population 1950–1979. Acta Orthop Scand Suppl. 1983;54(suppl 202):1–109

29. Landin LA. Epidemiology of children's fractures. J Pediatr Orthop 1997;6(2):79–83

30. Rose SH, Melton LJ, Morrey BF et al Epidemiologic features of humeral fractures. Clin Orthop Relat Res 1982;(168):24–30

31. Shrader MW. Proximal humerus and humeral shaft fractures in children. Hand Clin 2007;23(4):431–5

32. Caviglia H, Garrido CP, Palazzi FF, Meana NV. Pediatric fractures of the humerus. Clin Orthop Relat Res 2005;(432):49–56

33. King J, Diefendorf D, Apthorp J et al Analysis of 429 fractures in 189 battered children. J Ped Ortho 1988;8(5):585 9

34. Strait RT, Siegel RM, Shapiro RA. Humeral fractures without obvious etiologies in children less than 3 years of age: When is it abuse? Pediatrics 1995;96(4 Pt 1):667–1

35. Worlock P, Stower M, Barbor P. Patterns of fractures in accidental and non-accidental injury in children: a comparative study. Br Med J 1986;293(6539):100–2

36. Kowal-Vern A, Paxton TP, Ros SP et al Fractures in the under 3-year-old cohort. Clin Pediatr 1992;31(11):653–9

37. Rosenberg N, Bettenfield G. Fractures in infants: a sign of child abuse. Ann Emerg Med 1982;11(4):178–80

38. Williams R, Hardcastle N. Best evidence topic report. Humeral fractures and non-accidental injury in children. Emerg Med J 2005;22(2):124–5

39. Shaw BA, Murphy KM, Shaw A et al Humerus shaft fractures in young children: accident or abuse? J Pediatr Orthop 1997;17(3):293–7

40. Merten DF, Carpenter BC. Radiologic imaging of inflicted injury in the child abuse syndrome. Ped Clin North Am 1990;37(4):815–837

41. Swischuk LE. Emergency imaging of acutely or injured cChild. Williams and Wilkins, 3rd ed, 1994, 361–3

42. Dameron TB, Reibel DB. Fractures involving the proximal humeral epiphyseal plate. J Bone Joint Surg 1969;51(2): 289–97

43. Lemperg R, Liliequest B. Dislocation of the proximal epiphysis of the humerus in newborns. Acta Paediatr Scand 1970;59(4):377–80

44. Shulman BH, Terhune CB. Epiphyseal injuries in breech delivery. Pediatrics 1951;8(5):693–700

45. Camus M, Lefebvre G, Veron P et al Obstetrical injuries of the newborn infant. Retrospective study apropos of 20,409 births. J Gynecol Obstet Biol Reprod 1985;14: 1033–43

46. Gagnaire JC, Thoulon JM, Chappuis JP et al [Injuries to the upper extremities in the newborn diagnosed at birth.] [Article in French] J Gynecol Obstet Biol Reprod (Paris) 1975;4(2): 245–54

47. Dalldorf PG, Bryan WJ. Displaced Salter-Harris type I injury in a gymnast. A slipped capital humeral epiphysis? Orthop Rev 1994;23(6):538–41

48. Ahn JI, Park JS. Pathological fractures secondary to unicameral bone cysts. Int Orthop 1994;18(1):20–2

49. Barber DB, Janus RB, Wade WH. Neuroarthropathy: an overuse injury of the shoulder in quadriplegia. J Spinal Cord Med 1996;19(1):9–11

50. Lock TR, Aronson DD. Fractures in patients who have myelomeningocele. J Bone Joint Surg Am 1989;71(8): 1153–7

51. Reed MH, Letts RM, Pollock AN. Birth fractures. In Letts RM (ed). Management of pediatric fractures. Churchill Livingstone, 1994, 1049–61

52. Samardzic M, Grujicic D, Milinkovic ZB. Radial nerve lesions associated with fractures of the humeral shaft. Injury 1990;21(4):220–2

53. Reisdorff EJ, Roberts MR, Wiegenstein JG (eds). Pediatric Emergency Medicine. WB Saunders Co, 1993

54. Lawton L. Fractures of the distal radius and ulna. In Letts RM (ed). Management of pediatric fractures. Churchill-Livingstone, 1994, 345–68

55. Thomas EM, Tuson KW, Browne PS. Fractures of the radius and ulna in children. Injury 1975;7(2):120–4

56. Cheng JC, Shen WY. Limb fracture pattern in different pediatric age groups: a study of 3,350 children. J Orthop Trauma 1993;7(1):15–22

57. Johnson PG, Szabo RM. Angle measurements of the distal radius: a cadaver study. Skel Radiol 1993;22(4):243–6

58. Reed MH. Fractures and dislocations of the extremities in children. J Trauma 1977;17(5):351–4

59. Bailey DA, Wedge JH, McCulloch RG et al Epidemiology of fractures of the distal end of the radius in children associated with growth. J Bone Joint Surg Am 1989;71(8): 1225–31

60. Tredwell SJ, Van Peteghem K, Clough M. Pattern of forearm fractures in children. J Pediatr Orthop 1984;4(5):604–8

61. Brodeur AE, Monteleone JA. Child Maltreatment. A Clinical Guide and Reference. GW Medial Publishing, 1994, 32

62. Price CT, Mencio GA. Injuries to the shafts of the radius and ulna. In Beatty JH, Kasser JR (eds). Rockwood and Wilkins' Fractures in Children, Lippincott Williams en Wilkins, 5th ed, 2001, 433–82

63. Taitz J, Moran K, O'Meara M. Long bone fractures in children under 3 years of age: is abuse being missed in Emergency Department presentations? J Paediatr Child Health 2004;40(4):170–4

64. Maeda H, Yoshida K, Doi R et al Combined Monteggia and Galeazzi fractures in a child: a case report and review of the literature. J Orthop Trauma 2003;17(2):128–31

65. Perron AD, Hersh RE, Brady WJ et al Orthopedic pitfalls in the ED: Galeazzi and Monteggia fracture-dislocation. Am J Emerg Med 2001;19(3):225–8

66. Korner J, Hansen M, Weinberg A et al Monteggia fractures in childhood – diagnosis and management in acute and chronic cases. Eur J Trauma 2004;30(6):361–70

67. Thompson GH. Dislocations of the elbow. In Beaty JH, Kasser JR (eds). Rockwood and Wilkins' Fractures in children. Lippincott Williams en Wilkins, 5th ed, 2001, 705–39

68. Kasser JR, Beatty JH. Femoral shaft fractures. In Beatty JH, Kasser JR (eds). Rockwood and Wilkins'

Fractures in children. Lippincott Williams and Wilkins, 5th ed, 2001, 941–80

69. Hedlund R, Lindgren U. The incidence of femoral shaft fractures in children and adolescents. J Pediatr Orthop 1986;6(1): 47–50

70. Hinton RY, Lincoln A, Crockett MM et al Fractures of the femoral shaft in children. Incidence, mechanism, and sociodemographic risk factors. J Bone Joint Surg Am 1999;81(4): 500–9

71. Buess E, Kaelin A. One hundred pediatric femoral fractures: epidemiology, treatment, attitudes, and early complications. J Pediatr Orthop 1998;7(3):186–92

72. Scherl SA, Miller L, Lively N et al Accidental and nonaccidental femur fractures in children. Clin Orthop Relat Res 2000;(376):96–105

73. Frasier LD. Child abuse or mimic. Consultant for Pediatrians 2003;2:212–5

74. Schwend RM, Werth C, Johnston A. Femur shaft fractures in toddlers and young children: rarely from child abuse. J Pediatr Orthop 2000;20(4):475–81

75. Pierce MC. Bertocci GE, Vogeley E et al Evaluating long bone fractures in children: a biomechanical approach with illustrative cases. Child Ab Negl 2004;28(5):505–24

76. Gross RH, Stranger M. Causative factors responsible for femoral fractures in infants and young children. J Pediatr Orthop 1983;3(3):341–3

77. Silverman FN. Radiological aspects of the battered child syndrome. In Helfer R, Kempe R (eds). The battered child. University of Chicago Press, 4th ed, 1987, 214–46

78. Rex C, Kay PR. Features of femoral fractures in nonaccidental injury. J Pediatr Orthop 2000;20(3):411–3

79. Blakemore LC, Loder RT, Hensinger RN et al Role of intentional abuse in children 1 to 5 years old with isolated femoral shaft fractures. J Pediatr Orthop 1996;16(5): 585–8

80. Helfer RE, Slovis TL, Black M. Injuries resulting when small children fall out of bed. Pediatrics 1977;60(4):533–5

81. Daly KE, Calvert PT. Accidental femoral fracture in infants. Injury 1991;22(4):337–8

82. Loder RT. Pediatric polytrauma: orthopaedic care and hospital course. J Orthop Trauma 1987;1(1):48–54

83. Johnson K, Chapman S, Hall CM. Skeletal injuries associated with sexual abuse. Pediatr Radiol 2004;34(8): 620–3

84. Morris S, Cassidy N, Stephens M et al Birth-associated femoral fractures: incidence and outcome. J Pediatr Orthop 2002;22(1):27–30

85. Cumming WA. Neonatal skeletal fractures. Birth trauma or child abuse? J Can Assoc Radiol 1979;30(1):30–3

86. Fry K, Hoffer MM, Brink J. Femoral shaft fractures in brain-injured children. J Trauma 1976;16(5):371–3

87. Torwalt CR, Balachandra AT, Youngson C et al Spontaneous fractures in the differential diagnosis of fractures in children. J Forensic Sci 2002;47(6):1340–4

88. Katz JF. Spontaneous fractures in paraplegic children. J Bone Joint Surg Am 1953;35-A(1):220–6

89. Robin GC. Fractures in poliomyelitis in children. J Bone Joint Surg Am 1966;48:1048–54

90. Kleinman PK, Marks SC, Richmond JM et al Inflicted skeletal injury: a postmortem-radiologic-histopathologic study in 31 infants. Am J Radiol 1995;165(3):647–650

91. England SP, Sundberg S. Management of common pediatric fractures. Ped Clin North Am 1996;43(5):991–1012

92. Kleinman PK. Diagnostic Imaging of Child Abuse. Williams and Wilkins, 1987

93. Roffman M, Moshel M, Mendes DG. Bicycle spoke injuries. J Trauma 1980;20(4):325–6

94. D'Souza LG, Hynes DE, McManus F et al The bicycle spoke injury: an avoidable accident? Foot Ankle Int 1996;17(3): 170–3

95. Mellick LB, Milker L, Egsieker E. Childhood accidental spiral tibial (CAST) fractures. Pediatr Emerg Care 1999;15(5):307–9

96. Coffey C, Haley K, Hayes J et al The risk of child abuse in infants and toddlers with lower extremity injuries. J Pediatr Surg 2005;40(1):120–3

97. Nimkin K, Spevak MR, Kleinman PK. Fractures of the hands and feet in child abuse: imaging and pathological features. Radiology 1997;203(1):233–6

98. Kleinman PK. The upper extremity. In Kleinman PK. Diagnostic imaging of child abuse. Mosby, 2nd ed, 1998, 72–109

99. Park EA. The imprinting of nutritional disturbances in growing bone. Pediatrics 1964;33(suppl):815–62

100. Boyages SC, Halpern JP, Maberly GF et al A comparative study of neurological and myxedematous endemic cretinism in western China. J Clin Endocrinol Metab 1988;67 (6):1262–71

101. Rosen RA, Deshmukh SM. Growth arrest recovery lines in hypoparathyroidism. Radiology 1985;155(1):61–2

102. Bessler W. Vertebral growth arrest lines after Cushing's syndrome. A case report. Diagn Imaging 1982;51(6):311–5

103. Fiszman P, Ansell BM, Renton P. Radiological assessment of knees in juvenile chronic arthritis (juvenile rheumatoid arthritis). Scand J Rheumatol 1981;10(2):145–52

104. Schwartz AM, Leonidas JC. Methotrexate osteopathy. Skeletal Radiol 1984;11(1):13–6

105. Meister B, Gassner I, Streif W et al Methotrexate osteopathy in infants with tumors of the central nervous system. Med Pediatr Oncol 1994;23(6):493–6

106. Bar-On E, Beckwith JB, Odom LF, Eilert RE. Effect of chemotherapy on human growth plate. J Pediatr Orthop 1993;13(2):220–4

107. Silverman FN. Variants due to diseases of bone. In Silverman FN, Kuhn JP (eds). Caffey's pediatric x-ray diagnosis: an integrated imaging approach. Mosby, 9th ed, 1994, 1521–7

108. Patton RG, Gardner LI. Growth failure in maternal deprivation. Charles C Thomas, 1967, 25–51

109. Patton RG, Gardner LI. Influence of family environment on growth: the syndrome of 'maternal deprivation'. Pediatrics 1962;30(6):957–62

110. Khadilkar VV, Frazer FL, Skuse DH et al Metaphyseal growth arrest lines in psychosocial short stature. Arch Dis Child 1998;79(3):260–2

Accidental Trauma

6

6.1 Introduction

In children fractures are a regular occurring feature (see section 1.2). When a physician finds a fracture in a child, he can draw up a comprehensive differential diagnosis. In this chapter accidental childhood fractures are discussed.

6.2 Fractures Resulting from Birth Trauma

6.2.1 General Aspects of Birth Trauma-Related Fractures

In older children, pain is often an indicator for the presence of a fracture. However, in neonates it is difficult to establish pain. Often the presence of a fracture can only be established by behaviour, muscle tone, heart beat and symptoms such as nausea and vomiting or limited use of a body part [1]. Fractures resulting from birth are not always diagnosed immediately post-partum, unless there are obvious symptoms, such as a clearly visible swelling and/or abnormal position. It is quite likely that physicians will completely overlook some fractures due to the lack of obvious symptoms. Research by Morris et al. showed that there was a delay in diagnosis in the majority of children that had sustained a post-partum femur fracture (section 5.7.3.1) [2]. When there are no clinical symptoms, skull fractures are also frequently overlooked, even after vacuum extraction, unless a routine radiograph was made [3]. In this study Simonson et al. found a 5% incidence of skull fractures in children born by vacuum extraction. Clavicle fractures too are

often diagnosed as late as several weeks after birth, due to the then present callus formation [4].

This delay in diagnosis can lead to wrongfully suspected child maltreatment. To a certain extent it is possible to differentiate between birth trauma and other trauma by evaluating the presence of callus formation. Cumming reports that callus may be visible as early as 7 days after birth [5]. When a fracture is found at an unusual location, or when 11 days after birth there is no callus visible, child abuse should be considered a possible cause.

6.2.2 Incidence and Prevalence of Fractures Resulting from Birth

In the medical literature a great number of studies can be found on the origin of fractures during delivery (Table 6.1) [6–8]. Based on these publications it has been established that the clavicle fracture is most prevalent (Fig. 6.1), followed by fractures of the humerus (Fig. 6.2), femur (Fig. 6.3) and skull. Rib fractures are only reported in exceptional situations (see paragraph 3.5.1). Jaarsma considers the incidence of post-partum fractures to be 0.1–3.5%; however, this is an underestimation (see Sect. 6.2.1) [1].

Many of the fractures that can be caused by violence have also been reported post-partum; usually in case reports. Hence, it is essential that in the immediate post-partum period, a thorough obstetric anamnesis is taken. In their research population, Bhat et al. found a higher incidence of bone defects in cases without prenatal care, after a complicated delivery or after a Caesarean section [8].

In 2007, Groenendaal and Hukkelhoven drew attention in the Netherlands Journal of Medicine to the

R. A. C. Bilo et al., *Forensic Aspects of Pediatric Fractures*,
DOI: 10.1007/978-3-540-78716-7_6, © Springer-Verlag Berlin Heidelberg 2010

Table 6.1 Fractures resulting from delivery

Authors	Babies (n)	Fractures (n (%))	Location (n)
Rubin A [6]	15,435	51 (0.35%)	• Clavicle (43) • Humerus (7) • Skull (1)
Camus M, Lefevre G, Veron P, et al. [7]	20,409	123 (0.6%)	• Clavicle (105) • Humerus (7) • Skull (7) • Femoral shaft (2) • Epiphysis (2)
Bhat BV, Kumar A, Oumachigui A [8]	34,946	35 (0.1%)	• Clavicle (16) • Humerus (7) • Femur (5) • Skull (4) • Orbit (1) • Epiphysis distal femur (1) • Dislocation elbow (1)
Groenendaal, Hukkelhoven [9]	158,035	1174 (0.74%)	• Clavicle[a] • Humerus • Femur • No other fractures were mentioned

[a] Number of fractures not available

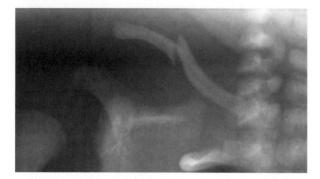

Fig. 6.1 One-day-old infant boy (birth weight 3,400 g) after uncomplicated delivery. At physical examination a swelling was seen at the site of the right clavicle. Radiograph showed a mid-clavicular fracture

prevalence of fractures in term births [9]. They used data from Perinatal Registration Netherlands which contains data on term neonates <28 days old (n = 158.035). In 1,174 children (0.74%) fractures were found. In 19% (n = 227) of cases, the cause of the fracture was not known: the vaginal birth had been either physiological and non-traumatic or there had been an uncomplicated Caesarean section; after the delivery there had been no cause for resuscitation and further diagnostics showed no indications for congenital bone diseases such as osteogenesis imperfecta or osteopenia. Twelve children had sustained a humerus fracture without known cause, and 3 a femur fracture. The remaining 212 children had sustained a fracture of the

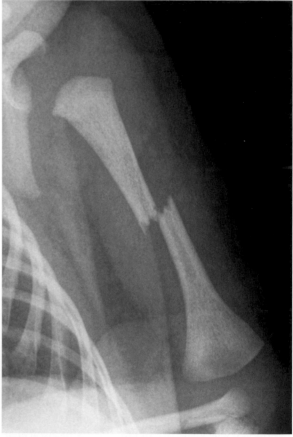

Fig. 6.2 One-day-old infant girl (birth weight 3,350 g) after vacuum extraction with shoulder dystocia. Radiograph showed a mid-shaft humerus fracture

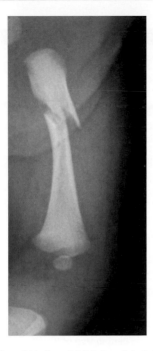

Fig. 6.3 One-day-old infant girl (birth weight 2,125 g) after primary Caesarean section for transverse presentation. At physical examination a swelling on the left femur was seen. Radiograph showed an oblique fracture of the proximal femur

clavicle. Groenendaal and Hukkelhoven suspect that the number of fractures in term neonates in The Netherlands is higher.

6.3 Accidental Fractures

6.3.1 Introduction

Physicians are expected to be able to distinguish between accidental and non-accidental injuries. However, this is not always easy. After regular diagnostic methods have established the nature and extent of the injury, physicians have four important aids to their disposal:

1. The anamnesis (the statement given by the parents/carers regarding the origin of the injury)
2. The level of development of the child
3. The theoretical interpretation of the skeletal injury based on biomechanical principles) see Chaps. 1–5)
4. Data from the scientific literature on the probability of injuries in specific accidents and falls

6.3.2 Anamnesis

In order to explain a particular injury, parents may mention an accident, whereas the physician is able to establish based on the level of development of the child and the scientific data that it is highly unlikely or even impossible for the sustained injury to result from the reported accident.

In an accidental injury, the anamnesis nearly always provides a conclusive explanation for the origin of the injury. Often, the patient history is supported by statements from witnesses. The presence of undisclosed congenital disorder such as osteogenesis imperfecta is the exception to this rule. Due to such diseases, fractures may be sustained in only minor trauma (see also paragraph 1.5.2).

6.3.3 The Level of Development of the Child

Based on a number of key ages, Table 6.2 provides a global overview of motor development in children up to 5 years of age. Key ages are a selection from many age levels and the most suitable frame of reference for diagnostic purposes. Every age mentioned in these fields of development are 'p50 aged'. This means that 50% of all children have reached that specific level of functioning at that age, and masters these functions at a more or less adult level. The table does not claim to be complete and only provides an indication of the general level of motor development of a child at a given age [10].

In non-mobile or partly mobile children it regularly occurs that the anamnesis reports that the child itself was responsible for the sustained fracture: for example, when it fell from the dressing table or out of bed. The question the physician should answer in these cases is whether at the moment of the reported incident, the child had the motor skills to fall in the manner described. This calls for careful assessment of the level of development of the child. This can take place based on the one hand on data in the anamnesis, and on the other hand on data from the infant welfare centre. When these data are not available, than a theoretical assessment of the motor skills can be made, based on scientific data. Hereby an important element is the moment at which a child can turn and crawl, since this creates the movement potential that makes falling feasible. Tables 6.3a–c and 6.4 provide an

Table 6.2 Overview key ages and their general motor development [10]

Age	Skill	General motor development
4 weeks	• Control muscles of the eye	• Positive head lag
16 weeks	• Balance head	• Stabile head balance • Symmetric posture
28 weeks	• Grip and manual manipulation	• Sits and leans forward supported on the hands • Stable stance when supported • Asymmetric neck reflex disappears (22–26 weeks)
40 weeks	• Control trunk and fingers: sitting, crawling and picking	• Sits without support • Crawls • Pulls up to stance • Grip reflex at the feet disappears (40 weeks–18 months)
52 weeks	• Control of legs and feet: the child stands erect and starts exploring	• Walks holding on to one hand • Walks along an object (such as coffee table or settee)
18 months	• Control of larynx function: words and word combinations	• Walks independently • Able to sit up independently
24 months	• Control of bladder and bowel functions	• Is capable of running • Can play football
36 months	• Speaks in sentences	• Can stand on one leg • Jumps from the bottom step of the stairs
48 months	• Understands numbers and shapes	• Hops well on one leg • Jumps forward on both legs
60 months	• Child ready for school and prepared to play with other children	• Hops equally well on either leg

Table 6.3a Overview of the reference values for supine-prone rotation [11]

Author	P value	Age (weeks)
Bayley	50	28
	95	43
BOS 2-30	5	19
	50	28
	95	41
D.O.S.	50	19
	90	38
Gesell	50	24
Helbrügge	–	30
Illingworth	–	28
Schlesinger	10	17
	50	24
	90	32
	99	39
	100	41

Table 6.3b Overview of the reference values of turning prone-supine [11]

Author	P value	Age (weeks)
Illingworth	–	24
Schlesinger	10	14
	50	23
	90	32

Table 6.3c Overview reference values for supine-prone and prone-supine rotation [11]

Author	P value	Age (weeks)
Schlesinger	10	22
	50	28
	90	36
Sheridan	–	26
Touwen	80	29–32

Table 6.4 Overview reference values for crawling along (abdomen touching the surface) [11]

Author	Similar characteristic	P value	Age (weeks)
Bayley	Pre-walking locomotion	50	31
		95	47
Gesell	Pulling self along on abdomen	50	<40
Helbrügge	Prone crawl position	–	39
Illingworth	Prone crawl position Crawls by pulling self forward with hands	–	40
Schlesinger	Crawls forwards, stomach touching the floor	10	28
		50	36
		90	46
		95	51
		98	53
		100	55
Sheridan	Attempts to crawl; sometimes succeeds	–	39
Touwen	Moves forward on stomach by using arms and legs	80	45–48

overview of reference values regarding the age at which such skills are present [11]. Based on these data it is possible to excluded that during the first few months of life a child is able to turn or crawl consciously (voluntary).

- Turning over from supine to prone is impossible as long as the asymmetrical tonic neck reflex (ATNR) is present. This reflex can be provoked by lying the child down on its back and from a symmetrical position turn the head to one side. The child will react by stretching the arm and the leg on the side towards which the head is turned, and will bend the arm and leg on the other side, as a result of this posture it is also known as the 'fencing reflex'. From the 4th to 5th month onwards, it is not all that easy to provoke the ATNR. From around the 6th month onwards, it is impossible to provoke the reflex in normal children. This reflex prevents the child from turning around from supine to prone.
- During the first months it is impossible for an infant to turn from a prone to a supine position. And if this happens in sporadic cases, it is not due to any conscious behaviour of the child. Children who show this behaviour are either very active or hypertonic. When the child lifts its head up high when lying prone and then turns its head around, it provokes an instable prone situation, which is followed by rotation (falling over).
- A change in position from lying sideways is possible in active children that end up in a opisthotonic position. In children that are inclined to be hypertonic,

this opisthotonic position may be a reflex caused by stimulation of the back of the head when lying on one side. This may also be the case in children with gastro-oesophageal reflux.

- Purposeful locomotion during the first few months is impossible. However, this does not imply that during that period the child cannot move forwards based on reflexes and involuntary movements. Children up to approximately 4 months of age have a Bauer reflex that may be provoked by pressing the soles of the feet when the child is lying prone (and hips and knees are bent). As a reaction the child moves forward with alternating movements (left–right). Sometimes the reflex occurs involuntary. It is probably due to the Bauer reflex that a child that has been laid down prone in the middle of his/her bed is found some time later transverse at the head the bed.

6.3.4 Data from the Literature

It appears that in their first year of life, approximately 50% of children will experience a fall over a limited distance [12]. This type of fall often necessitates a visit to the emergency department (approximately 1 in 100 children <1 year of age) [13]. Approximately 1 in 1,000 children will be hospitalised for such a fall, and approximately 1 in 250,000 children <1 year of age will die from such a fall [14].

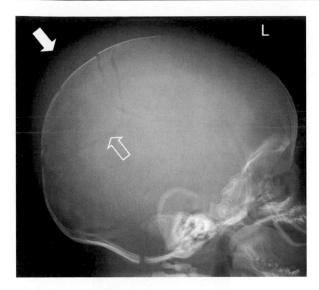

Fig. 6.10 Ten-year-old boy who fell out of his travel bassinet down the stairs (14 steps). After the fall he was drowsy, a radiograph of the skull showed soft-tissue swelling (*arrow*) and a linear biparietal fracture (*open arrow*)

Arnholz et al. describe bilateral skull fractures in a 6-week-old infant who fell from a distance of about 90 cm from a perambulator and landed with the top of the head on concrete stairs (Fig. 6.10) [52]. Two symmetrically located haemorrhages on the scalp were found as associated injuries.

6.8.3 Conclusions

A fall from a perambulator, in particular in children <1 year old, is not an unusual occurrence. Often children will fall on their head. Serious intracranial injuries (a typical impact injury: epidural haemorrhages) are only reported in case reports. Lasting damage is rare, as is death.

6.9 Fall from a High Chair

6.9.1 Introduction

From the moment that children are well able to sit up and eat solid food, parents/carers will usually place them in a high chair at the dining-room table. In spite of the straps in these chairs, children regularly fall out of them.

6.9.2 Data from the Literature

Watson and Ozanne evaluated the relation between accidents resulting from children's furniture and perambulators and the occurrence of injuries (see paragraph 6.8.2) [48].

By means of a questionnaire directed to the parents, Mayr et al. evaluated 103 children that had fallen from a high chair and presented at the emergency department [53]. Fifty percent of children wanted to stand up in the chair before they fell down, and 14% of accidents occurred because the high chair toppled over. Most children had suffered head injuries: contusions or haematomas on the head or lacerations of the scalp or face (68.9%), skull fractures (15.5%) and concussions (13.6%). The article does not mention any children that died as a result of the fall or ended up in a life-threatening situation.

Powell et al. carried out the most comprehensive (retrospective) study into injuries in children up to the age of 3 years old, related to a fall from a high chair (n=40,650, average age 10 months, over a period of 5 years) [54]. The purpose of the study was compile a report on the incidence of this type of accident, the circumstances and the types of injury. Over 5,000 children (13%) fell from a booster seat and over 4,000 children fell from a youth chair. Predominantly head (44%) and facial (39%) injuries were found: contusions and abrasions (36%), lacerations (25%), intracranial injuries (21%) and fractures (8%). Two percent of the children were hospitalised. The article does not mention any children that died as a result of the fall.

6.9.3 Conclusions

Children, in particular those <1 year old, regularly fall from high chairs. The (albeit limited) literature hardly ever mentions serious or even life-threatening injuries. Only the article of Watson mentions one child that died as a result of a fall from a high chair [48].

6.10 Fall from a Staircase

6.10.1 Introduction

Almost all parents have experienced that a child fell down the stairs. Consequently, the number of annual falls of this type should be high. Yet, the paediatric literature has but a few publications on this subject and on the injuries that may be sustained.

6.10.2 Data from the Literature

In a prospective study, Joffe and Ludwig describe 363 children from 1 month to nearly 19 years old with injuries resulting from a fall down the stairs (average age: 55 months) [55]. Fifty-four children were <1 year old. Ten children were being carried by their parent/carer. Twenty-four were in a baby walker when they fell down the stairs. Children who were victims of child abuse were excluded from the study.

The majority of children had superficial injuries, 73% sustained injuries to head and neck. Head injuries were more frequently seen in children <4 years of age. In 28%, injuries of the extremities were found, in particular distally. Only in 2% of children injuries to the trunk were seen, and 6% of children ($n=22$) had sustained fractures. Sixteen children had suffered a fracture of one of the extremities (15 of them were >4 years old). Six children had suffered a skull fracture (all <3 years old). Four of the six skull fractures were sustained in ten children who fell on the stairways from the hands of their parents/carers. None of the children showed rib, spinal, pelvic or hip fractures.

The group of children of 6–12 months old counted 40 injuries in total. Twenty-four of those injuries were seen in the 24 children that had fallen in their baby walker (see paragraph 6.5). Only 2.7% of children had sustained injuries to more than one body part.

Children who had fallen more than four steps down the stairs did not sustain more injuries than children who had fallen less than four steps down the stairs, irrespective of their age. Also, the injuries were of similar severity. Three percent was admitted. None of the children experienced a life-threatening situation. Also, none of the children was admitted to the intensive care unit, no intracranial haemorrhages or brain contusions were found, and none of the children died.

Joffe and Ludwig concluded that there was no relation between the number of steps a child falls down and the severity of the injury, and that a fall from a staircase is less serious than a free fall from the same height. When a child presents with multiple and severe injuries to the trunk or extremities, and according to the clinical history he/she has fallen down the stairs, then other causes should be considered (Fig. 6.11).

Chiaviello et al. also studied the effects of a fall down the stairs in 69 children of <5 years of age (average age

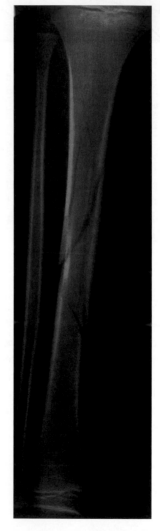

Fig. 6.11 Five and a half-year-old boy who sustained a spiral fracture after a fall down the stairs. The anamnesis showed that he had climbed over the stair barrier holding a toy in his hand, caught is leg in the railing and lost his balance. A police investigation at the site of the accident confirmed the clinical history.

2 years), including three children who had fallen together with their parent/carer [56]. Unlike Joffe, they excluded accidents with baby walkers. They also excluded children suspected to be victim of child abuse.

The majority of the injuries were not serious. Fifteen children had sustained serious injuries, such as: concussion (11 children, 16%), skull fracture (five children, 7%), brain contusion (two children, 3%), subdural haemorrhages (one child, 1%) and a fracture of the second cervical vertebra (one child, 1%). The three children that had been carried by their parent/carer who fell on the child against the staircase sustained the most serious injuries: two children suffered a skull fracture, and one of the children showed a small subdural haemorrhage and contusion. This was also the child who had sustained the fracture of the second cervical vertebra.

Chaviello et al. concluded that in the majority of falls there were no serious injuries. Injuries of head and neck prevailed. The incidence of an injury to more than one body part is rare.

6.10.3 Conclusions

Children fall regularly down the stairs. Usually there are few or no injuries. However, when injuries are sustained, they are usually seen to the head, neck and distal extremities (Fig. 6.12). Compared to the study of Joffe and Ludwig, the study of Chaviello et al. showed more severe injuries [55, 56]. Whether this difference is realistic or the result of a different use of diagnostic devices is not clear. Chaviello as well as Joffe conclude that a free fall inflicts more damage than a fall of the same height down the stairs.

6.11 Fall from a Shopping Trolley

6.11.1 Introduction

Children are often placed in shopping trolleys; in the designated seats as well as in the trolley itself.

A fall from a shopping trolley is a regular occurrence, possibly due to diminished attention of the parents while shopping.

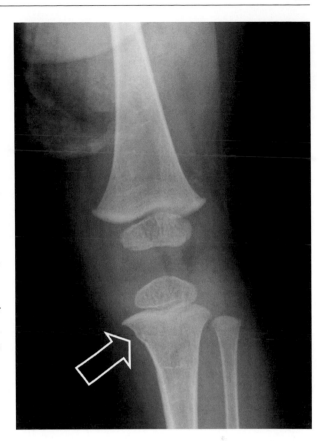

Fig. 6.12 Fourteen-month-old boy after witnessed fall down the stairs. The proximal tibia shows a torus fracture (*open arrow*)

6.11.2 Data from the Literature

Smith et al. evaluated retrospectively the emergency department data of over 75,000 shopping trolley-related injuries in children of 15 years old and younger (84% <5 years old) [57]. Head and neck injuries were most prevalent (74%). Of the children that had sustained injuries, 2.7% had to be hospitalised (93% <4 years old), mostly due to fractures (45%), followed by internal injuries (22%) and concussion (17%).

In another prospective study, Smith et al. evaluated 62 children from 4 months to 10 years old (average age 2.8 years), who had presented at the emergency department due to shopping trolley-related injuries over a period of 15 months [58]. Twelve children presented by ambulance. Forty-nine children (79%) were found to have sustained a head injury. Fractures were found in 11 children (18%: 5 skull fractures, two femur fractures, a metatarsal fracture, a clavicle fracture and a radius and ulna fracture). Nine children (14%) had sustained lacerations and 30 children (48%) had suffered superficial injuries. Most children sustained the injuries by falling from the trolley (58%), followed by toppling over of the trolley (26%). Injuries resulting from a fall out of the trolley occurred in all age groups, toppling over of the trolley was mostly seen in children <1 year old.

Smith et al. concluded that accidents with shopping trolleys may lead to serious and potentially life-threatening injuries, although there were no cases of serious (intra)cranial injury – in spite of a fall on a solid (often concrete) surface. No intracranial haemorrhages were found.

Parry et al. evaluated retrospectively 282 hospitalisations of children up to 15 years of age over a period of 10 years as the result of shopping trolley-related injuries [59]. Of the hospitalised children, 92% was less than 5 years old, 65% was less than 2 years old. Ninety percent of the injuries resulted from a fall out of the trolley. Eighty-four percent of the injuries were seen to the head or face. The physicians considered 22% of the injuries to be serious. None of the children died from the fall.

6.11.3 Conclusions

Although Smith et al. maintain that a fall from a shopping trolley may lead to life-threatening injuries, there are up to the present day no reports on children that died as a consequence of such a fall [57]. In the (albeit very limited) literature, there are also no reports on intracranial haemorrhages.

6.12 Fall from a Trampoline

6.12.1 Introduction

Most children who sustain injuries during trampoline jumping are older than the children that belong to the most vulnerable group for non-accidental injuries. However, there is an overlap between the youngest group of children with trampoline-related injuries (<5 years old) and the oldest victims with severe non-accidental injuries (2–5 years). Besides, here applies, the younger the child is that gets injured while trampoline

jumping, the more serious the injuries. In 2003, The American Academy of Orthopedic Surgeons counted 211,646 trampoline accidents in children of less than 19 years of age [60].

6.12.2 Data from the Literature

Woodward et al. report on 114 children with injuries due to trampoline accidents [61]. The average age was 8 years. The youngest children ran the highest risk for injuries. In 55% of children injuries of the extremities were found (Fig. 6.13). Head and neck injuries were seen in 37% of children. Seventy-five percent was X-rayed, 23% was hospitalised and 17% had to have an operation.

Chalmers et al. evaluated 2,098 hospitalisations and two deaths related to the use of trampolines over a period of 10 years [62]. Eighty percent of children fell from the trampoline on the ground. Fractures were the most prevalent injuries (68%). The arms were the most

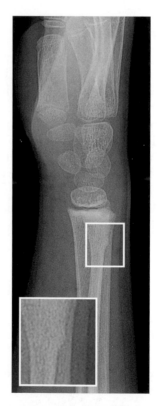

Fig. 6.13 Nearly 7-year-old girl who has fallen from the trampoline at the day-care centre. A radiograph of the right wrist shows a torus fracture (see inset)

commonly involved body part. The study did not show that serious head and neck injuries were seen on a regular basis.

Larson and Davis reported on 217 children and adults that had sustained trampoline injuries [63]. Their ages ranged from 18 months to 45 years of age (average age 10 years). Forty-three percent was between 5 and 9 years old. The following injuries were found: fractures (39%), sprains and strains (25%), lacerations (21%) and contusions (16%). The patients had sustained injuries to: elbow or lower arm (26%), head and neck (21%), ankle or foot (18%), knee or leg (15%), trunk or back (9%), shoulder or arm (6%) and wrist or hand (4%). None of the patients sustained lasting neurological damage.

McDermott et al. described retrospectively 88 children (33 boys and 55 girls, average age 8.6 years) who had presented over a period of 6 months at their local hospital with a fracture due to a trampoline accident [64]. Most fractures were located in the upper extremities (69%). Thirty-six children (41%) had to have a surgical intervention; the others could be treated conservatively. In 40% of cases, playing on the trampoline was supervised by a parent/carer.

The earlier-mentioned data were more or less confirmed by Hume et al. [65]. In the 114 cases they examined (95%, age <20 years) sprains and strains (40%) were the most frequently seen injuries. The legs were the most common place of injury.

Smith carried out a retrospective analysis in approximately 249,000 children of ≤18 years old who had been treated between 1990 and 1995 for a trampoline accident [66]. Well over 70% of injuries were found in the extremities. Smith found several age-specific injury patterns:

- There is an inversely proportional relation between the age of the child and the relative frequency of injuries to the upper extremities, fractures and dislocations.
- There is a proportional relation between the age of the child and the occurrence of skin lesions (haematomas, contusions) and injuries to the lower extremities.
- There is an inversely proportional relation between the age of the child and face, head and neck injuries and lacerations.

Hospitalisations were indicated in 3.3% of children. Main reasons for hospitalisation were fractures and dislocations (83%). Children who could go home after their visit to the emergency department had sustained predominantly skin lesions (53%), fractures and dislocations (30%) and lacerations (14%). Smith concludes that trampoline injuries are an important cause of (lethal) injuries.

Smith and Shield carried out a prospective study into trampoline accidents in 214 children from 1 to 16 years of age (average age: 9.4 years) [67]. Most injuries were found in the lower extremities (36%), followed by the upper extremities (31.8%), the head (14.5%), the trunk (9.8%) and the neck (7.9%). Most frequently seen were skin lesions (haematomas and contusions) (51.9%), followed by fractures (34.6%) and lacerations (11.7%). Fractures of the extremities were most often seen in the upper extremities. Skin lesions were seen predominantly in the lower extremities. Lacerations were most prevalent to the head and the face, especially in children <6 years of age. This was also the group with the largest number of skin lesions.

6.12.3 Conclusions

Most trampoline accidents do not result in life-threatening injuries. On average the age of children with trampoline injuries is higher than the age of children who are victims of non-accidental serious injuries.

6.13 Fall from a Considerable Height

6.13.1 Introduction

Most children that fall from a considerable height are <6 years old. They fall over a distance of 3–7 m (one to two floors), in or in the vicinity of their home, more often during the warm seasons [68–71].

6.13.2 Data from the Literature and Conclusions

As described in Chap. 2, a child who falls from a considerable height will in particular sustain injuries to the head and neck area [68, 70]. The most prevalent injuries are (in order of occurrence):

1. External and visible injuries [68–74]
2. Skull fractures, of the cranium as well as the base of the skull, possibly with intracranial abnormalities [68, 69, 72, 73]
3. Fractures of the extremities [68–70]
4. Fractures of the spine [69]

Only occasionally more than one body part is injured [68, 69].

A remarkable discovery in the study of Wang et al. is that orthopaedic and thoracic injuries (fractures of the extremities, lung contusion and pneumothorax) are more frequently seen in falls over a distance of more than 4–5 m, and that abdominal injuries (liver lacerations, visceral and spleen injuries) are more frequently seen in a fall of less than 4–5 m [74].

Although this type of fall carries a high morbidity, it seldom leads to lasting defects or death [68, 69]. Morbidity increases with fall distance, although a fall distance of less than 5 m can also be lethal [69, 72]. Hereby intracranial injuries are the main cause of death (Fig. 6.14a and b) [72].

6.14 Fractures Resulting from Daily Care and Medical Procedures

6.14.1 Introduction

In normal circumstances a child will not sustain injuries during daily care and due to medical treatments. However, in this section we present a number of cases in which this took place.

6.14.2 Daily Care

In the literature there are case reports on fractures that have allegedly been sustained in the day-to-day care of children. Hymel and Jenny describe a case in which a humerus fracture was sustained by an infant when the parents turned the child over from prone to supine (Fig. 6.15). The incident was recorded on video, which supports the plausibility of the story [75].

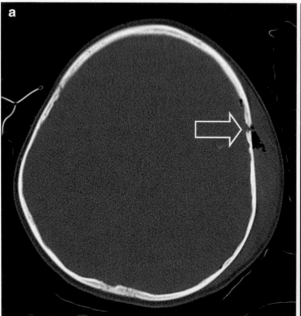
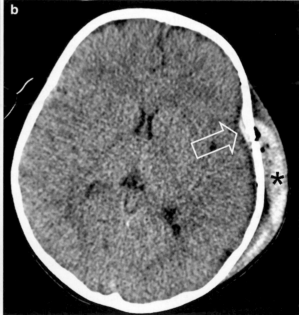

Fig. 6.14 (a) Twenty-two-month-old boy who had fallen from a 4 m high window. The skull CT shows a fracture of the parietal bone (*open arrow*). (b) CT at soft-tissue setting shows a small, probably epidural, haematoma (*open arrow*) and a soft-tissue haematoma (asterisk)

Fig. 6.15 Graphic representation of the mechanism of fractures as described by Hymel and Jenny

6.14.3 Medical Procedures

6.14.3.1 Use of Intra-Osseous Vascular Access Needles

Harty and Kao describe two children that presented at the emergency department for bone abnormalities [76]. According to the physicians, the abnormalities had possibly been caused by child abuse. In both children cortical bone defects were found in the proximal tibiae, which were thought to be healing fractures. In the end it appeared that in both children intra-osseous vascular access needles had been used.

Bowley describes a case of a 2-year-old child that had sustained an iatrogenic tibia fracture after the use of an intra-osseous vascular access needle [77]. In the discussion of their case they mention two more children that had sustained an iatrogenic fracture after a bone needle had been placed.

6.14.3.2 Physical Examination

The medical literature does not report any cases in which a fracture was sustained in a physical examination. However, the authors of this book have been confronted with a 3-day-old neonate that had sustained a mid-shaft femur fracture (Fig. 6.16). According to the mother the child showed pain when she changed the diaper. Patient history and follow-up examination did not show any signs of child abuse. Post-partum there were no indications for a fracture. On day 3, the paediatric resident performed an examination according to Ortolani. The resident wrote in the dossier that a little snap was heard and that the Ortolani was positive.

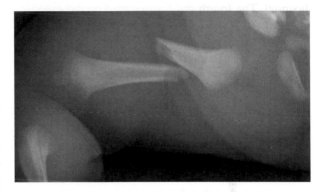

Fig. 6.16 Femur fracture in a neonate after incorrectly preformed Ortolani

After this examination the infant showed pain when the diaper was changed. A radiograph of the leg showed a mid-shaft oblique femur fracture. The successively made skeletal survey did not show any other fractures. The combined facts led to the conclusion that the femur fracture had to be the result of the examination according to Ortolani.

6.14.3.3 Physiotherapy

A number of articles refers to fractures sustained during physiotherapy [78–84]. There can only be confusion with fractures resulting from child abuse when the physiotherapy takes place outside the hospital and/or by the parents [79, 80].

Pickett et al. describe an ex-premature infant (pregnancy 33 weeks) in whom multiple defects to both legs were found at age 4 weeks: periosteal reactions around the knees combines with 'bucket-handle' fractures of both proximal tibiae, bilateral diaphyses and metaphyseal new-bone formation metaphyseal fragmentation of the tibiae, diaphyseal new-bone formation at the distal end of the left femur and metaphyseal corner fractures of the medial proximal part of both femurs [78]. The defect appeared to be limited to the joints treated for contractures by a physiotherapist.

Helfer et al. describe four children of <1 year old (three ex-prematures and one term infant) who, in their opinion, sustained serious bone damage due to passive exercises [79]. In the three ex-premature infants, the parents/carers executed the exercises advised by the hospital. The fourth child was started on the exercises on the initiative of the babysitter. Due to the results of the radiological examination, the physicians suspected these children to be abused.

Helfer et al. draw attention to the risk of this type of exercise for infants. It appeared that in all cases the parents executed the exercises far more strenuously than was intended. The context, as described by Helfer et al., does not always completely exclude child abuse. In one case, the father abused alcohol while in charge of the child. Only in one case the authors state specifically that after extensive investigation child abuse was excluded. In a letter, as reaction to this article London et al. emphasise the danger of including potentially maltreating families in (what is more or less) medical treatment such as passive exercises or physiotherapy in already vulnerable children [80].

Simonian and Staheli draw attention to fractures inflicted around the knee joint in passive exercising for contractures around the knee joint [81].

The occurrence of rib fractures resulting from physiotherapy has also been reported (see also paragraph 3.5.3). Chalumeau et al. describe five boy infants (average age 3 months) within a period of 4 years who were shown to have sustained a rib fracture after physiotherapy [82]. In a prospective study of Gorincour et al., there were six children of less than 2 years old that had sustained either lateral rib fractures or possibly had remains of rib fractures as a result of physiotherapy [83]. The authors maintain that in these children child abuse could be ruled out based on plausible grounds. Chanelière et al. described two children with lateral rib fractures after they had received physiotherapy for bronchiolitis [84].

6.15 Sports Fractures

6.15.1 Introduction

Over the last few decennia, the number of children who are engaged in sports has increased. The incidence of sports injuries in children of school age has been estimated to be 3–11%, in which the majority of sports injuries (such as distortions and contusions) is not serious and will heal quickly. Serious sports injuries are fractures and ruptures.

6.15.2 Data from the Literature

Fractures sustained while playing sports can be divided in acute and chronic injuries (overuse). [85, 86].

6.15.2.1 Acute Fractures

Fractures sustained while playing sports are of the same nature and severity as 'normal' accidental fractures, such as Salter-Harris fractures and shaft fractures, since the biomechanics are often the same. Possibly Salter-Harris fractures of the distal femur and fractures of the patella are more frequently seen in sports-related trauma.

Fractures sustained while playing sports are seldom suspect for non-accidental injuries, due to an adequate anamnesis and age. Moreover, often the trauma has been witnessed by a large number of people.

6.15.2.2 Chronic Osseous Injuries (Stress Injuries)

The radiological image of stress injuries may suggest non-accidental injury, especially when the anamnesis does not immediately point into the direction of overuse. One will find stress fractures and chronic avulsion fractures that are accompanied by ample callus formation, sclerosis and sometimes bone resorption.

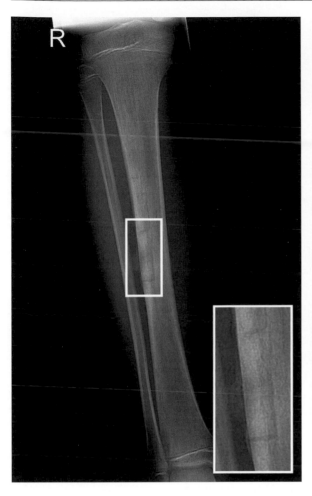

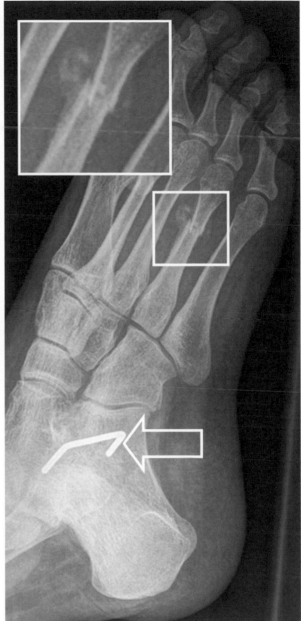

Fig. 6.17 Multiple fracture lines, cortical widening and sclerosis in the tibia shaft of a young kick-boxer, corresponding to stress fractures (see inset). After plaster immobilisation the abnormalities disappeared

Stress fractures are often seen in the feet (metatarsals 2 and 3), tibia and fibula (Figs. 6.17 and 6.18); chronic avulsion fractures are seen a.o. in the pelvis at the level where the muscles are attached to the anterior inferior and superior iliac spinous process and the ischial tuberosity.

Fig. 6.18 Stress fracture of metatarsal 4 (March fracture). Extensive callus formation (see inset). Status after stapled talocalcaneal arthrodesis (*open arrow*)

References

1. Jaarsma AS. Botbreuken bij pasgeborenen. Patient Care 2007;34(9):9–12
2. Morris S, Cassidy N, Stephens M et al Birth-associated femoral fractures: incidence and outcome. J Pediatr Orthop 2002;22(1):27–30
3. Simonson C, Barlow P, Dehennin N et al Neonatal complications of vacuum-assisted delivery. Obstet Gynecol 2007; 109(3):626–33
4. Joseph PR, Rosenfeld W. Clavicular fractures in neonates. Am J Dis Child 1990;144(2):165–7
5. Cumming WA. Neonatal skeletal fractures. Birth trauma or child abuse? J Can Assoc Radiol 1979;30(1):30–3
6. Rubin A. Birth injuries: incidence, mechanisms, and end results. J Obstet Gynecol 1964;23:218–21
7. Camus M, Lefevre G, Veron P et al Traumatismes obstétricaux du nouveau-né. Enquete retrospective à propos de

20409 naissances. J Gynecol Obstet Biol Reprod 1985;14(8): 1033–44

8. Bhat BV, Kumar A, Oumachigui A. Bone injuries during delivery. Indian J Pediatr 1994;61(4):401–5

9. Groenendaal F, Hukkelhoven C. Botbreuken bij voldragen pasgeborenen. Ned Tijdschr Geneeskd 2007;151(7):424

10. Bilo RAC, Voorhoeve HWA, Koot JM. Kind in ontwikkeling – een handreiking bij de observatie van jonge kinderen. Elsevier Tijdstroom, 7e druk, 2008

11. Brouwers-de Jong EA, Burgmeijer RJF, Laurent de Angulo MS. Ontwikkelingsonderzoek op het consultatiebureau – handboek bij het vernieuwde Van Wiechenonderzoek, 1996

12. Kravitz H, Driessen G, Gomberg R et al Accidental falls from elevated surfaces in infants from birth to one year of age. Pediatrics 1969;44(5)Suppl:869–76

13. Gallagher SS, Finison K, Guyer B et al The incidence of injuries among 87,000 Massachusetts children and adolescents: results of the 1980-81 Statewide Childhood Injury Prevention Program Surveillance System. Am J Public Health 1984;74(12):1340–7

14. Rivara FP, Alexander B, Johnston B et alPopulation-based study of fall injuries in children and adolescents resulting in hospitalization or death. Pediatrics 1993;92(1):61–3

15. Wheeler DS, Shope TR. Depressed skull fracture in a 7-month-old who fell from bed. Pediatrics 1997;100(6): 1033–4

16. Helfer RE, Slovis TL, Black M. Injuries resulting when small children fall out of bed. Pediatrics 1977;60(4):533–5

17. Nimityongskul P, Anderson LD. The likelihood of injuries when children fall out of bed. J Pediatr Orthop 1987;7(2): 184–6

18. Lyons TJ, Oates RK. Falling out of bed: a relatively benign occurrence. Pediatrics 1993;92(1):125–7

19. Tarantino CA, Dowd MD, Murdock TC. Short vertical falls in infants. Pediatr Emerg Care 1999;15(1):5–8

20. Bechtel K, Stoessel K, Leventhal JM et al Characteristics that distinguish accidental from abusive injury in hospitalized young children with head trauma. Pediatrics 2004; 114(1):165–8

21. Lueder GT. Retinal hemorrhages in accidental and nonaccidental injury. Pediatrics 2005;115(1):192; author reply 192

22. Warrington SA, Wright CM. Accidents and resulting injuries in premobile infants: data from the ALSPAC study. Arch Dis Chil 2001;85(2):104–7

23. Hennrikus WL, Shaw BA, Gerardi JA. Injuries when children reportedly fall from a bed or couch. Clin Orthop Relat Res 2003;(407):148–51

24. Johnson K, Fischer T, Chapman S et al Accidental head injuries in children under 5 years of age. Clin Radiol 2005; 60(4):464–8

25. Monson SA, Henry E, Lambert DK et al In-hospital falls of newborn infants: data from a multihospital health care system. Pediatrics 2008;122(2):e277–80

26. Trinkoff A, Parks PL. Prevention strategies for infant walker-related injuries. Public Health Rep 1993;108(6):784–8

27. American Academy of Pediatrics. Committee on Injury and Poison Prevention. Injuries associated with infant walkers. Pediatrics 2001;108(3):790–2

28. Fazen LE, Felizberto PI. Baby walker injuries. Pediatrics 1982;70(1):106–9

29. Kavanagh CA, Banco L. The infant walker: a previously unrecognized health hazard. Am J Dis Child 1982;136(3): 205–6

30. Wellman S, Paulson JA. Baby walker-related injuries. Clin Pediatr (Phila) 1984;23(2):98–9

31. Stoffman JM, Bass MJ, Fox AM. Head injuries related to the use of baby walkers. Can Med Assoc J 1984;131(6): 573–5

32. Rieder MJ, Schwartz C, Newman J. Patterns of walker use and walker injury. Pediatrics 1986;78(3):488–93

33. Partington MD, Swanson JA, Meyer FB. Head injury and the use of baby walkers: a continuing problem. Ann Emerg Med 1991;20(6):652–4

34. Coats TJ, Allen M. Baby walker related injuries - a continuing problem. Arch Emerg Med 1991;8(1):52–5

35. Chiaviello CT, Christoph RA, Bond GR. Infant walker-related injuries: a prospective study of severity and incidence. Pediatrics 1994;93(6 Pt 1):974–6

36. Mayr J, Gaisl M, Purtscher K et al Baby walkers – an underestimated hazard for our children? Eur J Pediatr 1994;153(7): 531–4

37. Petridou E, Simou E, Skondras C et al Hazards of baby walkers in a European context. Inj Prev 1996;2(2):118–20

38. Smith GA, Bowman MJ, Luria JW et al Babywalker-related injuries continue despite warning labels and public education. Pediatrics 1997;100(2):E1

39. Website Consument en Veiligheid: http://www.veiligheid.nl/ csi/websiteveiligheid.nsf/

40. Claydon SM. Fatal extradural hemorrhage following a fall from a baby bouncer. Pediatr Emerg Care 1996;12(6) :432–4

41. Farmakakis T, Alexe DM, Nicolaidou P et al Baby-bouncer-related injuries: an under-appreciated risk. Eur J Pediatr 2004;163(1):42–3

42. Davis C, Brown S. Penetrating intracranial trauma in an infant secondary to a modified baby bouncer. N Z Med J 2000;113(1118):406

43. Selbst SM, Baker MD, Shames M. Bunk bed injuries. Am J Dis Child 1990;144(6):721–3

44. MacGregor DM. Injuries associated with falls from beds. Inj Prev 2000;6(4):291–2

45. Mayr JM, Seebacher U, Lawrenz K et al Bunk beds – a still underestimated risk for accidents in childhood? Eur J Pediatr 2000;159(6):440–3

46. Johnson GF. Pediatric Lisfranc injury: 'bunk bed' fracture. Am J Roentgenol 1981;137(5):1041–4

47. Belechri M, Petridou E, Trichopoulos D. Bunk versus conventional beds: a comparative assessment of fall injury risk. J Epidemiol Community Health 2002;56(6):413–7

48. Watson WL, Ozanne-Smith J. The use of child safety restraints with nursery furniture. J Paediatr Child Health 1993;29(3):228–32

49. Couper RT, Monkhouse W, Busutil M et al Stroller safety. Med J Aust 1994;160(6):335–8

50. Lee AC, Fong D. Epidural haematoma and stroller-associated injury. J Paediatr Child Health 1997;33(5):446–7

51. Powell EC, Jovtis E, Tanz RR. Incidence and description of stroller-related injuries to children. Pediatrics 2002;110(5): e62

52. Arnholz D, Hymel KP, Hay TC et al Bilateral pediatric skull fractures: accident or abuse? Trauma 1998; 45(1):172–4

53. Mayr JM, Seebacher U, Schimpl G et al Highchair accidents. Acta Paediatr 1999;88(3):319–22

54. Powell EC, Jovtis E, Tanz RR. Incidence and description of high chair-related injuries to children. Ambul Pediatr 2002;2(4):276–8

55. Joffe M, Ludwig S. Stairway injuries in children. Pediatrics 1988;82(3 Pt 2):457–61

56. Chiaviello CT, Christoph RA, Bond GR. Stairway-related injuries in children. Pediatrics 1994;94(5):679–81

57. Smith GA, Dietrich AM, Garcia CT et al Epidemiology of shopping cart-related injuries to children. An analysis of national data for 1990 to 1992. Arch Pediatr Adolesc Med 1995;149(11):1207–10

58. Smith GA, Dietrich AM, Garcia CT et al Injuries to children related to shopping carts. Pediatrics 1996;97(2):161–5

59. Parry ML, Morrison LG, Chalmers DJ et al Shopping trolley-related injuries to children in New Zealand, 1988-97. J Paediatr Child Health 2002;38(1):51–4

60. American Academy of Orthopedic Surgeons Position Statement 1135 http://www.aaos.org/about/papers/position/1135.asp

61. Woodward GA, Furnival R, Schunk JE. Trampolines revisited: a review of 114 pediatric recreational trampoline injuries. Pediatrics 1992;89:849–54

62. Chalmers DJ, Hume PA, Wilson BD. Trampolines in New Zealand: a decade of injuries. Br J Sports Med 1994;28(4):234–8

63. Larson BJ, Davis JW. Trampoline-related injuries. J Bone Joint Surg Am 1995;77(8):1174–8

64. McDermott C, Quinlan JF, Kelly IP. Trampoline injuries in children. J Bone Joint Surg Br 2006;88(6):796–8

65. Hume PA, Chalmers DJ, Wilson BD. Trampoline injury in New Zealand: emergency care. Br J Sports Med 1996;30(4):327–30

66. Smith GA. Injuries to children in the United States related to trampolines, 1990-1995: a national epidemic. Pediatrics 1998;101(3 Pt 1):406–12

67. Smith GA, Shields BJ. Trampoline-related injuries to children. Arch Pediatr Adolesc Med 1998;152(7):694–9

68. Musemeche C, Barthel M, Cosentino C et al Pediatric falls from heights. J Trauma 1991;31(10):1347–9

69. Lallier M, Bouchard S, St-Vil D et al Falls from heights among children: a retrospective review. J Pediatr Surg 1999;34(7):1060–3

70. Vish NL, Powell EC, Wiltsek D et al Pediatric window falls: not just a problem for children in high rises. Inj Prev 2005;11(5):300–3

71. Mayer L, Meuli M, Lips U et al The silent epidemic of falls from buildings: analysis of risk factors. Pediatr Surg Int 2006;22(9):743–8

72. Kim KA, Wang MY, Griffith PM et al Analysis of pediatric head injury from falls. Neurosurg Focus 2000;8(1):e3

73. Murray JA, Chen D, Velmahos GC et al Pediatric falls: is height a predictor of injury and outcome? Am Surg 2000;66(9):863–5

74. Wang MY, Kim KA, Griffith PM et al Injuries from falls in the pediatric population: an analysis of 729 cases. J Pediatr Surg 2001;36(10):1528–34

75. Hymel KP, Jenny C. Abusive spiral fractures of the humerus: a videotape exception. Arch Pediatr Adolec Med 1996;150(2):226–8

76. Harty MP, Kao SC. Intraosseous vascular access defect: fracture mimic in the skeletal survey for child abuse. Pediatr Radiol 2002;32(3):188–90

77. Bowley DMG, Loveland J, Pitcher GJJ. Tibial Fracture as a complication of intraosseous infusion during pediatric resuscitation. Trauma 2003;55(4):786–7

78. Pickett WJ, Johnson JF, Enzenauer RW. Case report 192. Neonatal fractures mimicking abuse secondary to physical therapy. Skeletal Radiol 1982;8(1):85–6

79. Helfer RE, Scheurer SL, Alexander R et al Trauma to the bones of small infants from passive exercise: a factor in the etiology of child abuse. J Pediatr 1984;104(47):47–50

80. London R, Noronha PA, Levy HB et al Bone trauma caused by passive exercise (letter). J Pediatr 1984;105(1):172–3

81. Simonian PT, Staheli LT. Periarticular fractures after manipulation for knee contractures in children. J Pediatr Orthop 1995;15(3):288–91

82. Chalumeau M, Foix-L'Helias L, Scheinmann P et al Rib fractures after chest physiotherapy for bronchiolitis or pneumonia in infants. Pediatr Radiol 2002;32(9):644–7

83. Gorincour G, Dubus JC, Petit P et al Rib periosteal reaction: did you think about chest physical therapy? Arch Dis Child 2004;89(11):1078–9

84. Chanelière C, Moreux N, Pracros JP et al [Rib fractures after chest physiotherapy: a report of 2 cases] [Article in French]. Arch Pediatr 2006;13(11):1410–2

85. Carty H. Children's sports injuries. Eur J Radiol 1998;26(2):163–76

86. Kerssenmaker SP, Fotiadou AN, de Jonge M et al Sport injuries in the pediatric and adolescent patient: a growing problem. Pediatr Radiol. 2009 May;39(5):471–84

Normal Variants, Congenital and Acquired Disorders

7.1 Introduction

Although in the differential diagnosis of fractures sustained in childhood one should be particularly aware of accidental trauma, it was found that congenital and acquired defects regularly give rise to suspicions of child abuse (see Table 7.1). Based on a combination of patient history, laboratory tests and radiological examination, it is usually possible to reach the correct diagnosis. In this chapter we discuss the most important disorders of which the radiological images could fit the criteria for child abuse.

7.2 Normal Variants

When evaluating radiographs of children, there are a number of normal variants that may cause confusion, and even lead to a false accusation of child abuse. At a very young age, subperiosteal new-bone formation around the shaft of the femur, tibia and humerus may be seen in normal, healthy neonates and infants (Fig. 7.1). This newly formed bone, which may radiologically be mistaken for a healing fracture, is most prominently present in children from 1 to 6 months old. Subperiosteal newly formed bone is usually seen bilaterally [1]; however, it may be more prominently present unilaterally [2]. Generally, the most distinct signs will disappear around the age of 8 months [3]. In physiological, subperiosteal newly formed bone, there is no obvious uptake of isotopes in a bone scan [4].

Neither should normal metaphyseal variants be mistaken for child abuse. This category comprises thickened edges of the metaphyses (collar, step off) exactly where the epiphyseal plate is attached (Fig. 7.2a–c).

This collar is usually present in the proximal tibia, proximal fibula, distal femur, distal radius and distal ulna, and is regularly seen bilaterally [5]. In young children pointed metaphyseal 'spurs' can also be found, which to the untrained eye of a radiologist may look very similar to CMLs. This spur is made of cortical bone that grows under the perichondrial ring of the epiphyseal plate. Spurs may be seen in the distal femur (Figs. 7.1 and 7.2b), the lateral aspect of the distal radius, the medial aspect of the distal ulna and the metacarpals (Fig. 7.3) and metatarsals. In 25% of cases this image is seen bilaterally. Finally, the metaphysis may show medial widening, especially in the proximal tibia and the humerus (Fig. 7.4).

In 4% of children a cortical irregularity is seen on the medial side of the proximal tibia. In 25% of these children this is present in both legs [5]. This irregularity may look like a healing fracture and consequently lead to an incorrect diagnosis.

One of the most important properties of the childhood skeleton is growth. Besides the normal growth centers, accessory centers may be seen (Fig. 7.5a and b) [6], which may be interpreted erroneously as fractures, and as such lead to confusion. The sutures of the skull, where normal variants may be found (Fig. 7.6), may also lead to an erroneous diagnosis of skull fracture [7].

7.3 Osteogenesis Imperfecta

7.3.1 Introduction

Together with child abuse osteogenesis imperfecta (OI) is the most common cause for the presence of multiple fractures, often at various stages of healing,

Table 7.1 Differential diagnosis in disease-related fractures in infancy and childhood [162, 165, 166]

Fractures	
Disorders related to collagen production	Osteogenesis imperfecta Copper deficiency Menkes syndrome Bruck syndrome
Congenital mineralisation disorders	Prematurity: metabolic bone disease of prematurity Neuromuscular disorders Vitamin-D-resistant rickets (or hypophosphatemic rickets) X-linked hypophosphatemia Liver abnormalities, such as Alagille syndrome Malabsorption Familiar osteoporosis Osteopetrosis Cole Carpenter syndrome Congenital CMV infection
Acquired mineralisation disorders	Vitamin-D-deficiency based on malnutrition: rickets Use of diuretics, glucocorticoids and methotrexate Intoxications, such as lead Cerebral paresis and spasticity
Other increased-risk disorders	Congenital pain insensitivity disorders: • Spina bifida • Congenital pain insensitivity Muscular dystrophy
Periosteal reactions	
Radiological differential diagnosis in the absence of fractures	Normal variants: • Such as: physiological thickening of the long bones (femur, tibia, humerus) in neonates and infants Congenital syphilis Osteomyelitis Septic arthritis Osteoid osteoma and other tumours Leukaemia Vitamin-C deficiency: scurvy Caffey's disease: infantile cortical hyperostosis Hurler disease: mucopolysaccharidosis type I Sickle-cell anaemia Vitamin use-related disorders • hypervitaminosis A • vitamin-E therapy Prostaglandin-E treatment Metastases of a neuroblastoma The use of intra-osseous vascular access needles

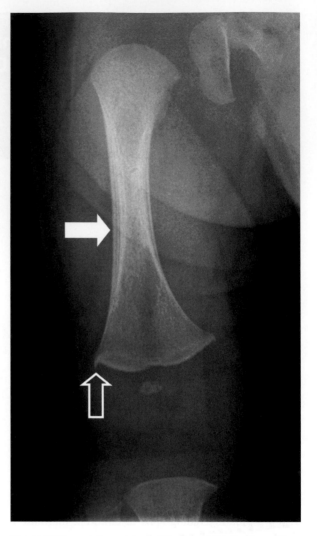

Fig. 7.1 Femur of a neonate, showing physiological subperiosteal new-bone formation (*arrow*) and metaphyseal spur (*open arrow*)

and without a plausible explanation (Fig. 7.7a and b). Hereby one should be well aware that OI is considerably less prevalent than child abuse.

7.3.2 Clinical Presentation

In OI there is a defect in the synthesis of type I collagen production. Type I collagen is an important protein in the extracellular matrix of many tissues. The disease is equally distributed between boys and girls, and is often seen in other family members, although spontaneous mutations do occur.

Fig. 7.2 (**a**) Physiological metaphyseal collar in the distal radius (*open arrow*). (**b**) Physiological metaphyseal collar (*open arrow*) and metaphyseal spur (*arrow*) in the distal femur metaphysis. (**c**) Physiological metaphyseal collar (*open arrow*) at the medial side of the istal fibula

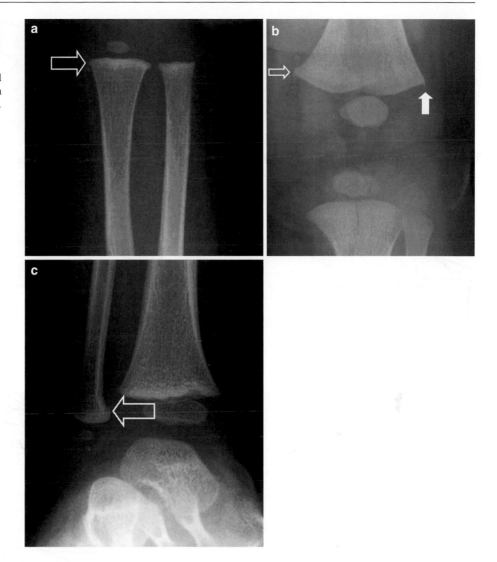

In the bones, a defect in the synthesis of type I collagen will lead to osteoporosis, which makes it possible for minimal trauma to cause multiple fractures (Fig. 7.8a–c). The protein is also present in ligaments, teeth, sclera and blood vessels. Consequently, the symptoms can occur to a higher or lesser degree in all these systems. Besides the defect in the synthesis of collagen type I, two more mutations have been reported; a mutation of the CRTAP gene, which causes a mild to severe recessive rhizomal form of OI [8]. Furthermore, mutations have been reported in CRTAP together with LEPRE1, which leads to an autosomal recessive form of OI [9, 10].

Sillence et al. provide a classification in four subtypes (see Table 7.2a) [11], based on the age at which the fractures occur, other physical symptoms and the way it is inherited. The incidence figures provided are based on research in Australian children. In 2004, Rauch and Glorieux published an overview in the Lancet in which they widened the Sillence classification to seven subtypes (see Table 7.2b) [12].

In 85% of children that have OI, fractures will heal at the same speed and in the same manner as in children without OI [13]. Children with OI types I and II (80% of all patients) usually present no diagnostic problem (Figs. 7.9a and b, 7.10a and b).

Young children without OI may also have blue sclerae [14]. Consequently, in abused children there may be the erroneous impression that they have pathological bone fragility that fits OI. The presence of

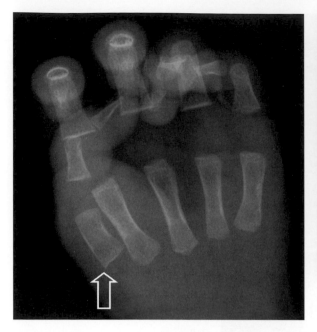

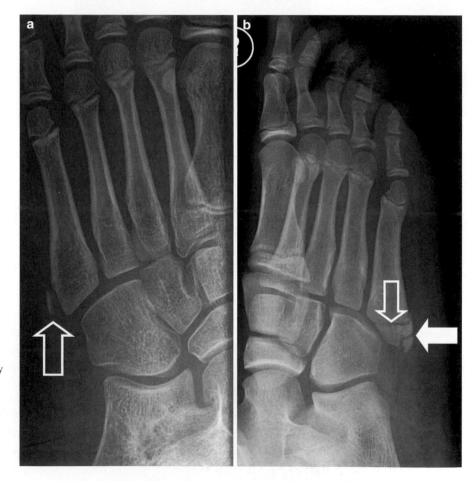

Fig. 7.3 Metaphyseal spur on the base of metacarpal 1 of the right hand (*open arrow*)

Fig. 7.4 Medial extension of the proximal metaphysis of the humerus (*open arrow*)

Fig. 7.5 (**a**) Accessory ossicle at the base of metatarsal 5 (*open arrow*). When one is not familiar with this phenomenon, it may be mistaken for an avulsion fracture. (**b**) Accessory ossicle at the base of metatarsal 5 (*arrow*). There is also a 'Jones fracture' visible at the base of metatarsal 5 (*open arrow*)

aberrant teeth (dentogenesis imperfecta) may either support or confirm the suspected OI. Rib fractures are frequently seen in all types, as is bowing of the lower extremities. Metaphyseal corner fractures may also be

seen in children with OI [13, 15]. Astley described metaphyseal corner fractures in seven children of a group of 41 children with OI [15]. He deems it impossible that one could erroneously suspect abuse in these children, because of the other noticeable signs fitting OI. On the other hand, Albin et al. are convinced that the presence of metaphyseal defects is pathognomic for child abuse, and that for this reason it is possible to differentiate between osteogenesis imperfecta and child abuse [16].

7.3.3 Additional Examinations

To experienced radiologists, the diagnosis OI will generally, in view of its characteristic lesions, not present many problems. When OI is suspected, radiological examination is essential. In prenatal ultrasound it is also possible to find characteristic defects, in those cases it often concerns type II.

In atypical cases, the biochemical analysis of the synthesis and structure of collagen may be used [17]. In order to differentiate with child abuse, a skin biopsy for the purpose of a fibroblast culture is not indicated. Steiner et al. concluded that based on clinical and radiological data, OI can be diagnosed in nearly all children. According to Steiner et al., biochemical

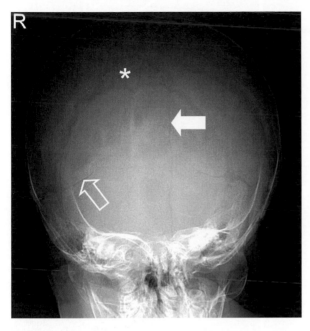

Fig. 7.6 Skull view showing multiple normal variants: suture mendosa (*open arrow*) and os inca (asterisk). There is also a sutura metopica visible (*arrow*)

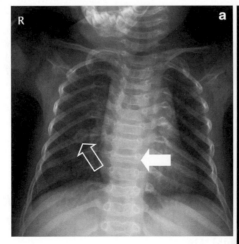

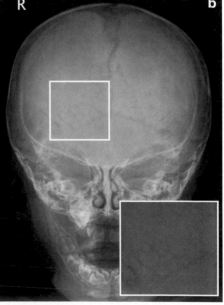

Fig. 7.7 (**a**) One-year-old boy who presented with a femur fracture after falling of the counter, in the presence of multiple witnesses. The chest radiograph shows old rib fractures (*open arrows*) and multiple collapsed vertebrae (*arrow*). (**b**) Skull view of the same patient shows multiple wormian bones (see inset). Osteogenesis perfecta was genetically

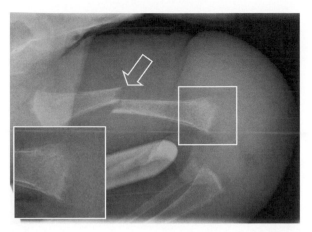

Fig. 7.14 Eight-month-old boy with a transverse mid-shaft femur fracture (*open arrow*) without evident trauma in the patient history. The distal femur metaphysis shows severe splaying, cupping and fraying, corresponding with rickets. Laboratory tests showed a vitamin-D deficiency

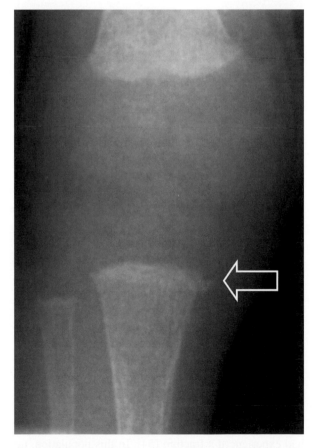

Fig. 7.15 Premature infant, born at 27 weeks' pregnancy. A radiograph at day 56 shows an irregular aspect of the proximal metaphysis of the tibia (*open arrow*). Laboratory test confirmed the diagnosis rickets. This anomaly could be interpreted as a metaphyseal corner fracture

7.5 Syndromes and Congenital disorders

7.5.1 Introduction

In the medical literature one can find case reports on suspected child abuse in skeletal abnormalities belonging to certain syndromes and congenital disorders. In this paragraph an overview is given. The overview does not claim to be complete.

7.5.2 Sickle Cell Anaemia

Sickle cell anaemia is an autosomal recessive inherited disease in which HbS is formed due to a disturbance in the production of haemoglobin. This results in sickle-shaped erythrocytes [47]. On a world-wide basis, millions of people suffer from sickle-cell disease. The disease is seen in particular in people (themselves or their ancestors) that hail from Africa, the Mediterranean countries and the Arabic peninsula, India and parts of South and Central America. Generally, the diagnosis can easily be made with a microscopic test. The symptoms of sickle-cell anaemia are due to abnormal erythrocytes that take on a sickle shape: early breakdown, which leads to anaemia. When the sickle-shaped cells occlude small vessels, it may cause pain and infection.

On a conventional radiograph, periostitis (Fig. 7.16) and radiolucencies with blurred margins are visible. These are present in bone infarcts as well as in osteomyelitis (which is more prevalent in patients with sickle-cell anaemia). After a period of time, the bone will start to show sclerosis. Since this image may resemble a healing fracture, it may cause confusion in the differential diagnosis [48]. Quite distinguishing for sickle-cell anaemia are the centrally located depression fractures of the vertebral corpora, which result in the signature H-shaped vertebrae (Fig. 7.17).

7.5.3 Alagille Syndrome

Alagille syndrome (arteriohepatic dysplasia) is an autosomal dominant disease with variable expression [49].

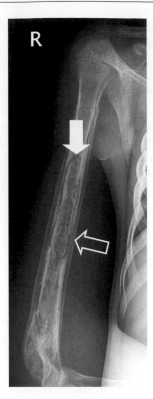

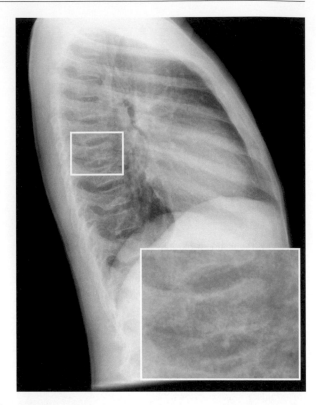

Fig. 7.16 Sixteen-year-old boy with confirmed patient history of sickle-cell anaemia presented at the emergency department with pain in the right upper arm. The radiograph shows extensive periosteal reaction (*open arrow*). Furthermore, there is an extensive anomaly in the medullary cavity, corresponding with a bone infarction (*arrow*)

Fig. 7.17 Eleven-year-old boy with a confirmed history of sickle-cell anaemia. Routine radiograph shows the characteristic H-shaped collapsed vertebra (see inset)

In this syndrome, various organs (liver, heart, kidneys, eyes and skeleton) may be affected. Furthermore, often typical facial features are seen (prominent forehead, hypertelorism, small chin and saddle nose). Mental retardation may also be present (mostly mild to moderate). In the United Stated, the incidence is approximately 1:100,000 live-born children.

Most children with Alagilles syndrome are seen for the first time when they are not even 6 months old for a neonatal jaundices based on cholestasis (70%) or cardiac symptoms (17%). Sometimes there is a deficiency of fat-soluble vitamins (A, D, E and K). The reported skeletal defects refer to the vertebrae, the so-called 'butterfly vertebrae', and to the ribs and arms/hands (shortened radius, ulna and digital phalanges) [50]. It is also possible that post-fracture bone deformations will not spontaneously correct itself [51].

The diagnosis is made based on the earlier-mentioned complaints, complemented with genetic and (if so required) pathological examinations (liver biopsy).

7.5.4 Duchenne Muscular Dystrophy

Duchenne muscular dystrophy is a recessive X-linked inherited progressive proximal muscular dystrophy with pseudohypertrophy of the calf muscles. It is the most prevalent form of muscular dystrophy seen in childhood and has an incidence of 1:3,500 boys. Usually onset is before the age of 3, and after a period of being wheelchair dependent, the patient generally dies before the age of 21 from respiratory failure [52]. The skeletal abnormalities are characterised mainly by the development of curvature of the spine [53]. McDonald et al. report on a population of 378 patients (average age 12 years; range 1–25 years). Of this group, 79 (20.9%) had experienced a fracture [54]. In this population, no rib fractures were reported. Since it is generally possible to make a firm diagnosis, the differential diagnosis should present no problems in these children.

7.5.5 Congenital Pseudarthrosis

Congenital pseudarthrosis of the tibia is a relatively rare defect, associated with neurofibromatosis type 1 (NF1). Fifty-five percent of patients with congenital pseudarthrosis also have NF1 [55]. Congenital pseudarthrosis is the result of segmental mesodermal dysplastic bone development. Although the defect is linked to neurofibromatosis, no neurofibromas are visible near the pseudarthrosis. In 99% of cases the defect is unilateral [55]. Because of segmental bone weakness, there is progressive anterolateral bowing of the tibia (often also fibula), which may finally break. Congenital pseudarthrosis of other bones is found to a lesser degree.

In case there is a fracture, it will happen in the first 2 years of life. After the fracture has been sustained, no spontaneous healing takes place, which results in a real pseudarthrosis. Treatment of the fracture is protracted, difficult and sometimes even without success, which will lead to amputation.

Crawford distinguishes four radiological types [56]. Typical anterolateral bowing is always present:

- Type I: Medullary cavity is normal.
- Type II: Medullary cavity is narrowed and there is cortical thickening.
- Type III: Presence of cysts, sometimes with a fracture.
- Type IV: Actual pseudarthrosis. After the fracture, a pseudarthrotic image develops in which the fracture ends may assume an osteolytic-like configuration.

Type II can simulate child abuse when the patents have not sought medical help, because the image can be interpreted as a healing fracture that has been badly reduced (Fig. 7.18a and b).

Type IV may be interpreted as pseudarthrosis due to non-immobilisation of the fracture in a neglected child (Fig. 7.18c).

7.5.6 Caffey's Disease

Caffey's disease (infantile cortical hyperostosis) is a little understood inflammatory disease which manifests itself by a gross periosteal reaction during infancy [57]. It mainly involves the long bones (often asymmetrically). However, the disease may also manifest itself in different locations, such as: the mandibles, ribs, scapulas and clavicles. Spine, phalanges and pelvis are hardly ever affected. Its autosomal dominant inheritance is reported to have variable expression [58]. Caffey's disease is self-limiting and by the age of 3 the clinical and radiological abnormalities have disappeared.

The patients have swollen and painful extremities, are irritable and show a sub(febrile) temperature. ESR and alkaline phosphates are often elevated. Conventional radiographs show extensive subperiosteal new-bone formation in the affected bones. In the extremities, the epiphyses and metaphyses are usually spared (Fig. 7.19a and b). As a result of subperiosteal haemorrhages, extensive subperiosteal new-bone formation can also be found in non-accidental injuries. Consequently, Caffey's disease can simulate child abuse and vice versa [59]. However, in child abuse fractures are a regular feature and the periosteal reaction is predominantly metaphyseal, contrary to the images in Caffey's disease.

Other disorders associated with pronounced periosteal reactions, and as such may cause differential diagnostic problems, are: hypervitaminosis A, prostaglandin-E1 medication in children with duct-dependent cardiac defects, leukaemia, syphilis, some storage-diseases (I-cell disease, mucolipidosis type II, GM gangliosidosis type I), vitamin-C deficiency and hypertrophic osteoarthopathy. These diseases can be differentiated from Caffey's disease on the basis of clinical, clinical-chemical and radiological results.

7.5.7 Menkes' Syndrome

Menkes' syndrome is a progressive neurodegenerative disease based on a congenital, X-linked recessive defect in copper metabolism [60]. Copper is required for enzymes essential to the formation of bone, nerve tissue and other structures.

The disease is seen nearly exclusively in boys. Yet, there are a few case reports on girls with this syndrome [61, 62]. The incidence is not well known. In Australia, Danks estimates it at 1:40,000 live births [63]. Over the period 1976–1987, Tonnesen et al. estimated the incidence in Denmark, France, The Netherlands, The United Kingdom and Germany to be 1:298,000 live births [64]. On the other hand, Gu et al. found a much lower incidence in Japan, 1:4.9 million boys [65].

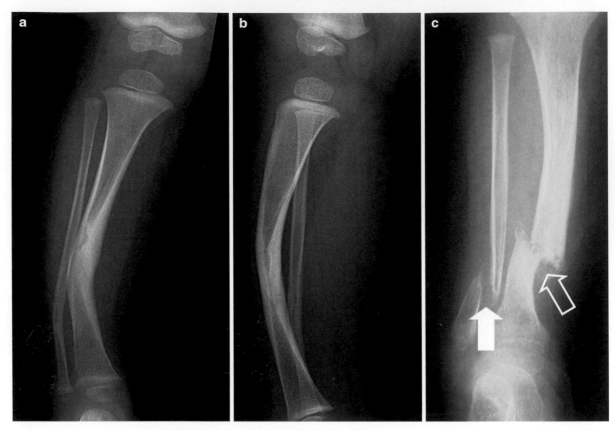

Fig. 7.18 (**a**) Congenital pseudarthrosis of the tibia, Crawford type II. Antero-posterior view of the lower leg. Anterolateral bowing with thickening of the cortical bone and narrowing of the medullary cavity. (**b**) Lateral view of the lower leg. (**c**) Crawford type IV with typical pseudarthrosis of the tibia (*open arrow*) and osteolytic-like pseudarthrosis of the fibula (*arrow*)

Fig. 7.19 (**a**) Two-month-old girl with Caffey's disease. Clinical presentation showed painful, slightly swollen limbs. Radiographs showed extreme periosteal reaction of the distal humerus without fractures. (**b**) Extreme periosteal reaction of along nearly the complete radius and ulna without fractures. After a year the girl was symptom-free and the bone anomalies had all but disappeared

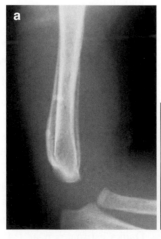

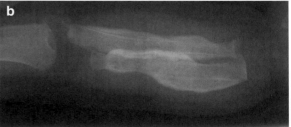

Onset of the disease occurs in the first weeks to months after birth. Initially, development progresses normally, after which there is a delay with loss of the earlier acquired skills. Hypotonia and convulsions may also be present, as is 'failure to thrive' [66]. The prognosis is poor: generally, the children will die before the age of 4, although sporadically there has been the odd child that survived longer, even past the age of 21 [66].

A striking feature is the hair anomaly, and not just of the scalp, but also of the lashes and eyebrows. In light-skinned people, the hair is often without colour and sometimes silver or steel-grey in colour. In black-haired ethnical groups, the hair may be blonde or brown in colour. It is sparsely present and fuzzy or stubbly to the touch. It is crinkly and breaks easily. It resembles glass wool. Consequently, Menkes' syndrome is also known as 'kinky hair disease' or 'steely hair disease'.

Besides the hair anomaly, the children often have growth problems, anterior rib defects (flaring) and 'wormian bones' on radiographs. Due to the disturbances in bone metabolism, which causes osteoporosis, there is a risk for fractures. Moreover, metaphyseal defects and periosteal reactions may be found. On radiographs, this set of anomalies is indistinguishable from fractures resulting from child abuse. However, the anamnesis, combined with the above-mentioned symptoms should make it possible to differentiate between disease and child abuse.

Jankov describes a neonate with a rapidly progressing fatal syndrome. The boy died on day 27. He has been seen because of an acute presentation with severe intra-abdominal bleeding, haemorrhagic shock and multiple fractures. The physicians made the diagnosis at autopsy, which was confirmed by copper accumulation in the fibroblast culture [67].

Grünebaum et al. described four children with copper deficiency who did not have Menkes' syndrome [68]. All four showed 'sickle-shaped metaphyseal spurs', two children showed fractures of these spurs'. This case report seems to indicate that the metaphyseal defects in Menkes' syndrome may be the result of copper deficiency.

7.5.8 Pain Insensitivity in Spina Bifida

In spina bifida there may be insensitivity to pain in the lower extremities. When there is incomplete paralysis, an effort will be made to have children with this disorder walk with devices such as splints. As a result, abnormal stress on the joints may lead to damage of the epiphyseal plate and the metaphysis, possibly resulting in a fracture. Moreover, patients with a severe form of spina bifida will develop immobilization-related osteoporosis. The combination of osteoporosis and pain insensitivity may lead to fractures that are only noticed at a later stage (Fig. 7.20).

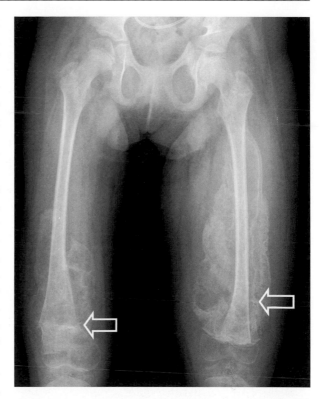

Fig. 7.20 Six and a half-year-old girl with spina bifida showed bilateral swollen knees at physical examination. Radiographs revealed bilateral distal metaphyseal femur fractures (*open arrows*) with extensive new-bone formation. Based on the anamnesis, child abuse was excluded

7.5.9 Congenital Pain Insensitivity

Congenital pain insensitivity is an autosomal recessive disease. Children with this disease have normal intelligence. The only aberrant neurological finding is their insensitivity to pain, which may lead to a plethora of unaccounted for injuries (Fig. 7.21). Especially in young children, repeated damage to the growing skeleton will not be noticed. This may cause defects to metaphyses and epiphyses. A meticulous neurological examination and careful anamnesis will make it possible to differentiate with child abuse [69, 70].

7.6 Skeletal Dysplasias

7.6.1 Introduction

Skeletal dysplasias are a heterogeneous group of disorders characterised by anomalies in bone and cartilage

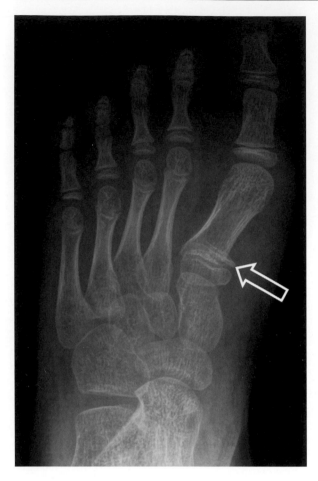

Fig. 7.21 Six-year-old girl with inherited sensitive-autonomous neuropathy (a serious defect in pain sensitivity) with a swollen left foot. A radiograph of the foot showed a torus fracture of metatarsal I (*open arrow*)

development and growth. Although the prevalence of skeletal dysplasias (350:1,000,000) is many times higher than that of bone tumours (20:1,000,000), trainee radiologists generally pay little attention to these disorders [71]. The resulting lack of knowledge may result in the unjust allocation of a radiological finding such as a metaphyseal spur in Jeune's 'asphyxiating thoracic dysplasia' (Fig. 7.22a and b, MIM %208500) to child abuse.

7.6.2 Metaphyseal Chondroplasia Type Schmid

Metaphyseal chondroplasia type Schmid is a rare autosomal dominant inherited skeletal dysplasia,

characterised by irregular margins of the metaphyses (Fig. 7.23, MIM #156500) [72, 73]. The metaphyseal defects cause bowing and shortening of the extremities during growth. The metaphyseal defects are very similar to rickets (see Sect. 7.4) and may be confused with metaphyseal corner fractures.

7.6.3 Spondylometaphyseal Dysplasia 'Corner Fracture Type'

Spondylometaphyseal dysplasia 'corner fracture type' (Sutcliffe type) is a rare skeletal dysplasia characterised by short stature and an aberrant, waddling gait (MIM %184255) [74, 75]. Often the diagnosis is not made until the age of 2–3 years, when an increasingly abnormal gait pattern is noticed.

From a radiological point of view, the most important anomalies are, as already indicated by its name, vertebral and metaphyseal anomalies, the latter having irregular margins. The metaphyses show triangular fragments, which may lead to the incorrect diagnosis 'metaphyseal corner fractures' when one is not familiar with this dysplasia (Fig. 7.24a–c).

7.7 Metabolic Disorders

7.7.1 Introduction

In the medical literature case reports can be found regarding suspected child abuse in skeletal abnormalities compatible with metabolic disorders. In this paragraph an overview is presented. The overview does not claim to be complete.

7.7.2 Osteopetrosis

The term osteopetrosis relates to a group of anomalies in which osteoclastic activity is suppressed, resulting in increased bone density (sclerosis) and ultimately in abnormal bone modelling [76].

From the point of view of a differential diagnosis concerning child abuse, it is important that infantile osteopetrosis is mentioned. In this disorder, the metaphyses may show a translucent area and have an irregular aspect

Fig. 7.22 (**a**) Neonate with a narrow chest. Radiographs of the knee showed a metaphyseal spur which may be confused with a metaphyseal corner fracture (*open arrow*). (**b**) Image of another patient with the same clinical presentation. Radiographs of spine and pelvis show a narrow chest and relatively short ribs. The pelvis shows spurs of the ileum (see inset). Based on o.a. the radiological examination, the diagnosis Jeune's asphyxiating thoracic dysplasia could be made

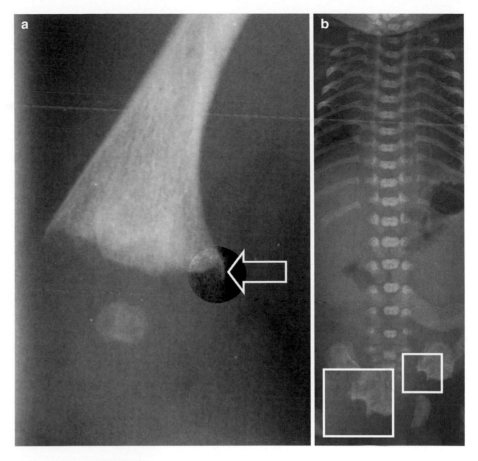

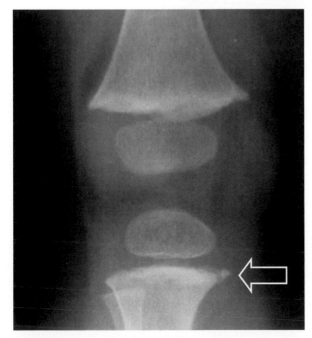

Fig. 7.23 Two-year old child with metaphyseal chondrodysplasia type Schmid. The irregularities of the proximal metaphysis of the tibia have a strong resemblance to metaphyseal corner fractures (*open arrow*)

(Figs. 7.25 and 7.26a and b). The presence of generalised skeletal sclerosis and metaphyseal undertubulation makes it possible to come to the correct diagnosis.

7.7.3 Osteoporosis

The World Health Organisation defines osteoporosis as a systemic disease characterised by low bone mass and micro-architectural regression of bone tissue, resulting in increased fragility of the skeleton and risk for fractures. Childhood osteoporosis may result from o.a. chronic disease, malnutrition, immobilisation and genetic defects (Table 7.7) [77, 78].

A specific form of childhood osteoporosis is idiopathic osteoporosis, a self-limiting primary osteoporosis of unknown origin, seen mainly in children in their second decade of life (Fig. 7.27a and b) [79]. The diagnosis of childhood osteoporosis is not always straightforward, since the commonly used techniques are validated for adults [80]. In osteoporosis the most frequently seen fractures are vertebral and metaphyseal.

Fig. 7.24 (**a**) Two-year-old child with spondylometaphyseal dysplasia, corner fracture type. The distal femur metaphysis as well as the proximal tibia metaphysis show anomalies that strongly resemble metaphyseal corner fractures (*open arrows*). (**b**) Hip radiograph of the same patient shows an anomalous aspect of the proximal metaphysis of the femur (*open arrow*). (**c**) Radiological image of the left hip at 13 years of age shows besides an irregular metaphysis (*open arrow*) with strong developmental retardation also deformation of the femoral head (asterisk)

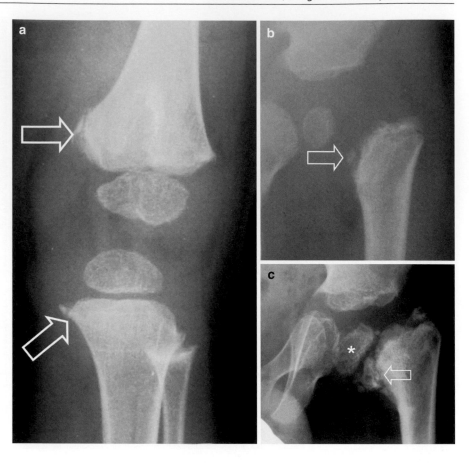

In children with multiple fractures osteoporosis should be excluded.

7.7.4 Dysostosis Multiplex Congenita

Dysostosis multiplex congenita is a group of storage diseases of complex proteins that have a large number of aspects in common. These include: mucopolysaccharidosis (such as Hurler disease and Hunter disease), gangliosidosis and mucolipidosis.

Clinical manifestation depends on the degree of storage and the organs in which the metabolite is stored. When storage occurs in the brain, progressive mental retardation will be the primary symptom. Other clinical symptoms are: typically course facial features, opaque corneas and organomegaly. Radiological lesion are: incomplete modelling of the long bones, epiphyseal dysplasia, broad ribs, abnormal configuration of the corpora vertebrae, in particular at the thoracolumbar

transition (so-called 'vertebral beaking' or 'hook-shaped vertebra'; Fig. 7.28). Periosteal reaction may be very pronounced in GM1 gangliosidosis and mucolipidosis II (I-cell disease) [81].

Suspected dysostis multiplex congenita is usually based on clinical and radiological anomalies and is confirmed by biochemical analysis of urine and blood for abnormal metabolites. However, the younger the child, the more difficult it is to make the diagnosis, since at a young age the clinical presentation has not yet fully developed, and consequently the radiographs may appear to be normal.

In patients with dysostosis multiplex, an injury may unjustly be suspected based on the periosteal reaction in GM1 gangliosidosis and mucolipidosis II (I-cell disease) [59]. Also, when observed cursory, the spinal anomalies may be considered spinal fractures after non-incidental injuries. The clinical presentation and the radiological anomalies in the remaining skeleton are usually sufficient to reach the correct diagnosis.

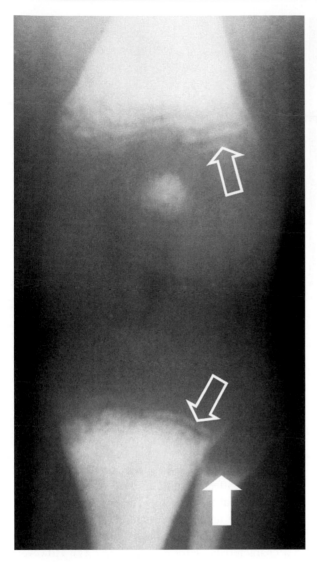

Fig. 7.25 Neonate with osteopetrosis. The distal femur and proximal tibia show irregular metaphyses (*open arrow*). In particular in the proximal metaphysis, the image could be confused with a bucket-handle fracture (metaphyseal corner fracture). The proximal fibula also shows an anomalous aspect

7.7.5 Hypophosphatasia

Hypophosphatasia is a rare disorder caused by a mutation of the gene coding for the enzyme alkaline phosphatase. The prevalence is estimated to be 1:100,000 [82]. There are six categories, depending on age: the perinatal (fatal), benign perinatal, infantile, child and adult forms and odontohypophosphatasia [82]. In the latter category only dental anomalies are present.

In young children decreased mineralisation of the cranium is seen with wide sutures, which later progresses to craniosynostosis, a noticeable bowing of the long bones, sometimes even angular (kyphomelia), fractures and pseudo-fractures and irregular metaphyseal ossification defects (Fig. 7.29a and b) [81]. Due to its heterogenic presentation, it may initially be difficult to diagnose, and the fractures, bowing and metaphyseal irregularities may even be reminiscent of non-accidental injury.

Moulin et al. describe a 9-year-old girl and her sister who frequently sustained fractures after trivial injuries. They had normal growth, normal sclerae, no rickets and only minor dental abnormalities. In the end, hypophosphatasia appeared to be the cause [83]. A clinical presentation of this kind may also look like non-accidental injuries within the home.

Ultimately, the diagnosis is made by DNA sequencing, measuring serum alkaline phosphatase activity, and proving an increased concentration of phosphoethanolamine and calcium in urine and pyridoxal 5'-phosphate and calcium in blood. By DNA sequencing, approximately 95% of mutations in severe hypophosphatasia (perinatal and infantile forms) can be found [82].

7.8 Infectious Diseases

7.8.1 Introduction

In the medical literature case reports can be found regarding suspected child abuse in skeletal anomalies compatible with infectious diseases. In this paragraph an overview is presented of the disorders. The overview does not claim to be complete.

7.8.2 Osteomyelitis

Osteomyelitis in childhood is a relatively rare diagnosis, with an estimated prevalence of 1:10,000 children under 12 years of age [84]. Since the course of the illness is often slow, it is often not diagnose until it reaches a well-advanced stage.

In osteomyelitis, metaphyseal abnormalities and periosteal reactions may be found (Fig. 7.30), which

in epileptic patients is three times that for the general population [135, 136]. The fractures are mostly fall-related and associated with an epileptic seizure. This risk increases in the presence of more risk-increasing factors such as spasticity and decreased bone density.

Sheth et al. report four mechanisms that apply to epilepsy-related fractures: the seizure itself or a fall related to the seizure, accidental trauma not related to the seizure, and a pathological fracture resulting from decreased bone density [135]. In newly diagnosed patients, the incidence of seizure-related fractures was very low, 5% [126].

Fractures caused by the seizure itself are rare. Schnadower et al. describe bilateral femur fractures in an adolescent with primary vitamin-D deficiency due to a hypocalcaemic seizure [133]. Presedo et al. pose that 2% of all fractures in spastic children may be the result of a seizure, but refrain from reporting whether it concerns a fracture by the seizure itself or a fracture due to seizure-related trauma (fall) [130].

In children with normal bone density (no anti-epileptica or inactivity osteopenia), no fractures of the extremities due to notably increased muscle tone during a seizure are known.

The prevalence of fractures in spastic children with an average age of 10 years is 6%, of which 45% has no identifiable cause, 32% is due to trauma, and 11% is caused by medical proceedings or physiotherapy [130]. It usually concerns the lower extremities (82%). The main risk factors are: immobility, osteoporosis and the use of anti-epileptica.

Lingam et al. described 5 spastic patients (10–19 years old) with five femur fractures and one cruris fracture without identifiable causal incident [129]. In this case the authors maintain it was a combination of inactivity osteoporosis, increased muscle tone with contractures and decreased muscle mass.

Anti-epileptica, such as phenobarbital, phenytoin, primidone, valproate, carbamazepine and oxacarbazepine cause decreased bone density [127, 131, 134]. Babayigit demonstrated this in 68 children who had been on anti-epileptica for over a year [127]. Sheth et al. found a pathological fracture due to reduced bone density in 15% of fractures in epileptic children [135].

There are no comprehensive studies known on fractures in spasticity and/or epilepsy in the age group up to 2 years old.

In conclusion, one may pose that patients with epilepsy and/or spasticity are at higher risk of fractures, especially of the lower extremities, in relatively minor trauma and sometimes even without identifiable cause. Of course this does not imply that there are no non-accidental injuries in this patient group. In each patient that presents with a fracture, this subject must be open for discussion.

After all, intentional or unintentional negligence in the medical treatment or care in these often institutionalised, fragile patients can also be considered non-accidental injury. Fractures in epileptic children of less than 2 years old without comorbidity should not just be ascribed to epilepsy and as such are suspect for child abuse.

7.11.3 Vitamine-C Deficiency

Infants are protected from congenital vitamine-C deficiency (scurvy) by vitamin-C storage in utero. They deplete this storage when after birth they receive vitamine-C-deficient artificial nutrition [137]. When postpartum there is total vitamin-C deprivation, it will still take at least 5 months before the supply has been depleted. Since severe vitamin-C deficiency in pregnant women results in early abortion, congenital vitamin-C deficiency is unknown [138].

Vitamin C is, amongst others, a catalyst in collagen formation. A disturbance in collagen formation results in many of the symptoms seen in vitamin-C deficiency: disturbance in wound healing, increased fragility of the capillary walls and osteoporosis.

Scurvy is hardly ever seen in children, especially in the Western industrialised world [138]. The last case report of a child in a Western industrialised country dates from 2001 and was a 15-month-old child that had been given deficient nutrition from the 4th months of life onwards (cow milk and oat meal). It showed all the classical symptoms of a vitamin-C deficiency [139]. In the nineties there were three case reports from France (1993), Italy (1992) and Spain (1991) [140–142]. In non-Western and non- or less industrialised countries, case reports and announcements on epidemics still surface regularly [143–150].

Even in the early stages, the radiological images are rather characteristic: limited density and irregularity of the epiphyseal lines, 'ringed' epiphyses (Wimberger rings) and slight osteoporosis (Fig. 7.42). At a later stage, examination may show swelling of the ends of the long bones, in particular the distal ends of the femur. These swellings are due to subperiosteal

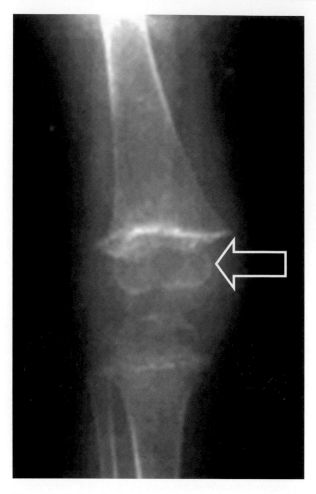

Fig. 7.42 Child with vitamin-C deficiency (scurvy). The radiograph shows an evident osteopenia with the characteristically exempt edge of the epiphysis (Wimberger ring – *open arrow*)

haemorrhages that will only in time be visible on radiographs. Externally, a shiny, livid (blue-black) skin will be visible at the location of the swelling.

If the child has already has incisors (at 7 months usually the incisors of the mandible), haemorrhagic areas will be found at their base. The gums are swollen. In adults, teeth may fall out when the deficiency has been present for a protracted period, which will reduce the state of the gums even further.

7.12 'Temporary Brittle-Bone Disease'?

In 1993, Patterson et al. described 39 children who presented with a set of symptoms that they considered to be a variant of osteogenesis imperfecta [151]. They called it

'temporary brittle-bone disease' (TBBD). As the name already implies, it supposedly was a temporary disease in which the presence of fractures is limited to the first year of life. The affected children would be susceptible to sustaining fractures after minor trauma for just a short period of time. The disorder heals spontaneously, without any visible pathology. Patterson et al. suspected that these symptoms were due to a temporary, self-limiting period of copper deficiency; although no evident proof was found in the limited study into serum copper contents.

Usually the disorder will starts with a period of vomiting, followed by diarrhoea, anaemia, hepatomegaly, incidences of respiratory arrest, neutropenia and oedema. The most common radiological findings were metaphyseal corner fractures, rib fractures, diaphyseal fractures and periosteal reactions along the long bones, anomalies at the costochondral junction and retarded bone age. Only 31% of children had a radiologically visible osteopenia.

It did not take long before doubt arose regarding the existence of TBBD, since children with confirmed copper deficiency hardly ever show fractures [152–154]. Not just the medical world criticised Patterson, also the legal world issued its comments [155–158]. One of the children in the series that Patterson described had sustained injuries as a result of child abuse. The authors did not report this in their article. This lead to concern that a full investigation into injuries in children would (no longer) take place, since the medical world could assume that one single disease could completely explain the anomalies.

In 2001, it was proclaimed in a court case in the United Kingdom that the testimony of an expert witness in the field of TBBD was not only inadmissible, but also that the scientific foundation was found to be inadequate. According to the judge, the study of the expert witness in question, doctor Patterson, was subjective, unreliable, unscientific and unproven [159, 160]. In 2004, the General Medical Council (GMC) retracted the qualifications of Patterson as pathologist. According to the GMC, he had failed as expert witness in two court cases in which the parents were accused of child abuse [161].

In 2005, the Society for Pediatric Radiology and the European Society for Paediatric Radiology jointly published an article [162]. Both societies maintain there is no scientific basis at all on which TBBD can be accepted a disease entity. Only a limited number of medical professionals believe, based on speculations, that TBBD exists. Moreover, they use conflicting ideas regarding the disorder and its origin. A few of the causes they put forward are:

- Bone or collagen pathology [151]
- Copper deficiency [151]
- Decreased in utero activity in children with reduced bone density [163, 164]

In his article, Mendelson concludes that there is no scientific foundation at all for the above-mentioned hypotheses as cause of TBBD. Consequently, this diagnosis should no longer be made [162].

References

1. Pergolizzi R, Oestrich AE. Child abuse fracture through physiologic reaction. Pediatr Radiol 1995;25(7):566–7
2. Shopfner C. Periosteal bone growth in normal infants: a preliminary report. Am J Roentgenol Radium Ther Nucl Med. 1966;97(1):154–63
3. Brill PW, Winchester P. Differential diagnosis of child abuse. In Kleinman PK (ed). Diagnostic imaging of child abuse. Williams & Wilkins, 1987, pag. 221
4. Conway JJ, Collins M, Tanz RR et al The role of bone scintigraphy in detecting child abuse. Semin Nucl Med 1993; 23(4):321–33
5. Kleinman PK, Belanger PL, Karellas A et al Normal metaphyseal radiologic variants not to be confused with findings of infant abuse. Am J Roentgenol 1991;156(4):781–3
6. Keats T, Anderson M. Atlas of normal roentgen variants that may simulate disease. Mosby, 8th ed, 2006
7. Weir P, Suttner NJ, Flynn P et al Normal skull suture variant mimicking intentional injury. Br Med J 2006;332(7548): 1020–1
8. Ward LM, Rauch F, Travers R et al Osteogenesis imperfecta type VII: an autosomal recessive form of brittle bone disease. Bone 2002;31(1):12–8
9. Barnes AM, Chang W, Morello R et al Deficiency of cartilage-associated protein in recessive lethal osteogenesis imperfecta. N Engl J Med 2006;355(26):2757–64
10. Cabral WA, Chang W, Barnes AM et al Prolyl 3-hydroxylase 1 deficiency causes a recessive metabolic bone disorder resembling lethal/severe osteogenesis imperfecta. Nat Genet 2007;39(3):359–65
11. Sillence DO, Senn A, Danks DM. Genetic heterogenecity in osteogenesis imperfecta. J Med Genet 1979;16(2):101–16
12. Rauch F, Glorieux FH. Osteogenesis imperfecta. Lancet 2004;363(9418):1377–85
13. Plotkin H. Osteogenesis imperfecta. eMedicine, 2008 http://www.emedicine.com/ped/topic1674.htm
14. http://www.wrongdiagnosis.com/symptoms/blue_sclerae/causes.htm
15. Astley R. Metaphyseal fractures in osteogenesis imperfecta. Br J Radiol 1979;52(618):441–3
16. Ablin DS, Greenspan A, Reinhart M et al Differentiation of child abuse from osteogenesis imperfecta. Am J Roentgenol 1990;154(5):1035–46
17. Gahagan S, Rimsza ME. Child abuse or osteogenesis imperfecta: how can we tell? Pediatrics 1991;88(5):987–91
18. Steiner RD, Pepin M, Byers PH. Studies of collagen synthesis and structure in the differentiation of child abuse from osteogenesis imperfecta. J Pediatr 1996;128(4):542–7
19. Kleinman PK. Diagnostic imaging of child abuse. Mosby, 2nd ed, 1998
20. Reece RM. Child abuse - medical diagnosis and management. Lippincott Williams & Wilkins 2001, pag 149–51
21. Knight DJ, Bennet GC. Nonaccidental injury in osteogenesis imperfecta: a case report. J Pediatr Orthop 1990;10(4): 542–4
22. Thacher TD, Fischer PR, Pettifor JM et al Radiographic scoring method for the assessment of severity of nutritional rickets. J Trop Pediatr 2000;46(3):132–9
23. Wauters IM, van Soesbergen RM. [Disease caused by lack of sunlight; rickets and osteomalacia]. Ned Tijdschr Geneeskd 1999;143(12): 593–7
24. Chesney RW. Rickets: the third wave. Clin Pediatr (Phila) 2002;41(3):137–9
25. Bachrach S, Fisher J, Parks JS. An outbreak of vitamin D deficiency rickets in a susceptible population. Pediatrics 1979; 64(6):871–7
26. Holick MF. Vitamin D deficiency. N Eng J Med 2007; 357(3):266–81
27. Gordon CM, DePeter KC, Feldman HA et al Prevalence of vitamin D deficiency among healthy adolescents. Arch Pediatr Adolesc Med 2004;158(6):531–7
28. Sullivan SS, Rosen CJ, Halteman WA et al Adolescent girls in Maine are at risk for vitamin D insufficiency. J Am Diet Assoc 2005;105(6):971–4
29. Gordon CM, Feldman HA, Sinclair L et al Prevalence of vitamin D deficiency among healthy infants and toddlers. Arch Pediatr Adolesc Med 2008;162(6):505–12
30. Bouillon R, Norman AW, Lips PN. Comment on Holick MF. Vitamin D deficiency. N Engl J Med. 2007;357(3):266–81. N Engl J Med. 2007 Nov 8;357(19):1980–1; author reply 1981–2
31. Baroncelli GI. Comment on Holick MF. Vitamin D deficiency. N Engl J Med. 2007;357(3):266–81. N Engl J Med 2007;357(19):1981; author reply 1981–2
32. Gartner LM, Greer FR. Section on Breastfeeding and Committee on Nutrition. American Academy of Pediatrics. Prevention of rickets and vitamin D deficiency: new guidelines for vitamin D intake. Pediatrics 2003;111(4 Pt 1): 908–10
33. Keller KA, Barnes PD. Rickets vs. abuse: a national and international epidemic. Pediatr Radiol 2008;38(11):1210–6
34. Slovis TL, Chapman S. Vitamin D insufficiency/deficiency - a conundrum. Pediatr Radiol 2008;38(11):1153
35. Slovis TL, Chapman S. Evaluating the data concerning vitamin D insufficiency/deficiency and child abuse. Pediatr Radiol 2008;38(11):1221–4
36. Chesney RW. Rickets or abuse, or both? Pediatr Radiol 2008;38(11):1217–8
37. Jenny C. Rickets or abuse? Pediatr Radiol 2008;38(11): 1219–20
38. Moncrieff M, Fadahunsi TO. Congenital rickets due to maternal vitamin D deficiency. Arch Dis Child 1974;49(10): 810–1
39. Kirk J. Congenital rickets – a case report. Aust Paediatr J 1982;18(4):291–3
40. al-Senan K, al-Alaiyan S, al-Abbad A et al Congenital rickets secondary to untreated maternal renal failure. Perinatol 2001;21(7):473–5
41. Mohapatra A, Sankaranarayanan K, Kadam SS et al Congenital rickets. J Trop Pediatr 2003;49(2):126–7
42. Ford JA, Davidson DC, McIntosh WB et al Neonatal rickets in Asian immigrant population. Br Med J 1973;3(5873):211–2
43. Zeidan S, Bamford M. Congenital rickets with maternal pre-eclampsia. J R Soc Med 1984;77(5):426–7

44. Zeiss J, Wycliffe ND, Cullen BJ et al Radiological case of the month. Am J Dis Child 1988;142(12):1367–8
45. Duncan AA, Chandy J. Case report: multiple neonatal fractures – dietary or deliberate? Clin Radiol 1993;48(2):137–9
46. Kleinman PK. Miscellaneous forms of abuse and neglect. In Kleinman PK. Diagnostic imaging of child abuse. Mosby, 2nd ed, 1998, pag. 343–61
47. Frenette PS, Atweh GF. Sickle cell disease: old discoveries, new concepts, and future promise. J Clin Invest 2007;117(4): 850–8
48. Madani G, Papadopoulou AM, Holloway B et al The radiological manifestations of sickle cell disease. Clin Radiol 2007;62(6):528–38
49. Brooks AS, Dooijes D. From gene to disease: arteriohepatic dysplasia or Alagille syndrome [article in dutch]. Ned Tijdschr Geneesk 2003;147(25):1213–5
50. Scheimann A. Alagille syndrome. Emedicine, 2006
51. de Halleux J, Rombouts JJ, Otte JB. Evolution of post-fracture bone deformities in an infant with hepatic osteodystrophy on Alagille syndrome [article in french]. Rev Chir Orthop Reparatrice Appar Mot 1998;84(4):381–6
52. Metules T. Duchenne muscular dystrophy. RN 2002 Oct;65(10):39–44
53. Karol LA. Scoliosis in patients with Duchenne muscular dystrophy. J Bone Joint Surg Am 2007;89(Suppl 1):155–62
54. McDonald DG, Kinali M, Gallagher AC et al Fracture prevalence in Duchenne muscular dystrophy. Dev Med Child Neurol 2002;44(10):695–8
55. Hefti F, Bollini G, Dungl P et al Congenital pseudarthrosis of the tibia: history, etiology, classification, and epidemiologic data. J Pediatr Orthop B 2000;9(1):11–5
56. Crawford AH. Neurofibromatosis in children. Acta Orthop Scand Suppl 1986; 218:1–60.
57. Caffey J. Infantile cortical hyperostosis; a review of the clinical and radiographic features. Proc R Soc Med 1957;50(5): 347–54
58. Saul RA, Lee WH, Stevenson RE. Caffey's disease revisited. Further evidence for autosomal dominant inheritance with incomplete penetrance. Am J Dis Child 1982;136(1):55–60
59. Ved N, Haller JO. Periosteal reaction with normal-appearing underlying bone: a child abuse mimicker. Emerg Radiol 2002;9(5):278–282.
60. Menkes JH, Alter M, Steigleder GK et al A sex-linked recessive disorder with retardation of growth, peculiar hair and focal cerebral and cerebellar degeneration. Pediatrics 1962;29:764–79
61. Kapur S, Higgins JV, Delp K et al Menkes syndrome in a girl with X-autosome translocation. Am J Med Genet 1987; 26(2):503–10
62. Abusaad I, Mohammed SN, Ogilvie CM et al Clinical expression of Menkes disease in a girl with X;13 translocation. Am J Med Genet 1999;87(4):354–9
63. Danks DM, Cartwright E, Campbell PE et al Is Menkes' syndrome a heritable disorder of connective tissue? (Letter) Lancet 1971;2(7733):1089
64. Tonnesen T, Kleijer WJ, Horn N. Incidence of Menkes disease. Hum Genet 1991;86(4): 408–10
65. Gu YH, Kodama H, Shiga K et al A survey of Japanese patients with Menkes disease from 1990 to 2003: incidence and early signs before typical symptomatic onset, pointing the way to earlier diagnosis. J Inherit Metab Dis 2005;28(4): 473–8
66. Chang CH. Menkes disease. Emedicine 2006 http://www.emedicine.com/neuro/topic569.htm
67. Jankov RP, Boerkoel CF, Hellmann J et al Lethal neonatal Menkes' disease with severe vasculopathy and fractures. Acta Paediat 1998;87(12):1297–300
68. Grünebaum M, Horodniceanu C, Steinherz R. The radiographic manifestations of bone changes in copper deficiency. Pediatr Radiol 1980;9(2):101–4
69. Akbarnia BA, Campbell RM. The role of the orthopedic surgeon in child abuse. In Morrissy RT, Winter RB. Lovell and Winter's Pediatric Orthopaedics. Lippincott, Williams and Wilkins Publ, 3rd ed, 1990
70. Spencer JA, Grieve DK Congenital indifference to pain mistaken for non-accidental injury. Br J Radiol 1990;63(748): 308–10
71. Offiah AC, Hall CM. Radiological diagnosis of the constitutional disorders of bone. As easy as A, B, C? Pediatr Radiol 2003;33(3):153–61
72. Spranger JW, Brill PW, Poznanski A. Bone dysplasias: An atlas of genetic disorders of skeletal development. Oxford University Press 2002, pag. 100–2
73. Elliott AM, Field FM, Rimoin DL et al Hand involvement in Schmid metaphyseal chondrodysplasia. Am J Med Genet A 2005;132A(2):191–3
74. Spranger JW, Brill PW, Poznanski A. Bone dysplasias: An atlas of genetic disorders of skeletal development. Oxford University Press 2002, pag. 236–8
75. Currarino G, Birch JG, Herring JA. Developmental coxa vara associated with spondylometaphyseal dysplasia (DCV/SMD): 'SMD-corner fracture type' (DCV/SMD-CF) demonstrated in most reported cases. Pediatr Radiol 2000;30(1): 14–24
76. Spranger JW, Brill PW, Poznanski A. Bone dysplasias: An atlas of genetic disorders of skeletal development. Oxford University Press 2002, pag. 460
77. Loud KJ, Gordon CM. Adolescent bone health. Arch Pediatr Adolesc Med 2006;160(10):1026–32
78. van der Sluis IM, de Muinck Keizer-Schrama SM. Osteoporosis in childhood: bone density of children in health and disease. J Pediatr Endocrinol Metab 2001;14(7):817–32
79. Lorenc RS. Idiopathic juvenile osteoporosis. Calcif Tissue Int 2002;70(5):395–7
80. van Rijn RR, van der Sluis IM, Link TM et al Bone densitometry in children: a critical appraisal. Eur Radiol 2003; 13(4):700–10
81. Spranger JW, Brill PW, Poznanski A. Bone dysplasia. An atlas of genetic disorders of skeletal development. Oxford University Press 2002, pag. 261–326
82. Mornet E. Hypophosphatasia. Orphanet J Rare Dis 2007; 2:40
83. Moulin P, Vaysse F, Bieth E et al Hypophosphatasia may lead to bone fragility: don't miss it. Eur J Pediatr 2008 [Epub]
84. Blyth MJG, Kincaid R, Craigen MAC et al The changing epidemiology of acute and subacute haematogenous osteomyelitis in children. J Bone Joint Surg Br 2001;83(1):99–102
85. Taylor MN, Chaudhuri R, Davis J et al Childhood osteomyelitis presenting as a pathological fracture. Clin Radiol 2008;63(3):348–51
86. Girschick H. Chronic recurrent multifocal osteomyelitis in children. Orphanet encyclopedia, March 2002. http://www.orpha.net/data/patho/GB/uk-CRMO.pdf
87. Brown T, Wilkinson RH. Chronic recurrent multifocal osteomyelitis. Radiology 1988;166(2):493–6
88. HK, Smith WL, Sato Y et al Congenital syphilis mimicking child abuse. Pediatr Radiol 1995;25(7):560–1

89. Solomon A, Rosen E. The aspect of trauma in the bone changes of congenital lues. Pediatr Radiol 1975;3(3): 176–8

90. Caffey J. Some traumatic lesions in growing bones other than fractures and dislocations: clinical and radiological features. Br J Radiol 1957;30(353): 225–38

91. SEER Cancer Statistics Review 1975-2005, National Cancer Institute http://seer.cancer.gov/csr/1975_2005/sections.html

92. McGregor LM, Metzger ML, Sanders R et al Pediatric cancers in the new millennium: dramatic progress, new challenges. Oncology (Williston Park) 2007;21(7):809–20

93. Crist WM, Pui CH. The Leukemias. In Behrman RE, Kliegman RM, Arvin AM (eds). Nelson Textbook of Pediatrics. Saunders, 1996, 15th ed.

94. Sinigaglia R, Gigante C, Bisinella G et al Musculoskeletal manifestations in pediatric acute leukemia. J Pediatr Orthop 2008;28(1):20–8

95. Miller SL, Hoffer FA. Malignant and benign bone tumors. Radiol Clin North Am 2001;39(4):673–99

96. Kransdorf MJ, Stull MA, Gilkey FW et al Osteoïd osteoma. Radiographics 1991;11(4):671–96

97. Berry M, Mankin H, Gebhardt M et al Osteoblastoma: a 30-year study of 99 cases. J Surg Oncol 2008;98(3): 179–83

98. Nakatani T, Yamamoto T, Akisue T et al Periosteal osteoblastoma of the distal femur. Skeletal Radiol 2004;33(2): 107–11

99. Leonard MB. Glucocorticoid-induced osteoporosis in children: impact of the underlying disease. Pediatrics 2007; 119(Suppl 2):S166–74

100. Meister B, Gassner I, Streif W et al Methotrexate osteopathy in infants with tumors of the central nervous system. Med Pediatr Oncol 1994;23(6):493–6

101. Schwartz AM, Leonidas JC. Methotrexate osteopathy. Skeletal Radiol 1984;11(1):13–6

102. Siegel NJ, Spackman TJ. Chronic hypervitaminosis A with intracranial hypertension and low cerebrospinal fluid concentration of protein. Two illustrative cases. Neurology 1972;11(10):580–4

103. Caffey J. Chronic poisoning due to excess of vitamin A. Description of the clinical and roentgen manifestations in seven infants and young children. Pediatrics 1950;5(4): 672–88

104. Gamble JG, Ip SC. Hypervitaminosis A in a child from megadosing. J Pediatr Orthop 1985;5(2):219–21

105. Frame B, Jackson CE, Reynolds WA et al Hypercalcemia and skeletal effects in chronic hypervitaminosis A. Ann Intern Med 1974;80(1):44–8

106. Mahoney CP, Margolis MT, Knauss TA et al Chronic vitamin A intoxication in infants fed chicken liver. Pediatrics 1980;65(5):893–7

107. Grissom LE, Griffin GC, Mandell GA. Hypervitaminosis A as a complication of treatment for neuroblastoma. Pediatr Radiol 1996;26(3):200–2

108. Eid NS, Shoemaker LR, Samiec TD. Vitamin A in cystic fibrosis: case report and review of the literature. J Pediatr Gastroenterol Nutr 1990;10(2):265–9

109. Kimmoun A, Leheup B, Feillet F et al Hypercalcemia revealing iatrogenic hypervitaminosis A in a child with autistic troubles [article in french]. Arch Pediatr 2008; 15(1):29–32

110. Olson JA. Recommended dietary intakes (RDI) of vitamin A in humans. Am J Clin Nutr 1987;45(4):704–16

111. Mendoza FS, Johnson F, Kerner JA et al Vitamin A intoxication presenting with ascites and a normal vitamin A level. West J Med 1988;148(1):88–90

112. Kerins DM, Murray R, FitzGerald GA. Prostacyclin and prostaglandin E1: molecular mechanisms and therapeutic utility. Prog Hemost Thromb 1991;10:307–37

113. Matzinger MA, Briggs VA, Dunlap HJ et al Plain film and CT observations in prostaglandin-induced bone changes. Pediatr Radiol 1992;22(4):264–6

114. Poznanski AK, Fernbach SK, Berry TE. Bone changes from prostaglandin therapy. Skeletal Radiol 1985;14(1): 20–5

115. Russell RG, Croucher PI, Rogers MJ. Bisphosphonates: pharmacology, mechanisms of action and clinical uses. Osteoporos Int 1999;9(Suppl 2):S66 80

116. Reszka AA, Rodan GA. Nitrogen-containing bisphosphonate mechanism of action. Mini Rev Med Chem 2004;4(7): 711–9

117. Boonen S, Vanderschueren D, Venken K et al Recent developments in the management of postmenopausal osteoporosis with bisphosphonates: enhanced efficacy by enhanced compliance. J Intern Med 2008;264(4):315–32

118. Glorieux FH. Treatment of osteogenesis imperfecta: who, why, what? Horm Res 2007;68(Suppl 5):8–11

119. Glorieux FH, Rauch F. Medical therapy of children with fibrous dysplasia. J Bone Miner Res 2006;21(Suppl 2): P110–3

120. Batch JA, Couper JJ, Rodda C et al Use of bisphosphonate therapy for osteoporosis in childhood and adolescence. J Paediatr Child Health 2003;39(2):88–92

121. Cimaz R. Osteoporosis in childhood rheumatic diseases: prevention and therapy. Best Pract Res Clin Rheumatol 2002;16(3):397–409

122. Andiran N, Alikaşifoğlu A, Küpeli S et al Use of bisphosphonates for resistant hypercalcemia in children with acute lymphoblastic leukemia: report of two cases and review of the literature. Turk J Pediatr 2006;48(3):248–52

123. Bateson EM. The relationship between Blount's disease and bow legs. Br J Radiol 1968;41(482):92–101

124. Thompson GH, Carter JR. Late onset tibia vara (Blount's disease): current concepts. Clin Orthop Rel Res 1990; (255):24–35

125. Henderson RC. Tibia vara: a complication of adolescent obesity. J Pediatr 1992;121(3):482–6

126. Appleton RE. Seizure-related injuries in children with newly diagnosed and untreated epilepsy. Epilepsia 2002; 43(7):764–7

127. Babayigit A, Dirik E, Bober E et al Adverse effects of antiepileptic drugs on bone mineral density. Pediatr Neurol 2006;35(3):177–81

128. Desai KB, Ribbans WJ, Taylor GJ. Incidence of five common fracture types in an institutional epileptic population. Injury 1996; 27(10):97–100

129. Lingam S, Joester J. Spontaneous fractures in children and adolescents with cerebral palsy. Br Med J 1994; 309(6949): 265

130. Presedo A, Dabney KW, Miller F. Fractures in patients with cerebral palsy. J Pediatr Orthop 2007;27(2):147–53

131. Samaniego EA, Sheth RD. Bone consequences of epilepsy and antiepileptic medications. Semin Pediatr Neurol 2007; 14(4):196–200

132. Blanco JS, Dahir G, McCrystal K. Bilateral femoral neck fractures secondary to hypocalcemic seizures in a skeletally immature patient. Am J Orthop 1999;28(3):187–8

133. Schnadower D, Agarwal C, Oberfield SE et al Hypocalcemic seizures and secondary bilateral femoral fractures in an adolescent with primary vitamin D deficiency. Pediatrics 2006;118(5):2226–30

134. Sheth RD. Bone health in pediatric epilepsy. Epilepsy Behav 2004; 5(Suppl 2):S30–5

135. Sheth RD, Gidal BE, Hermann BP. Pathological fractures in epilepsy. Epilepsy Behav 2006;9(4):601–5
136. Wirrell EC. Epilepsy-related injuries. Epilepsia 2006;47 (Suppl 1):79–86
137. Harnack GA von. Säuglings-Skorbut (Möller-Barlowsche Krankheit). In Harnack GA von. Kinderheilkunde. Springer Verlag, 1977, pag. 74
138. Finberg L. Concepts and diet analysis. In Finberg L. Saunders Manual of Pediatric Practice. WB Saunders Company, 1998, pag. 23
139. Riepe FG, Eichmann D, Oppermann HC et al Special feature: picture of the month. Infantile scurvy. Arch Pediatr Adolesc Med 2001;155(5):607–8
140. Hoeffel JC, Lascombes P, Mainard L et al Cone epiphysis of the knee and scurvy. Eur J Pediatr Surg 1993;3(3): 186–9
141. Maroscia D, Negrini AP, Salsano G et al Scurvy: a disease that has not yet disappeared. Apropos a case [Article in Italian] Radiol Med (Torino) 1992;83(4):462–4
142. Burches Greus E, Lecuona Lopez C, Ardit Lucas J et al Radiologic diagnosis of Moller-Barlow disease (scurvy). Apropos of a case [Article in Spanish] An Esp Pediatr 1991;34(3):243–6
143. Ratanachu-Ek S, Sukswai P, Jeerathanyasakun Y et al Scurvy in pediatric patients: a review of 28 cases. J Med Assoc Thai 2003;86(Suppl 3):S734–40
144. Paul DK, Lahiri M, Garai TB et al Scurvy persists in the current era. Indian Pediatr 1999;36(10):1067
145. Ahuja SR, Karande S. An unusual presentation of scurvy following head injury. Indian J Med Sci 2002;56(9): 440–2
146. Yilmaz S, Karademir S, Ertan U et al Scurvy. A case report. Turk J Pediatr 1998;40(2):249–53
147. Caksen H, Odabas D. Keratomalacia and scurvy in a severely malnourished infant. Pediatr Dermatol 2002;19(1): 93–5
148. Narchi H, Thomas M. A painful limp. J Paediatr Child Health 2000;36(3):277–8
149. Najera-Martinez P, Rodriguez-Collado A, Gorian-Maldonado E et al Scurvy. A study of 13 cases [Article in Spanish] Bol Med Hosp Infant Mex 1992;49(5):280–5
150. Cheung E, Mutahar R, Assefa F et al An epidemic of scurvy in Afghanistan: assessment and response. Food Nutr Bull 2003;24(3):247–55
151. Patterson CR, Burns J, McAllion SJ. Osteogenesis imperfecta: the distinction from child abuse and the recognition of a variant form. Am J Med Genet 1993;45(2): 187–92
152. Ablin DS, Sane SM. Non-accidental injury: confusion with temporary brittle bone disease and mild osteogenisis imperfecta. Pediatr Radiol 1997;27(2):111–3
153. Ablin DS. Osteogenesis imperfecta: a review. Can Assoc Radiol J 1998;49(2):110–23
154. Chapman S, Hall CM. Non-accidental injury or brittle bones. Pediatr Radiol 1997;27(2):106–10
155. Cazalet J. Note Re R (A Minor) (Expert Evidence) [1991] 1 FLR 291
156. Lynch MA. A judicial comment on temporary brittle bone disease [Letter]. Arch Dis Child 1995;73(4): 379
157. Wissow LS. Child abuse and neglect. N Engl J Med 1995;332(21):1425–31
158. Wall J. Re: AB (child abuse: expert witnesses) [1995] 1 FLR 181–200
159. Singer P. Non-Accidental Injury: Expert Evidence [2001] 2 FLR 1, 27. Royal Courts of Justice, Family Division
160. Dyer O. Doctor accused of misrepresenting evidence in child abuse cases. Br Med J 2004;328(7433):187
161. General Medical Council. Br Med J 2004;328:604
162. Mendelson KL. Critical review of 'temporary brittle bone disease'. Pediatr Radiol 2005;35(10):1036–40
163. Miller ME, Hangartner TN. Temporary brittle bone disease: association with decreased fetal movement and osteopenia. Calcif Tissue Int 1999;64(2):137–143
164. Miller ME. Hypothesis: fetal movement influences fetal and infant bone strength. Med Hypotheses. 2005;65(5): 880–6
165. Altman DH, Smith RL. Unrecognized trauma in infants and children. J Bone Joint Surg Am 1960;42-A: 407–13
166. O'Neill JA Jr, Meacham WF, Griffin PP et al Patterns of injury in the battered child syndrome. J Trauma 1973; 13(4):332–9
167. Sillence D. Osteogenesis imperfecta: an expanding panorama of variants. Clin Orthop 1981;(159):11–25
168. Sillence D, Butler B, Latham M et al Natural history of blue sclerae in osteogenesis imperfecta. Am J Med Genet 1993;45(2):183–6
169. Taitz LS. Child Abuse and metabolic bone disease: are they often confused? Br Med J 1991;302(6786):1244

Radiology in Suspected Child Abuse

8.1 Introduction

Even before Kempe published his now classic article on 'the battered child syndrome' in 1962 [1], radiologists drew attention to fractures that could really only be explained by the impact of external mechanical force. In 1946, Caffey was the first to describe the relation between the presence of multiple fractures of the long bones and subdural haematomas in six children in whom no previous trauma was known [2]. He thought it remarkable that in a number of children no new anomalies were found while hospitalised; however, some children showed new manifestations as soon as they returned home. Based on the fact that in children subdural haematomas are usually of traumatic origin, he suspected that this combination had a traumatic origin. In 1953, Silberman established that the combination of injuries as described by Caffey had to have a traumatic background [3]. In 1955, Woolley was the first to conclude that the found anomalies were the result of 'intentionally' inflicted physical injuries [4]. In 1957, 11 years after his original publication, Caffey concluded that abuse by either one or both parent(s) could be a possible explanation for this combination of injuries [5].

The importance of radiological examination when there are suspicions was not just demonstrated by the earlier-mentioned radiologists. Ellerstein performed routine radiological examinations in children suspected of being abused [6]. In 11.5% he found radiological indications for abuse. Approximately 20% of these children had fractures without any clinical manifestations.

Generally, fractures are the result of the more serious forms of abuse. The fractures seen in child abuse are similar to fractures sustained in an accident. Whether a fracture can be the result of child abuse is determined by a combination of:

- The type of fracture
- The age and level of development of the child
- The manner in which the fracture must have been sustained (according to established biomechanical data)
- The statement of the child, the parents or the carers, regarding the origin of the fracture

Abuse is likely when the first three factors are contradicted by the fourth. The role of (paediatric) radiologists is of great importance and often conclusive in determining whether child abuse is involved. In children below a certain age (see Sect. 8.2) who are suspected of being abused, it is indicated to do a skeletal survey. The purpose of the skeletal survey is:

- Detection of hidden fractures.
- To obtain additional information on clinically suspect abnormalities.
- To date fractures
- To diagnose the underlying skeletal abnormalities that may provide an increased risk for fractures.

In the following paragraphs, the existing guidelines and quality criteria that apply to a skeletal survey will be discussed.

8.2 Conventional Radiology

8.2.1 Guidelines

8.2.1.1 American College of Radiology

According to The American College of Radiology (ACR), the use of specific imaging techniques in child abuse will depend on the age of the child and the signs and symptoms presented [7]. For this purpose the ACR

R. A. C. Bilo et al., *Forensic Aspects of Pediatric Fractures*,
DOI: 10.1007/978-3-540-78716-7_8, © Springer-Verlag Berlin Heidelberg 2010

uses the following guidelines; for completeness, not just conventional radiology is mentioned:

1. Every child under the age of 2 years who is suspected of being abused, also without focal injuries.
   (a) A full skeletal survey (see Table 8.1)
   (b) In case the results of the full skeletal survey are negative, but a genuine clinical suspicion for abuse remains, a bone scintigraphy may be considered. Hereby one should be aware that skull fractures generally do not show increased radio-isotope up-take. A bone scintigraphy will specifically show fractures of the ribs, vertebrae, pelvis and acromion.
2. Every child under 2 years of age who has sustained head trauma, also when no focal or neurological abnormalities are present, and is suspected of being subjected to child abuse:
   (a) A full skeletal survey (see Table 8.1)
   (b) In case the results of the full skeletal survey are negative, but a genuine suspicion for abuse

remains, a MRI may be considered. An MRI has a much higher sensitivity for showing and dating intracranial injuries than a CT. Moreover, in this manner unnecessary radiation is avoided.
   (c) When there is still genuine clinical suspicion, a bone scintigraphy may be considered.
3. Every child under 5 years of age with neurological abnormalities, also without further focal abnormalities, in whom child abuse is suspected:
   (a) Thorough clinical examination. When the child presents seriously ill with symptoms indicating neurological injury, a CT scan of the brain without contrast is indicated. When no abnormalities are found that require acute neurological intervention, the child should be stabilised, directly followed by an MRI of the brain.
   (b) When the child is clinically stable and shows neurological symptoms (transient loss of consciousness, seizures, altered consciousness, retinal haemorrhages), the MRI can be used for initial neurological evaluation by imaging.

Table 8.1 Radiographic protocol for suspected child abuse [7, 14, 23, 48, 49]

	ACR	RCR and RCPCH
Skull[a]	AP Lateral Additional view when indicated: oblique or Towne view	AP Lateral Clinical basis (Towne view)
Cervical spine	Lateral AP	Lateral AP only when indicated[b]
Thorax	Routine AP and lateral Additional views when indicated: oblique views of the ribs	Routine AP including clavicles Oblique, left *and* right
Abdomen, lumbosacral spine, pelvis	AP abdomen AP lumbosacral spine Lateral lumbar spine and pelvis	AP, including pelvis and hips Lateral, if so required in different views When the quality of the views of chest and abdomen is not insufficient, an additional AP view of the spine
Upper extremities	Routine AP of the humerus, including shoulder and radius/ulna Additional views when indicated: specific views of the joints or lateral views	Routine AP view. Additional views when indicated: lateral in case of shaft fractures Lateral 'coned' views of elbows and wrists can show metaphyseal abnormalities in greater detail than AP views
Lower extremities	Routine AP of the femur, including hip and tibia/fibula Additional views when indicated: specific views of the joints or lateral views	Routine AP view. Additional views when indicated: lateral in case of shaft fractures Lateral 'coned' views of knees and ankles can show metaphyseal abnormalities in greater detail than AP views
Hands	PA	PA
Feet	AP/PA	AP
Follow-up		Repeat of the examination after 1–2 weeks of each fracture so as to facilitate dating of the fractures Chest/rib views after 2–3 weeks when the initial views appeared normal and there is still cause for concern

[a] Always part of a full examination, even if a head CT has been made. A linear skull fracture is not necessarily visible on the CT scan
[b] At this age, AP views of the cervical spine are hardly ever diagnostic and should only be made at the request of the radiologist

Hereby a comprehensive neuroradiological protocol is indicated.

(c) When the CT does not show a fracture, a full skeletal survey should be made of all children <2 years old, including a full skull series.

4. Every child, irrespective of age, with visceral injuries that do not correspond with the clinical anamnesis and in whom physical examination or laboratory tests do not provide a satisfactory explanation of the presentation. Visceral injuries comprise: a pseudocyst of the pancreas, haemorrhages of the adrenals, free air in the abdominal cavity after a blunt trauma to the abdomen, contusion or lacerations of viscera and traumatic perforation of the bladder. In this context, all the earlier-mentioned abnormalities should be considered signs of child abuse.

(a) A full skeletal survey of children <2 years old (see Table 8.1).

(b) A CT scan with orally or intravenously administered contrast.

In other words: when child abuse is suspected, radiological examination is always advised in children <2 years old, and in children >2 years only when there are further serious external or internal injuries.

When these images show any abnormalities, a view in a second plane should be made. Making images of details should certainly be considered.

8.2.1.2 The Royal College of Radiologists and the Royal College of Paediatrics and Child Health

In March 2008, The Royal College of Radiologists in collaboration with The Royal College of Paediatrics and Child Health formulated a British guideline for imaging when child abuse is suspected [8]. According to this guideline, a skeletal survey should be made in each child <2 years who is suspected of being subjected to child abuse. In view of the medical/legal implications of this examination, this skeletal survey should meet the highest technical standards and as such should be made by two trained radiographers. The examination should be performed under the supervision of a radiologist, who also safeguards the quality of the examination. The child is only allowed to leave the radiology department after the radiologist has approved the complete examination.

An important difference with the ACR protocol is the standard oblique view of the ribs (Fig. 8.1a and b).

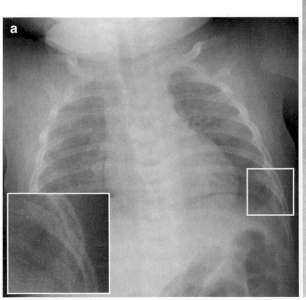

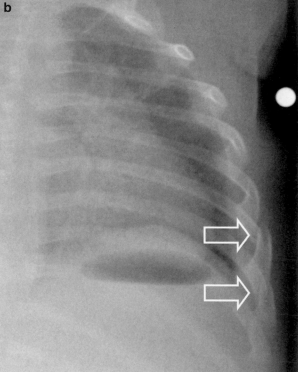

Fig. 8.1 (a) According to the parents, this 5-week-old girl had fallen from her crib. On the antero-posterior chest view a subtle abnormality of the 7th rib can be seen. (b) Oblique costal view shows lateral rib fractures on the left side, level 6th and 7th rib

Ingram et al. showed in a randomised control study that this increases the sensitivity of the detection of rib fractures by 17% (95% CI 2–36%) and the specificity by 7% (95% CI 2–13%) [9]. Hansen et al. described a series of 22 patients in which the oblique view changed the interpretation in 12 cases ($p = 0.02$) [10]. In these 12 cases, 19 rib fractures were found on the oblique views, and six fractures were excluded. All patients with rib fractures showed at least one fracture on the anterior-posterior and lateral views.

8.2.1.3 Examination on Indication

Besides the indications in the earlier-mentioned guidelines, there are also further situations in which imaging may be indicated.

Firstly, Smith et al. maintain that a full skeletal survey, as stated in Table 8.1, is also indicated in children between the ages of 2 and 5 who are seriously suspected of being subjected to child abuse. The indication will be void when only minimal signs are found or when the situation is such that they are regularly/daily seen by other persons outside the family, for example, in a kindergarten or school [11].

In children of 5 years and older, radiological examination is only indicated when at clinical examination abnormalities are found, such as areas of the bones that show pain on pressure or reduced mobility.

Secondly, studies have shown that physicians dealing with child abuse are of the opinion that when one child of a family is abused, this is sufficient reason to subject the other children in the family to medical examination (Fig. 8.2a and b)[12]. In a retrospective analysis of 759 siblings of 400 index children, it appeared that in 37% of cases abuse was directed to all children and in 20% to one or several children in the family [13]. The British Society for Paediatric Radiology maintains that in proven child abuse, all siblings of ≤3 years should be subjected to a full skeletal survey [14]. However, there are no studies that support this guideline.

Finally, children <5 who suddenly and inexplicably die should always undergo a full skeletal survey.

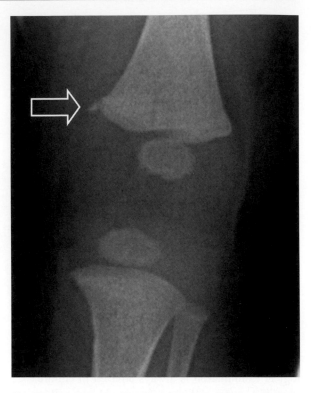

Fig. 8.2 Three-month-old girl whose older sister had allegedly fallen from a carseat. At physical examination bruising was noticed in this girl, the skeletal survey shows a metaphyseal corner fracture of the left distal femur (*open arrow*)

8.2.2 Adequacy of Examination

8.2.2.1 Number of Views

When child abuse is suspected, and the decision is made to continue with radiological examination, this should be conducted adequately. Hereby it should first be established that in young infants the so-called babygram (consisting of one anterior-posterior view and one lateral view) of the skeleton should be considered obsolete and an error of judgement (Fig. 8.3a and b). In diagnostic radiology, a babygram is inadequate when child abuse is suspected [15]. According to professional standards, this radiograph, preferably made on a mammograph, is only admissible in premature foetuses in which imaging is otherwise impossible. Due to the loss of detail, images of trunk and extremities in one view should also be avoided [14].

Fig. 8.3 (a) So-called babygram within the scope of a child abuse protocol. The use of a babygram for diagnostic purposes is obsolete when child abuse is suspected and should be considered a serious flaw with regard to living as well as deceased children. (b) Lateral view of a babygram

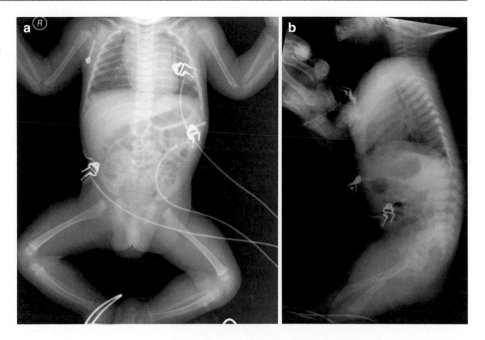

It regularly happens that the radiological examinations performed do not meet the required standard. Offiah and Hall studied the quality of radiological examinations performed within the scope of child abuse that were submitted for re-evaluation to Great Ormond Street Children's Hospital (London, UK) [16]. They used three exclusion criteria:

• Examinations in which only a selection of the produced radiographs was submitted for re-evaluation
• Examinations of less than three radiographs (excluding babygrams)
• Examinations of children ≥2 years

In total they admitted the skeletal surveys of 50 consecutive children to their study. Per child an average of 10 [2–13] radiographs was made. Hereby it should be mentioned that a professionally executed skeletal survey comprises 18–19 radiographs. In total, Offiah and Hall found 37 different combinations, including five babygrams. None of the examinations met the required standard. In general, hands and feet radiographs were absent.

A study of Kleinman et al. from the United States confirmed the findings of Offiah and Hall [17]. As part of their study they inquired, by means of a questionnaire, in 155 paediatric hospitals which radiological protocol was used when child abuse was suspected. Of

the 155 hospitals, 69% returned the questionnaire. Of these responders, 90.7% subscribed to the Society for Pediatric Radiology (SPR). Here too, a large variety was seen in the number of radiographs made.

Van Rijn et al. researched the Dutch practices with regard to the radiological examination used in suspected child abuse [18]. One of the most common mistakes was imaging the extremities on one single radiograph (Fig. 8.4). The results of this study were similar to the earlier published international studies.

Swinson et al. studied the effects of the publication of the guidelines of the British Society of Paediatric Radiology (followed by the guidelines for The Royal Collage of Radiologists and the Royal College of Paediatrics and Child Health) and compared their findings with the earlier-mentioned article of Offiah and Hall [19]. Their study still showed a considerable deviation in imaging, but significantly less so than in the earlier study. The publication of guidelines and education of the physicians involved seems to have a positive effect on the quality of imaging in cases suspected of child abuse.

8.2.2.2 Technique

Not only is it essential that the examination is complete, the techniques used are also of great importance.

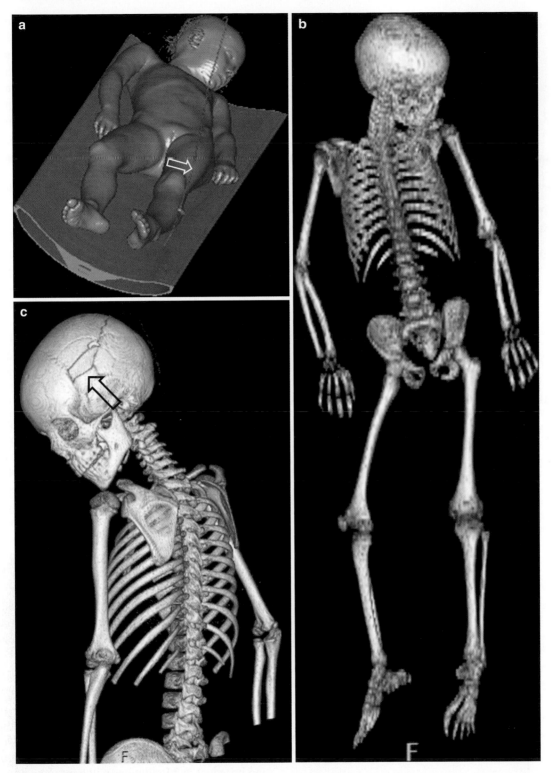

Fig. 8.16 (**a**) Six-year-old girl who died as result of a blow on the head with a hammer. Post mortem CT has been made with the body in a body bag. Reconstruction shows that in spite of the bag the body is still clearly visible. The zip of the body bag is visible as an artefact (*open arrow*). (**b**) Three-dimensional reconstruction of the whole skeleton. (**c**) Three-dimensional reconstruction of skull and chest. The fracture at the left side of the parietal bone (*open arrow*) that resulted from the hammer blow is clearly visible

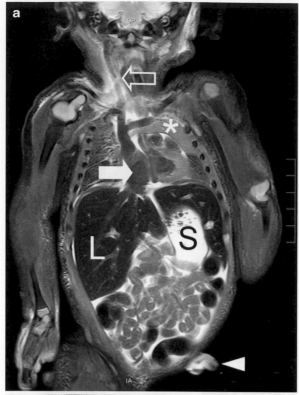

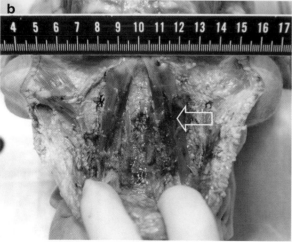

Fig. 8.17 (**a**) Deceased neonate, found in a refuse container. Postmortem T2-weighted MRI shows oedema around the blood vessels in the neck (*open arrow*). Also, the neonatal anatomy is clearly visible. (**=thymus; L=liver; S=stomach; arrow=right atrium; arrow point=umbilical cord.). (**b**) Autopsy (seen from above) shows a haematoma around the blood vessels on the right side of the neck (*open arrow*), possibly the result of strangulation

should be a standard part of the postmortem examination in children who die suddenly and inexplicably. In

these cases, skeletal abnormalities may be found that are suspect for an unnatural death.

In a retrospective study of McGraw et al. of 106 consecutive postmortem skeletal surveys, 14 children showed signs of child abuse [40]. Sperry and Pfalzgraf describe a 9-month-old child whose death was initially contributed to cod death [41]. However, postmortem examination showed healing clavicle fractures and a healing fracture of the humerus on the left.

Extensive investigation revealed that 4 weeks prior to death a non-qualified chiropractor had treated the child for a 'shoulder dislocation'. It was very likely that this treatment was the cause of the fractures.

Also, Ojima et al. describe the sudden and unexplained death of a child in whom fractures were found [42]. This child had undiagnosed osteogenesis imperfecta.

A relatively new development in clinical and forensic pathology is the use of postmortem CT (Fig. 8.16a–c) and MRI (Figs. 8.17a and b and 8.18a and b) [43–45]. The use of these, clinically widely used, techniques is evident; also, for laymen it produces an image they can understand (when reconstructions are used), and that is suitable for presentation in court cases. Furthermore, it provides calibrated three-dimensional measurements and long-term storage of images. However, postmortem imaging also has its disadvantages. Firstly, obviously there is no blood circulation, which makes it impossible to use contrast media. A possible solution to this problem has been developed by the 'Virtopsy project' in Bern, where after perfusion with paraffin oil and with the use of a heart-lung machine it was still possible to produce an angiography [46]. A second, even more important problem is the interpretation of the CT and MRI images. Where radiologists are experienced in evaluating the images of living patients and pathologists are experienced in the performing and interpreting autopsies, there is little or no overlapping knowledge. This may lead to problems in interpretation; for example, when air is seen in the portal system (Fig. 8.18). In living patients this is a rare finding, but in postmortem CTs of critically ill patients, this is regularly found. Shiotani et al. described portal air in 33% of 190 postmortem CTs [47].

Postmortem radiology is still in full development, and its values and limitations will have to be proven in the future. However, it seems obvious that after its successful introduction into the clinic, radiology will now also find its place in pathology.

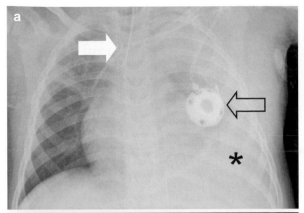

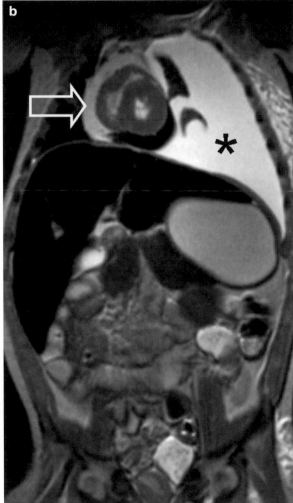

Fig. 8.18 (**a**) Two-year-old girl with thrombocytopenia in ALL who died from acute bradycardia, in spite of resuscitation. The chest radiograph shows opafication of the left side of the chest (asterisk) with a right-shifted mediastinum (easily recognisable by the deviation of the tracheal tube [*arrow*]). For administering chemotherapy a central line has been inserted (*open arrow*). (**b**) Postmortem T2-weighted MRI shows, conform chest radiograph, a left-sided haemothorax (asterisk). Furthermore, there is a clearly visible haemopericard (*open arrow*)

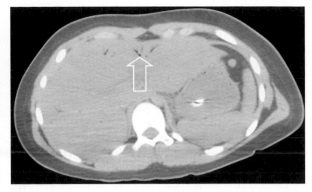

Fig. 8.19 Postmortem of a deceased 12-year-old girl. Autopsy revealed no anatomical cause of death. The axial slice through the liver shows evident air in the portal veins (*open arrow*)

References

1. Kempe CH, Silverman FN, Steele BF et al The battered child syndrome. JAMA 1962;181:17–24
2. Caffey J. Multiple fractures in the long bones of infants suffering from chronic subdural hematoma. Am J Roentgenol Radium Ther Nucl Med 1946;56:163–73
3. Silverman FM. The Roentgen manifestations of unrecognized skeletal trauma in infants. Am J Roentgenol Radium Ther Nucl Med 1953;69(3):413–26
4. Woolley PV, Evans WA. Significance of skeletal lesions in infants resembling those of traumatic origin. J Am Med Assoc 1955;158(7):539–43
5. Caffey J. Some traumatic lesions in growing bones other than fractures and dislocations: clinical and radiological features. Brit J Radiol 1957;30(353):225–38
6. Ellerstein NS, Norris KJ. Value of radiologic skeletal survey in assessment of abused children. Pediatr 1984;74(6): 1075–8
7. American College of Radiology. ACR Appropriateness Criteria Suspected Physical Abuse – Child. ACR, 2005 http://www.acr.org/
8. Intercollegiate report from the Royal College of Radiologists and the Royal College of Paediatrics and Child Health. Standards for radiological investigations of suspected non-accidental injury. RCR and RCPCH, 2008
9. Ingram JD, Connell J, Hay TC. Oblique radiographs of the chest in nonaccidental trauma. Emerg Radiol 2000;7(1): 42–6
10. Hansen KK, Prince JS, Nixon GW. Oblique chest views as a routine part of skeletal surveys performed for possible physical abuse--is this practice worthwhile? Child Abuse Negl 2008;32(1):155–9
11. Schmitt BD. The child with nonaccidental trauma. In Helfer RE, Kempe RS (eds). The battered child. University of Chicago Press 4th edition 1987, 178–96
12. Campbell KA, Bogen DL, Berger RP. The other children: a survey of child abuse physicians on the medical evaluation of children living with a physically abused child. Arch Pediatr Adolesc Med 2006;160(12):1241–6
13. Hamilton-Giachritsis CE, Browne KD. A retrospective study of risk to siblings in abusing families. J Fam Psychol 2005; 19(4):619–24
14. http://www.bspr.org.uk/nai.htm

15. Alexander R, Kleinman PK. Diagnostic imaging of child abuse – portable guides to investigating child abuse. US Department of Justice, 2000

16. Offiah AC, Hall CM. Observational study of skeletal surveys in suspected non-accidental injury. Clin Radiol 2003;58 (9):702–5

17. Kleinman PL, Kleinman PK, Savageau JA. Suspected infant abuse: radiographic skeletal survey practices in pediatric health care facilities. Radiology 2004;233(2):477–85

18. Van Rijn RR, Kieviet N, Hoekstra R et al Radiology in suspected Non Accidental Injury: theory and practice in the Netherlands. Eur J Radiol 2009;71:147–151

19. Swinson S, Tapp M, Brindley R et al An audit of skeletal surveys for suspected non-accidental injury following publication of the British Society of Paediatric Radiology guidelines. Clin Radiol 2008;63(6):651–6

20. Kleinman PK, Nimkin K, Spevak MR et al Follow-up skeletal surveys in suspected child abuse. Am J Roentgenol 1996;167(4):893–6

21. Prosser I, Maguire S, Harrison SK et al How old is this fracture? Radiologic dating of fractures in children: a systematic review. Am J Roentgenol 2005;184(4):1282–6

22. Zimmerman S, Makoroff K, Care M et al Utility of follow-up skeletal surveys in suspected child physical abuse evaluations. Child Abuse Negl 2005;29(10):1075–83

23. Kemp AM, Butler A, Morris S et al Which radiological investigations should be performed to identify fractures in suspected child abuse? Clin Radiol 2006;61(9):723–36

24. Scaglione M, Pinto A, Pedrosa I et al Multi-detector row computed tomography and blunt chest trauma. Eur J Radiol 2008;65(3):377–88

25. Sangster GP, González-Beicos A, Carbo AI et al Blunt traumatic injuries of the lung parenchyma, pleura, thoracic wall, and intrathoracic airways: multidetector computer tomography imaging findings. Emerg Radiol 2007;14(5):297–310

26. Provenzale J CT and MR imaging of acute cranial trauma. Emerg Radiol 2007;14(1):1–12

27. Geijer M, El-Khoury GY. MDCT in the evaluation of skeletal trauma: principles, protocols, and clinical applications. Emerg Radiol 2006;13(1):7–18

28. Stoodley N. Neuroimaging in child abuse: reducing the risk. Clin Radiol 2004;59(11):965–6

29. Hargaden G, O'Connell M, Kavanagh E et al Current concepts in wholebody imaging using turbo short tau inversion recovery MR imaging. Am J Roentgenol 2003;180(1):247–52

30. Kellenberger CJ, Epelman M, Miller SF et al Fast STIR whole-body MR imaging in children. Radiographics 2004; 24(5):1317–30

31. Kumar J, Seith A, Kumar A et al Whole body MR imaging with the use of parallel imaging for the detection of skeletal metastases in pediatric patients with small-cell neoplasms: comparison with skeletal scintigraphy and FDG PET/CT. Ped Radiol 2008;38(9):953–62

32. Stranzinger E, Kellenberger CJ, Braunschweig S et al Whole-body STIR MR imaging in suspected child abuse: an alternative to skeletal survey radiography? Eur J Radiol Extra 2007;63(1):43–7

33. Elterman T, Beer M, Girschick HJ. Magnetic Resonance Imaging in child abuse. J Child Neurol 2007;22(2):170–175.

34. Evangelista P, Barron C, Goldberg A et al MRI STIR for the evaluation of nonaccidental trauma in children. Pediatric Academic Societies annual meeting April 29–May 2, 2006, San Francisco, California, USA

35. Cohen MC, Whitby E. The use of magnetic resonance in the hospital an coronial pediatric postmortem examination. Forensic Sci Med Pathol 2007;3(4):289–96

36. Dedouit F, Guilbeau-Frugier C, Capuani C et al Child Abuse: practical application of autopsy, radiological, and microscopic studies. J Forensic Sci 2008;53(6):1424–9

37. Norman MG, Smialek JE, Newman DE et al The postmortem examination of the abused child. Pathological, radiographic and legal aspects. Perspect Pediatr Pathol 1984;8 (4):313–43

38. Kleinman PK, Marks SC, Richmond JM et al Inflicted skeletal injury, a postmortem radiologic-histopathologic study in 31 infants. Am J Radiol 1995;165(3):647–50

39. Harris VJ, Lorand MA, Fitzpatrick JJ et al Radiographic atlas of child abuse – a case studies approach. Igaku-Shoin 1996, 9–10

40. McGraw EP, Pless JE, Pennington DJ et al Postmortem radiography after unexpected death in neonates, infants, and children: should imaging be routine? Am J Roentgenol 2002;178(6):1517–21

41. Sperry K, Pfalzgraf R. Inadvertent clavicular fractures caused by 'chiropractic' manipulations in an infant: an unusual form of pseudoabuse. J Forensic Sci 1995;35(5): 1211–6

42. Ojima K, Matsumoto H, Hayase T et al An autopsy case of osteogenesis imperfecta initially suspected as child abuse. Forensic Sci Int 1994;65(2):97–104

43. Bollinger SA, Thali MJ, Ross S et al Virtual autopsy using imaging: bridging radiologic and forensic sciences. A review of the Virtopsy and similar projects. Eur Radiol 2008;18(2): 273–82

44. Stawicki SP, Gracias VH, Schrag SP et al The dead continue to teach the living: Examining the role of computed tomography and magnetic resonance imaging in the setting of postmortem examinations. J Surg Educ 2008;65(3): 200–5

45. Griffiths PD, Paley MNJ, Whitby EH. Post-mortem MRI as an adjunct to fetal or neonatal autopsy. Lancet 2005;365 (9466):1271–3

46. Grabherr S, Gygax E, Sollberger B et al Two-step postmortem angiography with a modified heart-lung machine: preliminary results. Am J Roentgenol 2008;190(2):345–51

47. Shiotani S, Kohno M, Ohashi N et al Postmortem computed tomography (PMCT) demonstration of the relation between gastrointestinal (GI) distention and hepatic portal venous gas (HPVG). Radiat Med 2004;22(1):25–9

48. American Academy of Pediatrics. Diagnostic imaging of child abuse. Pediatrics 2000;105(6):1345–8

49. Merten DF, Cooperman DR, Thompson GH. Skeletal manifestations of child abuse. In Reece RM (ed). Child abuse – medical diagnosis and management. Lea & Febiger 1992, 23–53

Fracture Dating

9.1 Introduction

Non-accidental fractures in children are signs of the application of severe external force. Hence, when non-accidental fractures are present, it is essential that they are identified as soon as possible.

Fractures inflicted by violence can be found throughout the whole skeleton, are often present in multiples and may be in various stages of healing [1–4]. These stages are visible as such, and can be identified on skeletal radiographs (Fig. 9.1a and b). Also, dating makes it possible to show inconsistencies between the more or less objective radiological dating and the subjective anamnestic dating and the reason provided for the injury [5].

Since in cases of abuse medical help is often sought late, further loading of the fracture by movement, additional injuries and newly sustained fractures may complicate the dating of an old fracture.

It is not always easy to differentiate between accidental and non-accidental fractures; however, it is essential to do so in order to enable a responsible intervention [6]. Adequate dating may help to establish whether the time given for the provided cause corresponds with the characteristics of the fracture.

Fractures can be dated in various ways:

- A fracture may hurt and limits movement in the initial phase, which may provide anamnestic information regarding the time it was sustained (see Sect. 9.2).

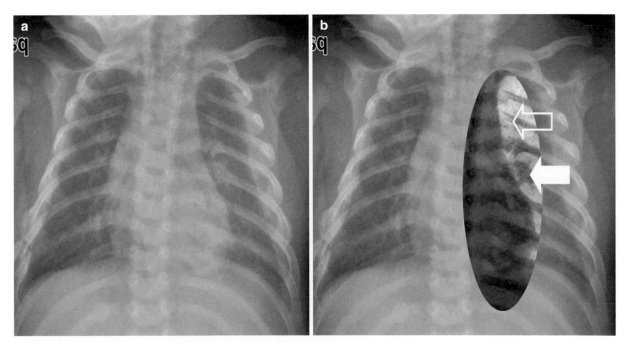

Fig. 9.1 (**a**) Chest radiograph of a 3-month-old boy shows several rib fractures (see also Fig. 3.9). (**b**) Radiograph after enhancement, improving the visibility of the fractures. There are fresh (*open arrow*) as well as healing (*arrow*) fractures

R. A. C. Bilo et al., *Forensic Aspects of Pediatric Fractures,*
DOI: 10.1007/978-3-540-78716-7_9, © Springer-Verlag Berlin Heidelberg 2010

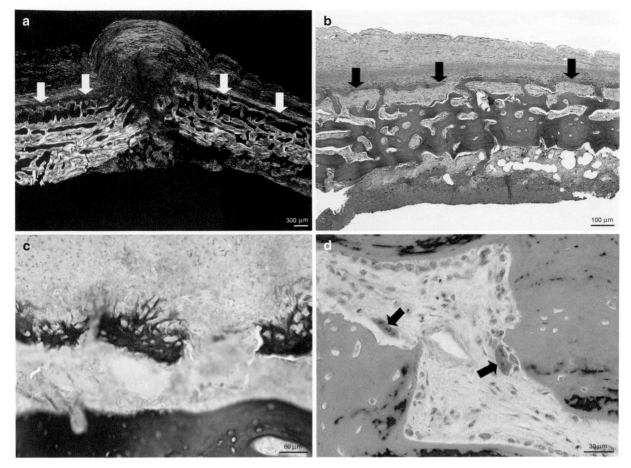

Fig. 9.6 (**a**) Discontinuity of the cranium with connective-tissue plug in the fracture cleft. Callus layer can still be separated from the marginal bone layer (*arrows*). Polarised light. (**b**) Detail of (a). Callus layer along the external trabecula of the cranium can still be separated (*arrows*). Haematoxiline-Eosine staining. (**c**) Depositions of primary bone tissue (disorganised), 'woven bones' in the callus layer. Lawson Van Gieson staining. (**d**) Howships lacunae with multiple-nuclear osteoclasts in the fracture cleft (*arrows*). Trichrome staining according to Goldner

closing cones (Fig. 9.7a) These are bone-tissue replacement systems that consist of a 'head' of osteoclasts that drills its way longitudinal through the cortex towards the fracture gap, and a 'tail' of osteoblasts that refills the (resorption) canal left behind by the 'head' with new-bone tissue. In this manner new Haversian systems (osteones) are formed which bridge the fracture as internal splints. A detail of such a 'head' (the cutting cone) clearly shows the features of Howships lacunae (Fig. 9.7b). Furthermore, Fig. 9.7a shows clearly that part of the primarily woven bone tissue has already been replaced by longitudinally running secondary lamellar bone tissue.

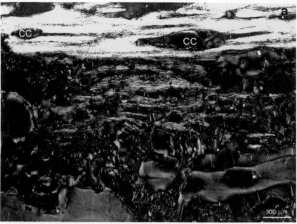
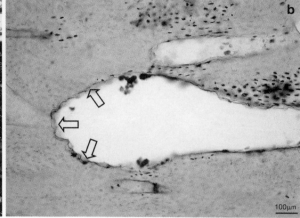

Fig. 9.7 (**a**) Cortical dry bone tissue with torpedo-shaped 'cutting and closing cones' at the top of the image (CC). Below, appositional callus tissue in which part of the primary bone (disorganised 'woven bone') has been replaced by longitudinal (here horizontally) shaped lamellar bone tissue (pale yellow).

Polarised light. (**b**) Detail of a 'cutting cone' in the cortex of the dry bone tissue of (a). The Howships lacunae, which had active osteoclasts during life, are shown as 'bites' taken from the bone tissue (*arrows*). Normal bright daylight. Unstained

References

1. Duhaime AC, Alario AJ, Lewander WJ et al Head injury in very young children: mechanisms, injury types, and ophthalmologic findings in 100 hospitalized patients younger than 2 years of age. Pediatrics 1992;90(2 Pt 1):179–85
2. Worlock P, Stower M, Barbor P. Patterns of fractures in accidental and non-accidental injury in children: a comparative study. Br Med J 1986;293(6539):100–2
3. Jeerathanyasakun Y, Hiranyavanitch P, Bhummichitra D et al Causes of femoral shaft fracture in children under five years of age. J Med Ass Thailand 2003;86 Suppl 3:S661–6
4. Leventhal JM, Thomas SA, Rosenfield NS et al Fractures in young children. Distinguishing child abuse from unintentional injuries. Am J Dis Child 1993;147(1):87–92
5. Kleinman P, Blackbourne B, Marks S et al Radiologic contributions to the investigation and prosecution of cases of fatal infant abuse. N Engl J Med 1989;320(8):507–11
6. Taitz J, Moran K, O'Meara M. Long bone fractures in children under 3 years of age: is abuse being missed in Emergency Department presentations? J Paediatr Child Health 2004;40(4):170–4
7. Lyons RA, Delahunty AM, Kraus D et al Children's fractures: a population based study. Inj Prev 1999;5(2):129–32
8. Akbarnia BA, Campbell RM. The role of the orthopedic surgeon in child abuse. In Morrissy RT, Winter RB. Lovell and Winter's Pediatric Orthopaedics. Lippincott, Williams and Wilkins Publ, 3rd ed, 1990
9. Barsness KA, Cha ES, Bensard DD et al The positive predictive value of rib fractures as an indicator of nonaccidental trauma in children. J Trauma 2003;54(6):1107–10
10. Merten DF, Radlowski MA, Leonidas JC. The abused child: a radiological reappraisal. Radiology 1983;146(2):377–81

11. Cadzow SP, Armstrong KL. Rib fractures in infants: red alert! The clinical features, investigations and child protection outcomes. J Paediatr Child Health 2000;36(4):322–6
12. Swischuk LE. Radiographic signs of skeletal trauma. In Ludwig S, Kornberg AE. Child Abuse - a medical reference. Churchill Livingstone 1992, 151–74
13. O'Connor JF, Cohen J. Dating fractures. In Kleinman PK. Diagnostic imaging of child abuse. Mosby, 2nd ed, 1998, 168–77
14. Pergolizzi R, Oestrich AE. Child abuse fracture through physiologic reaction. Pediatr Radiol 1995;25(7):566–7
15. Brodeur AE, Monteleone JA. Child Maltreatment. A Clinical Guide and Reference. GW Medical Publishing, 1994, 32
16. Hobbs C. Fractures. In Meadow R. ABC of child abuse. Br Med J 3rd ed, 1997, 9–13
17. Prosser I, Maguire S, Harrison SK et al How old is this fracture? Radiologic dating of fractures in children: a systematic review. Am J Roentgenol 2005;184(4):1282–6
18. Dreizen S, Spirakis CN, Stone RE. The influence of age and nutrition on 'bone scar' formation in the distal end of the growing femur. Am J Phys Anthropol 1964;22:295–306
19. Ham AW. A histological study of the early phases of bone repair. J Bone Joint Surg Am 1930;12:827–44
20. Cruess RL, Dumont J. Fracture healing. Can J Surg 1975;18(5):403–13
21. Campbell RM. Child abuse. In Beaty JH, Kasser JM. Rockwood and Wilkins' Fractures in children. Lippincott Williams and Wilkins, 5th ed, 2001
22. Kleinman PK, Nimkin K, Spevak MR et al Follow-up skeletal surveys in suspected child abuse. Am J Roentgenol 1996;167(4):893–6
23. Hobbs CJ, Hanks HGI, Wynne JM. Child abuse and neglect – a clinician's handbook. Churchill Livingstone, 1993, 57–65
24. Segall HD, McComb JG, Tsai FY et al Neuroradiology in head trauma. In Stanley G. Diagnostic imaging in pediatric trauma. Springer International, 1980, 18–63

25. Cameron JM. Radiological pathological aspects of the battered child syndrome. In Smith SM. The maltreatment of children. University Park Press, 1978, 69–81

26. Kleinman PK, Barnes PD. Head trauma. In Kleinman PK. Diagnostic imaging of child abuse. 2nd ed. Mosby, 1998, 285–342

27. Taveras JM, Wood EH. Diagnostic neuroradiology. Williams and Wilkins, 1964

28. Rosenthall L, Hill RO, Chuang S. Observation on the use of 99mTc-phosphate imaging in peripheral bone trauma. Radiology 1976;119(3):637–41

29. Cumming WA. Neonatal skeletal fractures. Birth trauma or child abuse? J Can Assoc Radiol 1979;30(1):30–3

30. Yeo LI, Reed MH. Staging of healing of femoral fractures in children. Can Assoc Radiol J 1994;45(1):16–9

31. Islam O, Sobeleski D, Symons S et al Development and duration of radiographic signs of bone healing in children. Am J Roentgenol 2000;175(1):75–8

32. Plenk H. Knochengewebe und Zähne. In Böck P (ed). Romeis Mikroskopische Technik. Urban und Schwarzenberg, 17e ed., 1989, 527–70

33. Bancroft JD, Stevens A. Theory and practice of histological techniques. Churchill Livingstone, 1996, 324–35

34. Burke CN, Geiselman CW. 1971. Exact anhydride epoxy percentages for electron microscopy embedding (Epon). J Ultrastruct Res 1971;36(1):119–26

35. Maat GJR. Dating of fractures in human dry bone tissue. The Berisha case. In Kimmerle E, Baraybar JP (eds). Identification of traumatic skeletal injuries resulting from human rights abuses and armed conflicts. Taylor and Francis (in print)

36. Maat GJR, van den Bos RPM, Aarents MJ. Manual preparation of ground sections for the microscopy of natural bone tissue. Update and modification of Frost's "rapid manual method". Int J Osteoarch 2001;11:366–74

37. Aegerter E, Kirckpatrick JA. 1968. The repair of fractures. In Aegerter E (ed). Orthopedic diseases. Physiology, pathology, radiology. Saunders, 1968, 257–79

38. Bennet GA. Bones. In Anderson WAD (ed). Pathology, volume 2. Mosby, 1966, 1300–5

39. Heppenstall RB. Fracture healing. In Heppenstall RB (ed). Fracture treatment and healing. Saunders, 1980, 41–64

40. Williams PL, Warwick R, Dyson M et al Gray's anatomy. The response of bone to injury. Churchill Livingstone, 37th ed, 1989, 313–5

41. Kleinman PK, Marks SC, Nimkin K et al Rib fractures in 31 abused infants: postmortem radiologic-histopathologic study. Radiology 1996;200(3):807–10

42. Buckwalter JA, Einhorn ThA, Bolander ME et al Healing of musculoskeletal tissues. In Rockwood ChA, Bucholz RW, Green DP et al (eds). Fractures in adults, vol 1. Lippincott-Raven, 4th ed, 1996, 267–83

43. Aufderheide AC, Rodriguez-Martin C. The Cambridge encyclopedia of human paleopathology. Cambridge University Press, 1998, 20–4

44. Schiller AL, Teitelbaum SL. Bones and joints. In Rubin E, Farber JL (eds). Pathology. Lippincott-Raven, 3rd ed, 1999, 1354–6

45. Vigorita VJ. Fracture healing. In Vigorita VJ (ed). Orthopedic pathology. Lippincott Williams and Wilkins, 1999, 85–96

46. Robbins SL, Cotran RS, Kumar V. Pathologic basis of disease. Saunders, 5th ed, 1991, 1227–9

47. Ortner D. Identification of pathological conditions in human skeletal remains. Academic Press, 2nd ed, 2003, 126–63

48. Klotzbach H, Delling G, Richter E et al 2003. Post-mortem diagnosis and age estimation of infants' fractures. Int J Legal Med 2003;117(2): 82–9

49. Saukko P, Knight B. Knight's forensic pathology. Hodder Arnold, 3rd ed, 2004, 181–9

50. Saukko P, Knight B. Knight's forensic pathology. Hodder Arnold, 3rd ed, 2004, 281–95

References

1. Duhaime AC, Alario AJ, Lewander WJ et al. Head injury in very young children: mechanisms, injury types, and ophthalmologic findings in 100 hospitalized patients younger than 2 years of age. Pediatrics 1992;90(2 Pt 1):179-85
2. Worlock P, Stower M, Barbor P. Patterns of fractures in accidental and non-accidental injury in children: a comparative study. Br Med J 1986;293(6539):100-2
3. Jeerathanyasakun Y, Hiranyavanitch P, Bhummichitra D et al. Causes of femoral shaft fracture in children under five years of age. J Med Ass Thailand 2003;86 Suppl 3: S661-6
4. Leventhal JM, Thomas SA, Rosenfield NS et al. Fractures in young children. Distinguishing child abuse from unintentional injuries. Am J Dis Child 1993;147(1):87-92
5. Kleinman P, Blackbourne B, Marks S et al. Radiologic contributions to the investigation and prosecution of cases of fatal infant abuse. N Engl J Med 1989;320(8):507-11
6. Taitz J, Moran K, O'Meara M. Long bone fractures in children under 3 years of age: is abuse being missed in Emergency Department presentations? J Paediatr Child Health 2004;40(4):170-4
7. Lyons RA, Delahunty AM, Kraus D et al. Children's fractures: a population based study. Inj Prev 1999;5(2):129-32
8. Akbarnia BA, Campbell RM. The role of the orthopedic surgeon in child abuse. In Morrissy RT, Winter RB. Lovell and Winter's Pediatric Orthopaedics. Lippincott, Williams and Wilkins Publ, 3rd ed, 1990
9. Barsness KA, Cha ES, Bensard DD et al. The positive predictive value of rib fractures as an indicator of nonaccidental trauma in children. J Trauma 2003;54(6):1107-10
10. Merten DF, Radlowski MA, Leonidas JC. The abused child: a radiological reappraisal. Radiology 1983;146(2):377-81
11. Cadzow SP, Armstrong KL. Rib fractures in infants: red alert! The clinical features, investigations and child protection outcomes. J Paediatr Child Health 2000;36(4):322-6
12. Swischuk LE. Radiographic signs of skeletal trauma. In Ludwig S, Kornberg AE. Child Abuse - a medical reference. Churchill Livingstone 1992, 151-74
13. O'Connor JF, Cohen J. Dating fractures. In Kleinman PK. Diagnostic imaging of child abuse. Mosby, 2nd ed, 1998, 168-77
14. Pergolizzi R, Oestrich AE. Child abuse fracture through physiologic reaction. Pediatr Radiol 1995;25(7):566-7
15. Brodeur AE, Monteleone JA. Child Maltreatment. A Clinical Guide and Reference. GW Medical Publishing, 1994, 32
16. Hobbs C. Fractures. In Meadow R. ABC of child abuse. Br Med J 3rd ed, 1997, 9-13
17. Prosser I, Maguire S, Harrison SK et al. How old is this fracture? Radiologic dating of fractures in children: a systematic review. Am J Roentgenol 2005;184(4):1282-6
18. Dreizen S, Spirakis CN, Stone RE. The influence of age and nutrition on 'bone scar' formation in the distal end of the growing femur. Am J Phys Anthropol 1964;22:295–306
19. Ham AW. A histological study of the early phases of bone repair. J Bone Joint Surg Am 1930;12:827-44
20. Cruess RL, Dumont J. Fracture healing. Can J Surg 1975; 18(5):403-13
21. Campbell RM. Child abuse. In Beaty JH, Kasser JM. Rockwood and Wilkins' Fractures in children. Lippincott Williams and Wilkins, 5th ed, 2001
22. Kleinman PK, Nimkin K, Spevak MR et al. Follow-up skeletal surveys in suspected child abuse. Am J Roentgenol 1996;167(4):893-6
23. Hobbs CJ,Hanks HGI, Wynne JM. Child abuse and neglect – a clinician's handbook. Churchill Livingstone, 1993, 57-65
24. Segall HD, McComb JG, Tsai FY et al. Neuroradiology in head trauma. In Stanley G. Diagnostic imaging in pediatric trauma. Springer International, 1980, 18-63
25. Cameron JM. Radiological pathological aspects of the battered child syndrome. In Smith SM. The maltreatment of children. University Park Press, 1978, 69-81
26. Kleinman PK, Barnes PD. Head trauma. In Kleinman PK. Diagnostic imaging of child abuse. 2nd ed. Mosby, 1998, 285-342
27. Taveras JM, Wood EH. Diagnostic neuroradiology. Williams and Wilkins, 1964.
28. Rosenthall L, Hill RO, Chuang S. Observation on the use of 99mTc-phosphate imaging in peripheral bone trauma. Radiology 1976;119(3):637-41
29. Cumming WA. Neonatal skeletal fractures. Birth trauma or child abuse? J Can Assoc Radiol 1979;30(1):30-3
30. Yeo LI, Reed MH. Staging of healing of femoral fractures in children. Can Assoc Radiol J 1994;45(1):16-9
31. Islam O, Sobeleski D, Symons S et al. Development and duration of radiographic signs of bone healing in children. Am J Roentgenol 2000;175(1):75-8
32. Plenk H. Knochengewebe und Zähne. In Böck P (ed). Romeis Mikroskopische Technik. Urban und Schwarzenberg, 17e ed., 1989, 527-70

33. Bancroft JD, Stevens A. Theory and practice of histological techniques. Churchill Livingstone, 1996, 324-35

34. Burke CN, Geiselman CW. 1971. Exact anhydride epoxy percentages for electron microscopy embedding (Epon). J Ultrastruct Res 1971;36(1):119-26

35. Maat GJR. Dating of fractures in human dry bone tissue. The Berisha case. In Kimmerle E, Baraybar JP (eds). Identification of traumatic skeletal injuries resulting from human rights abuses and armed conflicts. Taylor and Francis (in print)

36. Maat GJR, van den Bos RPM, Aarents MJ. Manual preparation of ground sections for the microscopy of natural bone tissue. Update and modification of Frost's "rapid manual method". Int J Osteoarch 2001;11:366-74.

37. Aegerter E, Kirckpatrick JA. 1968. The repair of fractures. In Aegerter E (ed). Orthopedic diseases. Physiology, pathology, radiology. Saunders, 1968, 257-79

38. Bennet GA. Bones. In Anderson WAD (ed). Pathology, volume 2. Mosby, 1966, 1300-5

39. Heppenstall RB. Fracture healing. In Heppenstall RB (ed). Fracture treatment and healing. Saunders, 1980, 41-64

40. Williams PL, Warwick R, Dyson M et al. Gray's anatomy. The response of bone to injury. Churchill Livingstone, 37th ed, 1989, 313-5

41. Kleinman PK, Marks SC, Nimkin K et al. Rib fractures in 31 abused infants: postmortem radiologic-histopathologic study. Radiology 1996;200(3):807-10

42. Buckwalter JA, Einhorn ThA, Bolander ME et al. Healing of musculoskeletal tissues. In Rockwood ChA, Bucholz RW, Green DP et al (eds). Fractures in adults, vol 1. Lippincott-Raven, 4th ed, 1996, 267-83

43. Aufderheide AC, Rodriguez-Martin C. The Cambridge encyclopedia of human paleopathology. Cambridge University Press, 1998, 20-4

44. Schiller AL, Teitelbaum SL. Bones and joints. In Rubin E, Farber JL (eds). Pathology. Lippincott-Raven, 3rd ed, 1999, 1354-6

45. Vigorita VJ. Fracture healing. In Vigorita VJ (ed). Orthopedic pathology. Lippincott Williams and Wilkins, 1999, 85-96

46. Robbins SL, Cotran RS, Kumar V. Pathologic basis of disease. Saunders, 5th ed, 1991, 1227-9

47. Ortner D. Identification of pathological conditions in human skeletal remains. Academic Press, 2nd ed, 2003, 126-63

48. Klotzbach H, Delling G, Richter E et al. 2003. Post-mortem diagnosis and age estimation of infants' fractures. Int J Legal Med 2003;117(2): 82-9

49. Saukko P, Knight B. Knight's forensic pathology. Hodder Arnold, 3rd ed, 2004, 181-9

50. Saukko P, Knight B. Knight's forensic pathology. Hodder Arnold, 3rd ed, 2004, 281-95

Index

Printing and Binding: Stürtz GmbH, Würzburg